WORLD® AIR POWER

JOURNAL

Aerospace Publishing Ltd

Airtime Publishing Inc.

Published quarterly by
Aerospace Publishing Ltd
179 Dalling Road
London W6 0ES
UK

ISSN 0959-7050

Aerospace ISBN 1 874023 36 0
                (softback)
                1 874023 37 9
                (hardback)
Airtime ISBN   1-880588-07-2
                (hardback)

Published under licence in USA and
Canada by AIRtime Publishing Inc.,
10 Bay Street, Westport,
CT 06880, USA

Editorial Offices:
WORLD AIR POWER JOURNAL
Aerospace Publishing Ltd
3A Brackenbury Road
London W6 0BE UK

Publisher: Stan Morse
Managing Editor: David Donald
Editor: Jon Lake
Sub Editor: Karen Leverington
Design: Barry Savage
        Robert Hewson
Typesetting: SX Composing Ltd
Origination and printing by
    Imago Publishing Ltd
Printed in Singapore

Europe Correspondent:
    Paul Jackson
Washington Correspondent:
    Robert F. Dorr
USA West Coast Correspondent:
    René J. Francillon
Asia Correspondent:
    Pushpindar Singh

The editors of WORLD AIR
POWER JOURNAL welcome
photographs for possible publication,
but cannot accept any responsibility for
loss or damage to unsolicited material.

The publishers gratefully acknowledge
the assistance given by the following
people:
The Public Affairs Officers of the A-10
operating wings for their help with
'Fairchild A-10: Fighting Warthog'

**World Air Power Journal is
published quarterly and is available
by subscription and from many fine
book and hobby stores.**

**SUBSCRIPTION AND BACK
NUMBERS:**

**UK and World (except USA and
Canada) write to:
Aerospace Publishing Ltd
FREEPOST
PO Box 2822
London
W6 0BR
UK**

**(No stamp required if posted in the
UK)**

**USA and Canada, write to:
AIRtime Publishing Inc.
Subscription Dept
10 Bay Street
Westport
CT 06880
USA
Toll-free order number in USA:
1 800 359-3033**

**Prevailing subscription rates are as
follows:
Softbound edition for 1 year:
        $58.00
Softbound edition for 2 years:
        $108.00
Softbound back numbers (subject
to availability) are:
$17.95 each. All rates are for
delivery within mainland USA,
Alaska and Hawaii. Canadian and
overseas prices available upon
request. American Express,
Mastercard and Visa accepted.
When ordering please include your
card number, expiration date and
signature.**

**Publisher, North America:
    Melvyn Williams
Subscription Director:
    Linda de Angelis
Retail Sales Director:
    Jill Brooks
Charter Member Services
Managers:
    Janie Munroe
    Monica A. Virag**

WORLD AIR POWER ®

AIR POWER

J O U R N A L

CONTENTS

Military Aviation Review

International

Four ER 33 Mirage **F1CR**s are detached to Treviso-Istrana to support Deny Flight operations. They are fully equipped with **SLAR**, tactical Elint and defensive systems.

Industry funds Eurofighter

Germany's immediate funding problems with the Eurofighter 2000 appeared to have been resolved in mid-1993, but may return to haunt this and other military programmes in the years to come. As the result of under-funding for Eurofighter in the 1993 defence budget, DASA, the German aircraft manufacturer, will provide the cash to continue work on the EFA for the remainder of the year and is to be reimbursed from the defence budget after 1995. However, the postponed cash shortage will be further compounded from next year when the already shrinking German defence budget will have to meet the costs of any out-of-area operations (such as humanitarian missions) instead of the Treasury's contingency fund. This caused alarm in France, which fears that the Eurofighter's slightly improved fortunes will be at the expense of the Franco-German Tiger/Gerfaut combat helicopter.

Germany has also been under pressure from its EFA partners to re-allocate the industrial share of the programme. Italy, Spain and the UK claim that their part of Eurofighter work is disproportionately small as a result of Germany cutting its procurement target from 250 to about 140 since work shares were first agreed. Germany refuses to give up any of its allocated 33 per cent and has made the unlikely suggestion that some of its Tornados could be prematurely replaced by Eurofighters in order to restore purchases to somewhere near the original balance.

As a means of further short-term cost saving in the Eurofighter programme, BAe proposed during the spring that the first production batch should comprise 30 two-seat trainers built on prototype jigs at only one assembly plant. This represents only a slight change from present plans, which call for 26 of the first 30 machines to be trainers. Only with the second batch, suggests BAe, should assembly on all lines be upgraded with production jigs to be funded from additional money.

Gerfaut follows Tiger

A second prototype of the Eurocopter Tiger – in Gerfaut escort helicopter configuration for the French army – made its initial flight at Marignane on 22 April following transfer from the German assembly centre at Ottobrunn. PT2, registered F-ZWWY, was shown statically at Paris in June, while its predecessor, which had amassed some 200 hours since 27 April 1991, participated in the daily flying programme. The third helicopter, PT3 (also German-assembled), was due to fly at Marignane in the fall of 1993 as the prototype for the anti-tank version known as PAH-2 Tiger in Germany and Tigre HAC in France. Two more prototypes will follow.

NATO command changes

A re-organisation of NATO's Allied Command Europe (ACE) under way in 1993-94 will result in disbandment of UK Air Forces at High Wycombe. Comprising most of the RAF squadrons assigned to NATO from home bases (and commanded by the AOC-in-C RAF Strike Command), UKAF is being combined with Allied Forces Northern Europe (Kolsass, Norway) as Allied Forces Northwest Europe, which will remain at High Wycombe. On the continent, the 2nd and 4th Allied Tactical Air Forces have been disbanded and their aircraft have been placed directly under Allied Air Forces Central Europe (AIRCENT), whose commander is also head of USAFE. The same has happened with NATO armies of the former Northern and Central Army Groups, which are directly subordinate to Allied Land Forces Central Europe. Reflecting disbandment of Allied Forces Baltic Approaches, Denmark is now classified as part of central Europe, although the air and surface units of the Command will be re-assigned to AF Northwest Europe at High Wycombe. Allied Command Channel, a naval formation, will disband and pass its functions to ACE. The third element of ACE, Allied Forces Southern Europe, will not undergo any major changes.

Operating from Lübeck on target facilities for the German forces is this IAI 1124 Westwind.

Western Europe

BELGIUM:

Army aviation re-organised

On 19 May, the three Germany-based squadrons of army aviation (Groepering Lichte Vliegtuigen/Groupement d'Avions Légers) were redesignated as battalions. These are now 16 Battalion (Liaison) at Butzweilerhof with 15 Alouette IIs; 17 Battalion (Anti-tank) at Merzbrück; and 18 Battalion (Anti-tank) at Werl. The two last-mentioned units are re-equipping with Agusta A 109s and will each have two anti-tank companies with seven armed and two observation A 109s, and one observation platoon with a further five. Nos 16-18 squadrons will withdraw to Bierset, Belgium, in September 1995, mid-1994 and mid-1995 respectively.

Magister retirement possible

Disbandment of 33 Squadron at Brustem appears possible in mid-1994, terminating the long career of Belgium's Fouga CM.170 Magisters. The unit's principal role is the provision of continuation flying for officers undertaking a ground tour, but this requirement was to cease after 1 July 1994. It is probable that pilots will in future take a refresher course on Alpha Jets after completing ground tours.

FRANCE:

Rafale delays

Deliveries of Rafales to the French air force appear have been postponed until 1999, although the Aéronavale still plans to receive its first 16 before 1999. These will be to SU 0 standard with reduced air-to-air capability. Between 1999 and 2002, 22 will be delivered to the air force in SU 1 configuration, having air-to-ground weaponry but still lacking full air combat equipment. Finally, the fully equipped SU 2 version will enter production at the rate of 24 per year in 2002, first deliveries to the navy following two years later. Flight-testing of a prototype with SU 2 avionics will begin in 1995. Having flown only on 30 April, the first two-seat Rafale, B01, made its initial public appearance at the Paris air show in June.

First Tucanos

A year of acceptance trials for the first two EMBRAER EMB-312F Tucano turbo-prop trainers was begun in June after the aircraft had been on show at Paris. Gaining their 'F' suffix by reason of incorporating French avionics, the pair made their first flights in Brazil on 7 April (No. 439) and 8 April (No. 438 - *sic*) before being handed over to Escadrille d'Expérimentation et de Transport 6/330 'Albret', part of the CEAM trials unit at Mont-de-Marsan. The next 20 Tucanos are to be delivered between July 1994 and July 1995 to GI 312, the Ecole de l'Air, at Salon de Provence, and 28 more will follow in the next 12 months. Although they have yet to be funded, 30 more are due by May 1998, mostly for base comms flights.

The French Jaguar fleet celebrated 20 years' service on 5 June at St Dizier. Aircraft from EC 7 and EC 11 received a special scheme.

On Deny Flight sorties over Bosnia, the F-15Cs of the 36th FW carry a telescopic sight to aid positive identification of slow-flying targets.

Flying training begins on the Tucano in January 1995, using a new syllabus. Hitherto, officer pilots destined for fighters have trained on Epsilons, Magisters and Alpha Jets, while prospective NCO pilots took a longer Epsilon course before attending the Alpha Jet school (GE 314) at Tours to gain their wings. In future, all will have 70 hours on Epsilons with GE 315 at Cognac; 53 on Tucanos of GI 312; and 85 on Alpha Jets. This represents a slight reduction in total flying, the current time to a pilot's brevet being 229 hours for officers and 207 for NCOs. Those selected for transport flying will progress straight from the Epsilon to GE 316 at Avord for 125 hours on EMBRAER Xingus.

Air force restructure

Having been slower than other Western air forces to announce post-Cold War defence cuts, the Armée de l'Air made up for lost time in mid-1993 with a series of structural changes and disbandments. Farthest ranging of these is the new command structure that will result in the disappearance by 1996 of all wing HQs (EC 3 at Nancy is expected to be the last). Thereafter, Tactical, Strategic and Transport Commands will control their squadrons directly, instead of through an intermediate HQ at each base. As squadrons are numbered as a component of their wing (1/3, 2/3 and 3/3, for example), the whole basis of the numbering system is undermined. It is likely that squadrons will retain their existing designations for historical reasons.

The Strategic Air Force implemented the new command chain *en bloc* on 31 July when HQs of 4, 91 and 93 Wings all disbanded. The Mirage 2000N, Mirage IVPs and C-135FRs which these wings previously commanded continue to fly, as before, with squadrons 1/4, 2/4, 3/4, 1/91, 2/91, 1/93 and 3/93. One disbandment associated with the rationalisation was of Escadron de Ravitaillement en Vol 2/93 'Sologne' at Avord on 1 August. Its two assigned C-135FR tankers were distributed among the other two tanker squadrons: ERV 1/93 'Aunis' and 3/93 'Landes'.

In Tactical Command, the 33 Escadre de Reconnaissance lost its third squadron, ER 3/33 'Moselle'. The squadron, equipped with Mirage F1CRs at Strasbourg, ceased operational flying on 1 July and officially disbanded on 31 July. Also on 31 July, EC 2/30 'Normandie-

Niemen' flying Mirage F1Cs at Reims, and EC 3/2 'Alsace' with Mirage 2000Cs at Dijon, were both disbanded. 'Normandie-Niemen' is one of the most famous squadrons in the French air force and it is likely to re-emerge following the redesignation of another unit.

Strength will not be reduced as much as these disbandments suggest, as tactical squadrons are being increased in size from 15 to 20 aircraft each at the same time that wings are reducing from three to two squadrons. In consequence, fighter bases will operate 40 aircraft, rather than the previous 45, with the exception of Nancy, which is to have three squadrons totalling 60 Mirage 2000Ds by 1996. The 20-aircraft squadrons are gaining a third flight (*escadrille*) to accommodate the additional crew. This happened at Strasbourg on 31 July when, as noted above, ER 3/33 'Moselle' and the wing HQ (00/033) both disbanded and the remaining squadrons adopted an extra flight each. These are now:

Escadron de Reconnaissance 1/33 'Belfort'

1re Escadrille: SAL 33 'Hache' (battle axe, as before)
2^e Escadrille: EALA 9/72 'Petit Prince' (as adopted in 1986)
3^e Escadrille: BR 244 'Leopard' (new; a leopard standing upon a letter B)

Escadron de Reconnaissance 2/33 'Savoie'

1re Escadrille: SAL 6 'Mouette' (seagull, as before)
2^e Escadrille: BR 11 'Cocotte (paper bird, ex ER 3/33, on disbandment)
3^e Escadrille: SPA BI 53 'C 53' (new; a pennant with '53' inside a letter C)

Further complications have arisen as a consequence of the traditional application of an escadrille badge to opposite sides of an aircraft's fin. With three badges to be applied in the proportions 13:13:14 to the 40 faces available on 20 fins, some squadrons have elected to adopt a more complex permutation of markings. Mirage 2000N squadrons have been the first to face this problem, with the result that at least three left-and-right combinations of badges are to be found on aircraft of a single unit.

New units formed

Amid the many disbandments two new units formed on 1 August, including Escadron de Transport Léger 1/62 'Vercors' at Creil, which will operate the air force's eight CN.235 light transports (the first two of which have been undergoing trials at Mont-de-Marsan since January 1991). Originally, it had been stated that the operating squadron would be at Bordeaux. Base Aérienne 110 'Lieutenant Colonel Guy la Horie' at Creil/Senlis was an air defence station until EC 10 disbanded there on 1 April 1985. It was reactivated on 1 March 1990, but only as an administrative unit. ET 62 disbanded as a Noratlas wing on 1 July 1978. ETL 1/62 will be expanded on September 1994 when it acquires the last three DHC-6 Twin Otters operated by the VIP transport

squadron, GAEL at Villacoublay.

Coincident with disbandment of HQ 4 Wing (OO/004) at Luxeuil, the Section d'Acceuil, Liaison et d'Entrainement 09/116 formed at the same base on 1 August. It has inherited the Magisters used for liaison and training and may also acquire the CiTAC 339 fleet of Falcon 20s, Jaguars and loaned Alpha Jets.

Second Mirage F1CT squadron

EC 3/13 'Auvergne', the second and last of Colmar-based 13 Wing's three squadrons to re-equip with Mirage F1CTs, made its first sortie with the new equipment on 23 April when Cdt Hervé Buchler was airborne on No. 245 '13-SA'. The squadron was due to complete conversion in October and achieve operational status in April 1994. The remaining squadron, EC 2/13 'Alpes' with Mirage 5Fs, will disband in June 1994 at the same time that EC 3/3 'Ardennes' at Nancy relinquishes its Mirage IIIEs and begins Mirage 2000D conversion. These two squadrons are the last in France to operate the first-generation Mirage III/5.

Elint aircraft refit

Thomson-CSF revealed that its ASTAC electronic intelligence system will be fitted in the second-generation DC-8 SARIGUE NG aircraft of France's 51 Escadron Electronique. EE 51 currently uses DC-8 Srs 53 45570 as its sole SARIGUE (Systeme Aéroportée de Recueil des Informations de Guerre Electronique) system, but this ageing aircraft

This Mirage IIIE was the last Armée de l'Air aircraft to go through overhaul. It wears an air defence scheme and the markings of EC 3/3.

will be replaced with a DC-8 Srs 72 when the type is supplanted in the transport role by Airbuses. Conversion of the SARIGUE Nouvelle Génération will be undertaken jointly by Air France and the Armée de l'Air at Clermont Ferrand. ASTAC also equips the two Transall C.160 GABRIEL aircraft of EE 54 and is available in podded form for Japanese RF-4EJ Phantoms.

GERMANY:

Lead-in training unit

As the result of retiring Alpha Jets from the front line, the Luftwaffe announced a new designation for the former OCU for the type, JBG 49 at Fürstenfeldbruck. This will disband on 1 April 1994 and become Fluglehrgruppe Fürstenfeldbruck (Air Training Group) with a diminished strength comprising the last 30 Alphas in service.

Last Skyservant

Phase-out of the Dornier Do 28D-2 Skyservant light transport from Luftwaffe service was completed on 11 July when 5829 flew its final sortie. Between January 1970 and January 1974, four Do 28D-1/S and 101 Do 28D-2 Skyservants were received, mainly for base flights. Economies began thinning the fleet from 1983 onwards,

This anniversary scheme on AMX MM7149 commemorates 50 years of 103° Gruppo.

AMI MB 339A trainers have adopted overall grey paint with high-conspicuity panels on the tip tanks.

Spanish miscellany: above left is a Cessna 560 Citation II (local designation TR.20) on delivery to Esc 403 at Cuatro Vientos. The fairing on the side is a survey camera. Above is one of Ala 12's smart RF-4Cs (CR.12), while at left is one of the eight Sikorsky S.76Cs (HE.24) used by Ala 78 at Granada for rotary wing training.

in less advanced states of completeness. It was envisaged that a second Gripen would be handed over in November 1993, followed by a third early in 1994. Squadrons will not receive a JAS 39B two-seat trainer until 1998, however.

when transfers were initiated to Greece, Turkey and civilian operators. Naval aviation continues to operate 20 of the type.

Navigation aids checker

3/JBG 32, the ECM training squadron equipped with Hansa Jets at Lechfeld, added former East German An-26SM 5209 to its complement. The aircraft continues to fly from Dresden/ Klotsche on navaids calibration duties as a parallel to the civilian-registered aircraft also based at Lechfeld with the Gemeinsame Flugvermessungsstelle.

GREECE:

New deliveries

Deliveries began in June of five Alouette IIIs (possibly fabricated in India) ordered from Eurocopter France by the Greek navy. They join four dating from 1976, naval aviation also having 11 Bell 212s, comprising nine for anti-submarine operations and two in the electronic warfare role. The number of ex-USAF F-4E Phantoms delivered to the Greek air force in 1992 has been confirmed as 28, all for 339 MPK at Andravidha. Deliveries were continuing between September 1992 and April 1994 of 27 ex-Luftwaffe RF-4Es for 348 MTA at Larissa.

ITALY:

Last F-104Gs

Italy's 28° Gruppo of 3° Stormo at Villafranca was stood down in June on retirement of its Orpheus recce pod-equipped RF-104G Starfighters. The unit is now converting to the AMX – still in the reconnaissance role – and will join co-located 132° Gruppo, which already operates that aircraft. The only 'G' versions of Starfighter remaining in service with the AMI are two-seat trainers.

Starfighter stretch-out mooted

Faced with further delays to the Eurofighter 2000 programme, the AMI devoted the spring to considering means by which it could retain an effective interceptor force until the early years of the next century. As an alternative to the preferred solution of leasing stop-gap aircraft – the Panavia Tornado ADV, Lockheed F-16 Fighting Falcon and McDonnell Douglas F/A-18 Hornet being among those examined – Italy was offered a further upgrade to 106 of its 140 Lockheed F-104S/ASA Starfighters. The last to receive the ASA modifications returned to service only in February 1993, but the mooted ASA-M (for Maintainability) would gain a further 10-15 years of life through the addition of some systems from the Tornado, plus rewiring and a partial rebuild for the GE J79 engine. A high/low mix of leased fighters and a smaller number of F-104s was also receiving thought.

Avanti delivered

As a partial replacement for ageing PD-808s and P.166s, the Italian air force received the first of three Piaggio P.180 Avanti executive turboprop twins on 14 May and has taken an option on a similar number.

NETHERLANDS:

Hercules introduction plans

The KLu expects to receive the first of its two Lockheed C-130H-30 Super Hercules early in 1994, but the aircraft will initially operate from Melsbroek, Belgium, where crews will be trained by the BAF. The second machine will be delivered directly to 334 Squadron at Eindhoven in 1995. During the spring of 1993, Major Maarten Kuijpers completed conversion to the KC-10A at Seymour Johnson AFB as the first KLu pilot destined for the two DC-10s being converted to tankers for 334 Squadron. The initial DC-10 crew, also trained in the US, will be operational in 1995.

SWEDEN:

New air force structure

A new organisation for the Flygvapen came into effect on 1 July 1993, coincident with disbandment of F13 (Viggen) and in anticipation of the similarly equipped F6 disappearing on 31 December. Main changes are at higher level and involve disbandment of the First Air Division (F7 and F15 with attack-tasked Viggens, plus the Hercules transport force) and one of the four regional air defence sectors. The last-mentioned have been reorganised into three Tactical Air Commands (Northern, Central and Southern) incorporating, where geographically appropriate, the assets of 1st AD.

Gripens grounded

Having been the first delivery to the air force, on 8 June, the second production JAS 39 Gripen (39102) was lost two months later, on 8 August, while displaying to crowds at the Stockholm water festival. One person on the ground suffered slight burns as the aircraft crashed into the suburb of Sodermalm. Saab test pilot Lars Radestrom described loss of control symptoms which clearly implicated the flight control computer, as in the June 1989 crash of the first prototype, which was also being flown by Radestrom. All Gripens were grounded pending investigation of the crash.

At the time of its delivery, 39102 had flown 24 hours in 31 sorties, bringing total Gripen airborne time to 854 hours in 1,115 flights. Aircraft 39103 to 39108 were in final assembly and 39109 to 39122

Army replaces AB 204s

Replacement of the army's dozen aged AB 204Bs is in prospect following the placing of an order in mid-1993 for an initial five AB 412s to be delivered in 1994. Options are held on a further 12.

Sk 60 upgrade for 2010

Details of re-engining for the 134 Saab Sk 60 light jet trainer/communications/ attack aircraft were being finalised in the summer in time for an upgrade to begin in 1995. Also including new avionics, of which satellite navigation is one feature, the upgrade will be applied to 100 aircraft, with an option held on the remainder. Candidates for replacing the existing two Turboméca Arbisque engines are the Williams/R-R F129 and Garrett F109. A structural modification programme was undertaken on the Sk 60 fleet in 1988-91, increasing the g limitation from 4.5 to 6.0 and extending service life beyond 2000. The new programme will take the aircraft to 2010, at least.

SWITZERLAND:

Hunter squadrons reduced

Withdrawal of those Swiss Hunter F.Mk 58s not capable of carrying Maverick ASMs continued with disbandment of 2 Escadrille on 6 May. The unit stood down at Turtmann although its war station is believed to have been Ulrichen. Six Hunter squadrons remain, one of them equipped with two-seat trainers.

UNITED KINGDOM:

Air defence bears brunt of White Paper cuts

Reductions in the UK air defence force was the key item in the 1993 Statement on the Defence Estimates, published on 5

The inactivation of F13 has seen the ECM and Elint units at Malmen become parented by F16, under the unit designation F16M. The J 32 Lansens (top) fly target facilities work, while the Tp 102 Gulfstream (above) is a staff transport . Two more Tp 102s are on order for F16M to replace the two Elint Caravelles.

July. The fact that it was as long ago as 6 September 1991 that the last CIS aircraft made an unannounced penetration of the UK Air Defence Region persuaded the government that it is safe to reduce the operational strength of the RAF's No. 11 Group and its supporting elements. Accordingly, Leeming-based No. 23 Squadron (Tornado F.Mk 3) is to be disbanded by April 1994; one of No. 8 Squadron's Sentry AEW.Mk 1s is to be placed on unestablished strength at Waddington, although Staff Requirement (Air) 920 for a Radar System Improvement Programme will continue; and three VC10 C.Mk 1K tankers are to be consigned to limbo as soon as they leave the conversion line at Bournemouth. In the same vein, it was not unexpected that plans for posthumous replacement of the Bloodhound SAM force have been shelved. Instead, the RAF has long-term thoughts for a medium-range SAM to enter service next century, perhaps in mobile form for use by rapid-reaction forces and almost certainly with anti-ballistic missile capability.

The White Paper shed little further light on the future of the Tornado GR.Mk 1's mid-life update, except to say that it will probably go ahead with reduced numbers and/or a lower standard of new equipment. The prototype Mk 4, a conversion of ZD708, made its first flight at Warton on 29 May. SR(A) 1244 for replacement of the WE177 free-fall nuclear bomb by a stand-off missile is being back-pedalled and the White Paper remarked only that the whole role of tactical nuclear strike is being examined. One explanation put forward unofficially was that the largely redundant fleet of Trident-launching submarines currently under construction will be given smaller war-

heads of a pre-strategic capability and the Tornado's nuclear role will disappear with WE177 early in the next century. SR(A) 1238 – the long-running selection of a stand-off anti-armour weapon - is still being pursued and SR(A) 1242 for a new 'smart' bomb is also on target.

Modernisation of the transport force is expected to involve orders in future years for new helicopters (any permutation of EH.101s, Black Hawks or Chinooks) and 30 transports to replace half the Hercules. The 'C-130J' which Lockheed has on offer for export seems most probable here and is almost certain to pick up the follow-on contract when (if) the other 30 are replaced later. Refurbishment of the existing aircraft has not been ruled out, however.

Operational strength of the RAF is set to fall from 743 in 1990, through 595 as envisaged in the 'Options for Change' defence review, to a new low of 567 plus a squadron or so of extra transport helicopters. These figures, representing only aircraft actually in squadrons and OCUs, reflect a cut of 22 Tornado F.Mk 3s, 22 Sidewinder-armed Hawks, one Sentry, 36 Tornado GR.Mk 1s, 22 Harriers, all 30 Buccaneers, all 65 Phantoms, eight Nimrod MR.Mk 2s and four tanker/transports. Chinook upgrades to Mk 2 have been reduced to 32 by the decision not to repair one damaged helicopter. The Navy's operational strength of Sea Harriers, cut from 24 to 22 by 'Options', remains at the latter level.

In detail, the data are:

	In 1990	'Options' plan	Current plan
Tornado GR.Mk 1	148	112	112
Tornado F.Mk 3	92	122	100
Phantom	65	0	0
Hawk T.Mk 1A	72	52	50
Sentry	0	7	6
Harrier	74	52	52
Jaguar	40	40	40
Buccaneer	30	0	0
Operational helicopter	93	90	90
Tanker/transport	94	83	90
Total	**743**	**595**	**567**

Tanker changes

The initial VC10 K.Mk 4 tanker made its first flight at Filton on 30 July after conversion from civil airliner configuration by BAe and was due to be delivered to No. 101 Squadron at Brize Norton in November 1993 after trials at the A&AEE at Boscombe Down. ZD242 was ferried to Filton on 27 July 1990 after nine years of storage at Abingdon, later being joined on the conversion line by ZD240, ZD230, ZD242 and ZD235, in that order. On the minus side, the RAF's six Hercules C.Mk 1K tankers will be withdrawn by 1996. They are prematurely approaching the end of their fatigue lives as a result of the non-standard nature of the modifications hastily incorporated for the 1982 Falklands War.

The first operational use of the VC10 C.Mk 1K tanker conversion occurred on 19 June 1993 when Wing Commander Al Stuart and his crew were despatched to Saudi Arabia to support Operation Jural over southern Iraq. By that time, No. 10 Squadron had received two aircraft from re-work and had trained three crews for the newly-acquired tanking role.

Tornado GR.Mk 1 squadrons are to acquire their own 'buddy' tanking capability through the addition of FRL Mk 20 pods taken from redundant Victors and donated by the disbanding Buccaneer force. Service entry is expected in 1996-97 of a few aircraft in each of the overland strike/attack squadrons. The two maritime units (Nos 12 and 617) due on line in 1994 are intended to have their own 'buddy' system based on the 15 SFC 28-300 pods bought from the German navy during the Gulf War. At least nine aircraft were modified for SFC pods at St Athan early in 1991, although this was a Special Trial Fit (STF 238) and will either have to be deleted or reworked as a fully-approved modification when the aircraft are converted to Sea Eagle missile-carrying GR.Mk 1Bs.

Communications cuts

Reductions in the RAF's communications fleet were announced during the summer. No. 32 Squadron at Northolt was programmed to lose all its seven Andovers between November 1993 and 1 April 1994. Current strength is four CC.Mk 2s and three E.Mk 3As, several of which have

The Slingsby T-3A has been chosen by the USAF for its primary training syllabus. This aircraft was shown at the official roll-out ceremony at Kirbymoorside.

adopted an overall light grey colour scheme since September 1992. According to unconfirmed reports, the squadron's four BAe 125 CC.Mk 1s and two CC.Mk 2s are targeted for later withdrawal, leaving only the six CC.Mk 3 variants and four Gazelle HT.Mk 3s in service. All but one of the 125s were grey by mid-1993.

Harrier stand–down

Operational service of the first-generation Harrier with the RAF ended on 6 July when No. 1417 Flight stood down in Belize, 16 years to the day after its predecessor (a detachment of No. 1 Squadron) had arrived. First installed in 1975 to meet an invasion threat from Guatemala to what was then British Honduras, six Harriers were withdrawn after five months. The second deployment was reduced to four aircraft in 1978 and became No. 1417 Flight under Squadron Leader John Finlayson on 1 April 1980. Finlayson was also the last CO and led three GR.Mk 3s (XZ971, ZD667 and ZD670) back to Wittering on 7-8 July via Goose Bay. The fourth Harrier will be preserved locally. Harrier GR.Mk 1s entered RAF service in May 1969 and No. 1 Squadron became the world's first operational V/STOL unit on 1 October that year. The GR.Mk 3 flew its last operational European mission (with No. IV Squadron in Germany) on 7 December 1990, although a small pool was retained at the Wittering OCU to supply the Belize detachment.

In all, three UK units are to be disbanded as a result of the decision to withdraw forces from Belize by the middle of 1994. After the Harrier departure, defences of the Central American republic comprised No. 1563 Flight operating Puma HC.Mk 1s, half a squadron of Rapier SAMs on rotation, and the Army's 25 Flight with four Gazelle AH.Mk 1s.

Army aviation moves

A new unit of the Army Air Corps, 6 Flight, formed at RAF Shawbury on 3 June with two of an eventual four Gazelle AH.Mk 1s. It is assigned to support the Army's Wales & Western District and, like the similarly-equipped 3 Flight at Edinburgh/Turnhouse, is staffed by the Territorial Army. Personnel include nine pilots.

As planned, 3 Regiment, AAC, officially moved into Wattisham Barracks on 9 June. Formerly based at Soest, Germany, the unit comprises 653, 662 and 663 Squadrons, all equipped with a mixture of Gazelles and Lynxes. In 1995, 4 Regiment (654, 659 and 669 Squadrons) will arrive

Above: British Aerospace flew the first Tornado GR.Mk 4 on 29 May. Note the new undernose sensors.

Below: For the 1993 display season, the CFS painted this Tucano T.Mk 1 in an all-blue scheme.

from Detmold. 656 Squadron is to transfer from Netheravon (7 Regiment) to Dishforth early in 1994, joining 9 Regiment. The squadron is currently converting from six Lynx AH.Mk 1s to six AH.Mk 7s, but will retain its six Gazelle AH.Mk 1s. Following the move, 9 Regiment will comprise 656 Squadron, 657 Squadron (Lynx AH.Mk 1/Gazelle), 664 Squadron (Lynx AH.Mk 9/Gazelle) and 672 Squadron (Lynx AH.Mk 9).

Canberra B.Mk 2 withdrawn

Phase-out of the venerable Canberra came closer on 7 July when the last B.Mk 2 version in the RAF made its final flight, ending 42 years of service. Following disbandment of No. 231 OCU at Wyton on 24 April 1993, the final Mk 2, WJ731, was transferred to No. 360 Squadron (Canberra T.Mk 17/17A), together with the remaining three T.Mk 4s and two PR.Mk 7s. One of the trainers will go to Marham when No. 39 Squadron moves its five PR.Mk 9s to that base in December 1993. After No. 360 disbands in October 1994, No. 39 will inherit all the PR.Mk 7s and possibly one or two more T.Mk 4s. Retention of the Mk 7 is in association with its duty of calibrating UK air defence radars, rather than any photographic capability.

On a related note, the second of Germany's three Canberra B.Mk 2s was withdrawn on 27 May 1993 when 9935 was delivered to Gatow, Berlin, where it will wait for the Luftwaffe Museum, currently at Uetersen, to catch up with it after the RAF moves out in 1994. The final aircraft, 9934, will be withdrawn in December 1993.

Synthetic aperture radar

A BAe One-Eleven of the Defence Research Agency is to begin flight trials in

1995 of a GEC-Marconi synthetic aperture radar as the next stage in the long-running ASTOR programme – SR(Land-Air) 925 – to acquire an equivalent to the USA's E-8C J-STARS. If successful, the project will lead to the service entry in 2003 of five aircraft equipped with electro-optical sensors and a radar capable of locating moving ground targets. The operational platform has yet to be selected, but its ceiling will have to be about 55,000 ft (16765 m), suggesting an executive jet in the class of the Gulfstream V. The same platform may be adopted as a replacement for the three Elint Nimrod R.Mk 1s currently used by No. 51 Squadron.

Through the looking glass

Eight new pilots (including one RN) received their wings at No. 4 FTS, Valley, on 3 June, becoming the first group in the RAF to complete the new 100-hour 'Mirror Image' flying training and weapons course. Candidates had arrived at Valley on 21 September 1992 for five weeks of ground school before joining No. 234 (Reserve) Squadron. Previously, following the Tucano or Jet Provost, students would fly a total of 132 hours on the Hawk at an FTS and TWU, gaining their wings at the half-way point.

'JP' withdrawn

The veteran Jet Provost officially departed from RAF pilot training on 4 June with the graduation of Course 125 at No. 1 FTS, Linton-on-Ouse, although it was later in the same month before Flight Lieutenant Nigel Curtis completed his training as the last student to fly the JP on a basic training course. The Mk 5 remained as a navigator trainer with No. 6 FTS at Finningley for a few weeks longer, until the unit held a private reunion and farewell on 14 August. The public version of the event was held at Finningley on 18 September. Experimental use of a batch of

10 Hunting Percival Jet Provost T.Mk 1s began in August 1955, and after the concept of all-through jet training had been validated, orders were placed for 200 T.Mk 3s, 187 T.Mk 4s and 110 pressurised T.Mk 5s for the RAF. The Mk 3 was issued to No. 2 FTS at Syerston in June 1959 and remained in service for 35 years. Between 1973 and 1976, 84 Mk 3s and 93 Mk 5s were converted with upgraded avionics to Mk 3A and Mk 5A. The Mk 4, which had a shorter fatigue life, had been withdrawn from pilot training before the upgrade programme began.

Return of the blimp

Surveillance in Northern Ireland is understood to be the role for the Westinghouse Skyship 600 airship purchased by the UK MoD in June. Presumably to be operated

1 FTS ended its last Jet Provost course in June, the unit having flown the type since August 1960. 6 FTS was the last RAF JP operator.

by the RAF, this will be the first military non-rigid airship since the submarine-patrolling 'blimps' of World War I.

Hercules upgrades

A retrofit has been ordered by the RAF for 30 of its Hercules, which will receive an upgraded navigation system. This will be an improved version of the kit fitted to six aircraft in 1990 for undercover operations from the UAE during the Gulf War. The six, which will be included in the 30 retrofits, gained an inertial navigation system, global positioning system and an air data computer.

Eastern Europe

CZECH REPUBLIC:

Aero L-139 debut

Only a month after its maiden flight on 10 May, the prototype Aero L-139 (5501) was making daily appearances in the flying display at the Paris air show. Based on the well-established L-39 Albatros, the L-139 is intended to compete in Western markets and accordingly has a Garrett TFE731-4 turbofan in place of the Ivchenko AI-25. The main prize in Czech sights is the USAF/USN JPATS competition but, with no US partner firm, the aircraft has little chance of success.

HUNGARY:

MiG-29s ordered

Despite an expressed preference for a Western aircraft as its next fighter, the Hungarian air force was forced by the twin constraints of finance and immediacy to order 28 MiG-29 'Fulcrums' during the spring. The urgent need for an interceptor more potent than the MiG-23MF 'Flogger-Bs' which equip a single squadron at Papa results from frequent violations of Hungarian airspace since the start of the Yugoslav civil war. All the MiGs were due to have been delivered by October 1993

to the Dezsö Szentgörgyi Regiment at Kecskemét, in preparation for which a group of 20 pilots from the base transferred to Krasnodar, Russia, where they began flying two-seat MiG-29UBs in August. The Szentgörgyi Regiment has (or had) two squadrons of MiG-21MFs named Puma (Puma) and Dongo (Wasp). Hungary continues to look at the Lockheed F-16, Dassault Rafale and Saab JAS 39 as possible contenders in a later fighter competition.

POLAND:

Uprated Orlik

Highest-powered Turbo-Orlik yet, the prototype PZL-130TC (SP-PCE) flew for the first time on 2 June. Fitted with a 950-shp (708-kW) Pratt & Whitney PT6A-62 turboprop, Bendix-King avionics and Martin-Baker Mk 15A ejection seats, the -130TC can carry up to 1,763 lb (800 kg) of weapons on six hardpoints. In addition to two PZL-130TM prototypes, the Polish air force plans to obtain 48 production Turbo-Orliks. All were expected to be the PZL-130TB with Motorlet M 601 engine and Eastern European avionics, but a subsequent report claimed that the contract has been modified to include 28 -130TCs.

New helicopters

Naval Aviation, the Morskie Lotnictwa Wojskowe, recently received an infusion of new equipment in the form of six locally-built PZL W-3RM Anakonda light helicopters for SAR duties with the 18 Eskandra. Testing has begun of another version of the helicopter, designated W-3SP Anakonda Special and fitted with Western avionics, including Bendix-King radar. A prototype was delivered early in 1993 to the 103 Pulk Lotniczy, a unit belonging to the Ministry of the Interior.

RUSSIA:

Second-generation 'stealth'

A Russian equivalent of the Lockheed F-22 has been built, but not flown, according to Mikoyan's chief designer, Rostislav Belyakov. Speaking in May, Belyakov said the aircraft, designated MiG-1.42, urgently needed funds for test flying in order to maintain the progress of Russian aircraft design. The 1.42 has twin tails and a blended body design like the F-22, but is not totally dedicated to stealth, like the F-117. Nevertheless, it has special shaping and radar-absorbent surface materials to minimise radar reflectivity. Belyakov also confirmed that production of the MiG-29 'Fulcrum' has ended, leaving the factory with some 100 'white-tail' aircraft which the VVS does not require and has not paid for.

MiG production data

The apparently never-ending series of revelations from behind the former Iron Curtain continued at the Paris air show in June when the Mikoyan bureau published production figures for its designs. These reveal that the former USSR built 604 MiG-9s in 11 variants; 12,000 MiG-15s in 17 variants; over 8,000 MiG-17s in 21 variants; over 2,000 MiG-19s in 27 variants; about 10,000 MiG-21s in 32 variants; over 5,000 MiG-23s in 10 variants; over 800 MiG-24s (export MiG-23s) in eight variants; more than 1,200 MiG-25s in 16 variants; some 2,000 MiG-29s; and over 500 MiG-31s. Of these, more than 10,000 continue in service with 40 countries, including slightly under half the CIS.

Withdrawals continue

Russian departures from former satellite states in early 1993 included naval Sukhoi Su-24 'Fencers' of 240th Bomb Regiment from Tukums in Latvia and 170th Bomb Rgt from Suukula in Estonia, the latter being the final Russian air units in that country. In Germany, 'Fencer Es' of 11th Recce Rgt left Welzow on 15 June (the unit's MiG-25 'Foxbats' having already gone), while on the same day MiG-29s of the 31st Fighter Rgt departed Falkenberg, following the similarly-equipped 787th Fighter Rgt which left Finow on 11 May. Completing the latest round of withdrawals, Su-25 'Frogfoots' of 368th Attack Rgt left Demin also on 15 June, but stopped overnight at Templin before clearing German airspace. Opening the prospect of improved relations with Japan, some 40 MiG-23MLD 'Flogger-Ks' were withdrawn from Burevestnik on the island of Etorfu (Iturup) in the Kuril chain, it was announced on 23 July. The southern Kurils were occupied by the USSR in the closing days of World War II and their occupation has been a source of dispute in subsequent years.

Sukhoi Su-30MK

A ground-attack version of the 'Flanker' made its Western debut at Paris in the

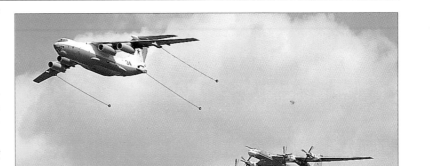

form of the Su-30MK (previously Su-27PU). Although the example displayed was 'converted' from an Su-27UB trainer demonstrator, the two-seat Su-30MK was a formidable spectacle, with 12 weapon pylons for up to eight tonnes of advanced armaments as part of its 33-tonne maximum take-off weight. With aerial refuelling, the aircraft is able to extend its 1,620-nm (3,000-km) range to 3,777 nm (6,990 km), equivalent to 10 hours in the air. Sample weaponry comprised the X-25LD (AS-10 'Karen') laser-guided ASM; X-29L/T (AS-14 'Kedge') laser- or TV-guided ASM; X-31R (AS-17 'Krypton') counter to the West's Patriot SAM; and X-59M (AS-18) TV-guided cruise missile. Additionally, the Su-30MK retains its considerable air-to-air capability with six each of R-27 (AA-10 'Alamo') and R-73E (AA-11 'Archer') AAMs which will soon be capable of replacement by the active radar homing R-77 'AMRAAM-ski'.

Attack helicopter havoc

The protracted Russian attack helicopter competition appeared to have ended in farce after Mil objected to the selection of Kamov's Ka-50 'Hokum' and succeeded in having its Mi-28 'Havoc' ordered for parallel production. The Ka-50 was expected to enter service late in 1993, to

be followed by its former rival in 1995. Both helicopters are seeking export orders, for which reason they appeared at Paris in June, their first joint exhibition at a Western show. Western experts have questioned the wisdom of the original selection in view of the high workload expected of the Ka-50's single occupant. Intriguingly, among countries showing interest in the Ka-50, the US Special Forces have begun negotiations for eight.

Yak trainer chosen

The Yakovlev bureau announced at Paris that its Yak-UTS jet trainer has been selected by the Russian air force against competition from MiG and Sukhoi. Aircraft will be designated Yak-130 and developed in conjunction with Aermacchi.

TAJIKSTAN:

Aircraft orders

First known order for the newly-formed Tajikstan air force was placed for at least 10 Mil Mi-8TBM 'Hip-C' helicopters.

Above and left: The IDF/AF flies a sizeable fleet of C-47s, many on electronic missions. Some have been repainted in a light grey.

Below: Still flying from Ben Gurion in May was the IAI Lavi TD demonstrator, operating on trials in company with a Kfir.

Middle East

LEBANON:

Israeli attacks

Responding to border attacks with Katyusha vehicle-mounted rocket systems, Israel launched a seven-day series of raids, Operation Accountability, on Lebanese territory on 25 July both to seek the elusive launchers and to strike at camps and command posts of the Hizbollah Islamic fundamentalist group. Lockheed F-16 Fighting Falcons and McDonnell Douglas F-4 Phantoms used laser-guided and free-fall bombs, while armed sweeps were made by McDonnell AH-64 and MD500 Defender and Bell AH-1 Cobra armed helicopters. In conjunction with artillery barrages, these measures succeeded in driving large numbers of Lebanese from their villages in the south of the country and swamping Beirut with refugees. The IDF/AF flew an average of 50 sorties per day and had dropped 1,000 bombs by the fifth day of operations.

KUWAIT:

Mirage F1 withdrawal

Spanish officials visited Kuwait on 10 May to negotiate terms for the possible purchase of 14 Mirage F1s which the Kuwait air force withdrew from Nos 18 and 61 Squadrons in July 1993. No direct replacement for the Mirage had been achieved by Kuwait apart from 10 additional McDonnell Douglas F/A-18C Hornets due to be supplied in 1994 to complement the 40 aircraft of Nos 9 and 25

Squadrons, the last of which was scheduled for delivery in December 1993. Kuwait expected to retire the last of its McDonnell Douglas A-4KU Skyhawks in 1993, but was preparing to form No. 19 Squadron with Shorts Tucanos. In storage in the UK since the Iraqi invasion, the aircraft received pre-delivery modifications in early 1993, while Kuwaiti instructors began a conversion course on RAF Tucanos at No. 3 FTS, Cranwell. Other Kuwaiti squadrons in operation during 1993 comprised No. 12 flying BAe Hawks; Nos 31 and 32 with Aérospatiale Pumas; Nos

33 and 34 using Eurocopter Gazelles; No. 41 with Hercules; No. 42 with a DC-9 and MD 83; and No. 62 operating Cougars.

The air force also, belatedly, issued details of its participation in Desert Storm. Skyhawks flew 621 sorties (970.8 hours), Mirage F1s 128 sorties (200.0 hours) and Gazelles 100 sorties (41.9 hours). For the whole period between regrouping in Saudi Arabia and liberation, Skyhawks generated 1,326 sorties and 1,796.8 hours; Mirages 634 and 700.0; Gazelles 203 and 127.3; Cougars 281 and 406.7; and Pumas 218 and 244.3.

Southern Asia

INDIA:

New aircraft deliveries

Developments in military aviation reported during mid-1993 included replacement of the ageing Breguet Alizés of INAS 310 at Dabolim by the first of a planned 24 HAL-built Do 228-201 maritime reconnaissance aircraft. The Antonov An-12 Cub finally departed IAF service after replacement by Ilyushin Il-76

'Candids' in Nos 25 and 44 Squadrons, although the type has been outlived by the ageless Douglas C-47 Dakota, at least three of which are still in use. India received 53 An-12s, of which only four were lost in over 30 years of service. At Hindustan Aeronautics Ltd (HAL), the SEPECAT Jaguar has returned to licensed production after a short break to provide a further 15 aircraft for the IAF's attack squadrons. The order, placed in 1988 but deferred on cost grounds the following year, brings Jaguar

deliveries to 131, including 40 built in the UK but not including the 18 borrowed from the RAF. Following interminable delays, HAL is hoping to bring forward by six months the first flight of its Light Combat Aircraft. Prototype DD1 is now programmed to fly in June 1996.

PAKISTAN:

F-16s remain in storage

A refund was demanded in July for the 11 Lockheed F-16s held in storage at Davis-

Monthan AFB since being built for the PAF. Embargoed as a result of US suspicions that Pakistan is developing nuclear weapons, the aircraft (six F-16As and five F-16Bs) keep company with three Lockheed P-3C Orions on which air force and navy personnel have already completed their training. A follow-on order for 60 more F-16s has not been started. In connection with the arms embargo, Pakistan made approaches to Turkey during May in an attempt to obtain Sikorsky UH-60 Black Hawk utility helicopters from the TAI production line. A successful outcome appears unlikely, as US permission is still required for third-party sales.

Far East

Multi-sensor Defender order

During July, an undisclosed Far Eastern country placed an order for three Pilatus/Britten-Norman Defenders in MSSA (Multi-Sensor Surveillance Aircraft)

configuration. Deliveries, for border and maritime patrol, will begin in the second quarter of 1994. MSSA equipment includes a prominent nose-mounted Westinghouse AN/APG-66 radar (as in F-16 Fighting Falcons, but modified with the addition of a moving target indicator for tracking vehicles) and a Westinghouse WF-360 infra-red camera in the belly.

SOUTH KOREA:

PC-9 requirement stalled

A decision on 7 May by the RoKAF that it would buy an initial batch of 20 Pilatus PC-9s as BAe Hawk lead-in trainers brought about a new round of political breast-beating in Switzerland, where there

is a policy of not exporting combat material to countries which might wish to use it for its intended purpose. The government in Geneva insisted that, as with the South African PC-7 order (which it approved on 2 June), wing hardpoints of any PC-9 sold to Korea should be rendered incapable of carrying weapons. This, of course, is purely for political face-saving reasons, as any competent aircraft engineer can design

Left: *A pair of Operation Warden Harriers lifts off from Incirlik for a sortie over northern Iraq. The Harriers from No. 4 Sqn have been fitted with the 100 per cent LERX; those from No. 3 retain the original.*

Above: *Providing the muscle for the USAF contingent in Turkey for the Provide Comfort detachment are the F-111Fs from the 27th FW at Cannon. This aircraft carries a GBU-24 LGB.*

a counter to such disarmament measures in a matter of moments. Korea was alleged to have appointed FN of Belgium to arm the PC-9s it proposes to buy.

MALAYSIA:

Twin fighter requirement

Combat aircraft from East and West are to re-equip the air force during 1994-96 as a result of orders to be finalised towards the end of 1993. On 29 June, it was officially announced that Malaysia would buy 18 MiG-29M 'Fulcrums' for air defence, at least partly replacing the Northrop F-5E Tiger IIs of 11 and 12 Skuadrons at Butterworth. Additionally, a commitment was made to eight McDonnell Douglas F/A-18D Hornets configured for two-seat attack missions (as per US Marine Corps). Malaysia's aircraft will have the latest standard of equipment, including Hughes AN/APG-73 radar and uprated General Electric F404-402 engines.

More trainers

Twenty MDB Flugtechnik/Datwyler MD3 Swiss Trainers were ordered in July for primary training, presumably as replacements for the BAe Bulldogs used by the Voluntary Pilot Training school at

Simpang. The aircraft will be assembled locally by SME, which has bought the design rights.

TAIWAN:

New Hawkeyes required

Having originally planned to upgrade four USN-surplus Grumman E-2B Hawkeyes for its own use, Taiwan agreed instead to buy four new E-2Cs. These will be to the current (post-1991) USN standard with General Electric AN/APS-145 radar, but the retention of the E-2T designation suggests undisclosed specific modifications as the aircraft. Deliveries will begin in May 1994 for training to start in the US two months later. The remainder will follow in July, September and November 1994 and the force will become operational in August 1995.

Second Hercules order

A repeat batch of 12 Lockheed C-130H Hercules was approved for Taiwan early in 1993 to continue the process of converting the Pingtung-based 6th Troop Carrier & Anti-Submarine Combined Wing from ageing Fairchild C-119s. No. 101 Squadron has already been equipped, and Nos 102 and 103 are expected to follow.

South America

ARGENTINA:

Turbo-Tracker conversions

Following a protracted rebuild, begun when it was delivered to Israel in November 1989, the first Israel Aircraft Industries turboprop S-2UP conversion of Grumman Tracker made its public debut at Paris in June. Powered by Garrett TPE331-15AW engines, 0702 will be followed by the remaining five aircraft of 1ª Escuadrilla Aeronaval Antisubmarina, which are to be converted in Argentina.

BRAZIL:

Super Tucano flies

EMBRAER flew the prototype EMB-312H Super Tucano (PT-ZTV) at Sao José dos Campos on 15 May and a second aircraft (PT-ZTF) two months later. The two are being used to develop new versions of the aircraft for possible use in Brazil as well as for the USAF/USN JPATS competition, in which EMBRAER is teamed with Northrop. Changes from the standard Tucano are considerable and include a 4-ft 6-in (1.37-m) fuselage stretch allied to a strengthened airframe and 1,600-shp (1195-kW) Pratt & Whitney PT6A-68/1 engine with five-bladed propeller.

Lynx purchase

Debt rescheduling by the UK government allowed Brazil to firm up in July its proposed order for more Westland Lynx. Eight Super Lynx will be delivered to the Forca Aéronaval de Marinha from 1996 onwards and six survivors of the nine Lynx Mk 21s supplied in 1978 are to be similarly upgraded for service with the 1° Esquadrao de Helicópteros de Ataque at Rio de Janeiro.

PERU:

Naval aviation expands

Maritime patrol assets will be augmented early in 1994 through a mid-1993 order placed in Brazil for three EMBRAER EMB-111 Bandeirantes. The source of the aircraft will be of interest, as manufacture of the EMB-110/111 has ended. An EMB-120 Brasilia light transport is included in the purchase.

Under the designation HM-1, the Brazilian army operates 36 Eurocopter AS 565UA Panthers from Taubaté. The final 10 were assembled locally by Helibras from kits supplied by Eurocopter.

Central America

MEXICO:

Training changes

Following the delivery to Mexico's navy in 1992 of 13 Maule MX7-180 lightplanes for training, the air force was also reported to be receiving an unknown number during early 1993. The naval Maules are in service with the Escuela Aviación Naval at Badajas, Vera Cruz, replacing Cessna 152s in the Escuadrón Primario, while the school's Escuadrón Avanzado appears to have replaced at least some of its six Beech Barons by four Valmet L-90TPs (originally believed to have gone to the air force). Although delivered only in 1982, the 20 Mudry CAP 10s serving the Escuela Militar de Aviación are also being withdrawn in favour of MX7s.

Two commemoratives from Canada: above is 441 Squadron's Hornet special for the 50th anniversary of D-Day, complete with invasion stripes and 'JE-J' codes for Johnny Johnson, who commanded 126 Wing, and below is 434 Sqn's 50th anniversary bird – 'Schooner 50'.

North America

UNITED STATES:

First C-17 airlifter delivered to US Air Force

The first production Douglas C-17 Globemaster III (89-1192), known as P-6, was delivered to the US Air Force on 14 June 1992. The first C-17 unit will be the 17th Airlift Squadron, part of the 437th Airlift Wing at Charleston AFB, South Carolina, which currently flies the ageing Lockheed C-141B StarLifter. Air Force chief of staff General Merrill ('Tony') McPeak was at the controls of P-6 when it arrived at Charleston. Plans call for the first squadron of 12 C-17s to be operational with the 437th by the beginning of 1995.

P-6 is the sixth production aircraft and the seventh built in all. Five other Globemasters – T-1, the test aircraft, and production aeroplanes P-l through P-4 – are currently in the flight test programme at Edwards AFB, California. They have recorded more than 1,450 flying hours on more than 400 missions since T-1's first flight on 15 September 1991. P-5, the fifth production C-17, is undergoing simulated lightning strike tests at the Naval Air Warfare Center, Patuxent River, Maryland.

The first operational Globemaster is painted in Air Mobility Command's recently-adopted grey paint scheme and nicknamed 'Spirit of Charleston' (although not yet painted with the yellow tail flash and palmetto tree found on Charleston's C-141Bs). P-6 had made its first flight only on 8 May 1993. This C-17 made an appearance at Air Mobility Command's annual competition, the Rodeo, at Little Rock AFB, Arkansas, on 10-11 June. A subsequent stop was made at Pope AFB, North Carolina where General McPeak boarded the C-17 for its delivery flight to Charleston.

At the delivery ceremony were South Carolina Senators Strom Thurmond and Ernest Hollings, Air Mobility Command chief General Ronald Fogleman, and 437th commander Brigadier General Thomas Mikolajcik. Before the C-17 delivery, Mikolajcik acknowledged that "we're going to have to see a resolution of the structural problem before we can bring [the C-17] on line," referring to questions about the strength of the aircraft which arise from the destruction of a static test article. Since then, Douglas has started to repair the static test article, added 700 lb (317 kg) to the aircraft wing (aluminium stringer segments and steel strap reinforcements), and stiffened ribs and spars in several areas of the wing. This will add one per cent to the wing's total weight of 60,000 lb (27215 kg) and is unlikely to raise new questions about the weight.

Mobility 'Rodeo' held at Little Rock AFB

The 440th Airlift Wing, Air Force Reserve, a C-130 Hercules operator based in Wisconsin, took the best overall wing title in AMC's Rodeo '93 competition. Held at Little Rock AFB, Arkansas, during 7-12 June 1993, Rodeo has been an annual event since 1979. The 1993 event was the 13th competition and the first not to be held at Pope AFB, North Carolina, which is no longer an AMC base.

Rodeo '93 was also the second competition to be held since AMC was formed on 1 June 1992. The event came on the heels of a USAF announcement that its fleet of C-130 Hercules, one of the most numerous and busiest aircraft in AMC, is to be transferred to Air Combat Command on 1 October 1993.

Rodeo '93 brought together 69 teams, representing active-duty US Air Force, US Air Force Reserve, Air National Guard and US Marine Corps units, and 10 other nations. Numerous other awards went to US and foreign operators of C-130, C-141B, and Alenia G222 aircraft. The British team came with C-130 Hercules from RAF Lyneham.

In 1993, Rodeo participants included 66 aircraft, 69 teams and 1,500 people (the figures for 1992 were 54, 48 and 991). C-5 Galaxies competed for the first time. Tanker crews were teamed up with airlift competitors, except for KC-10 Extenders, which were paired with other KC-10s. A readiness training exercise, Rodeo is designed to emphasise the ability to use aerial refuelling operations and airdrop delivery methods to resupply ground forces. Aircrews competed for the best scores when air refuelling cargo aircraft, and when airdropping Army paratroopers and container delivery system loads onto drop zones near Little Rock. The competition also included short field landings, cargo loading, aircraft navigation, and (for KC-135 crews) response to wartime alert procedures.

The 1994 Rodeo will be held at McChord AFB, Washington, without the C-130 Hercules which have been a familiar sight at the competitions.

VIP Boeing VC-137 retired in Andrews ceremony

In a ceremony at Andrews AFB, Maryland, on 14 June 1993, the US Air Force retired a Boeing VC-137B VIP transport (58-6970) after nearly a quarter-century of service. Based on the Boeing 707-320B airliner and originally designated VC-137A, ship 58-6970 became operational on 12 June 1959 and was the first jet aircraft in USAF inventory specifically designed for the transport of personnel.

Though not earmarked as a presidential aircraft, this VC-137 carried American chief executives on numerous trips from 26 August 1959, when Dwight D. Eisenhower on a European trip became the first president to travel by jet. Presidents Kennedy, Johnson, Nixon and Bush travelled on the aircraft.

Now that two VC-137C models have been released from White House duties due to a shift of the presidential commitment to the Boeing VC-25A (or Boeing 747-200B), it became possible to retire 58-6970, which is destined for the US Air Force Museum in Dayton, Ohio.

VISTA F-16

The VISTA (Variable Stability In-flight Simulator Test Aircraft) F-16, equipped with a General Electric axisymmetric, pitch/yaw thrust-vectoring engine nozzle, began flight tests at Fort Worth on 2 July 1993, with Joe Sweeney and Major Mike Gerzanics making the 26-minute first flight. The VISTA/F-16 is a variable-stability F-16D developed originally to replace the USAF's NT-33A (the USAF's oldest operational aircraft, hence its acronym). Tests with the thrust-vectoring system are to continue at Edwards AFB, California, in a five-month programme to assess nozzle performance.

S/MTD F-15B Eagle resumes flying

The McDonnell S/MTD (STOL Manoeuvrability Technology Demonstrator) F-15B Eagle resumed flying on June 1993 at St Louis after 22 months in stor-

A recent participant in a Red Flag exercise at Nellis was the 416th Bomb Wing, flying B-52Hs from Griffiss AFB, New York.

An operational squadron has returned to Nellis AFB in the form of the 561st FS, one of two CONUS squadrons which survive with the F-4G 'Wild Weasel'.

age, flown by test pilots Gary Jennings (in the front seat, making his first flight in the aircraft) and the very experienced Larry Walker in the back seat. The flight was one hour long and the aircraft reached a speed of Mach 1.5.

The modified F-15B is serving as ACTIVE (Advanced Control Technology for Integrated Vehicles) testbed in a joint USAF/NASA programme to assess the aerodynamic effects of axisymmetric, pitch/yaw thrust-vectoring engine nozzles. The S/MTD F-15B is currently equipped with conventional nozzles and will begin a six-12 month flight test programme with the thrust-vectoring nozzles in October 1994. F100-P-229s will be fitted for further tests.

US Navy and Marine Corps squadron changes

HS-9 'Sea Griffins', a Sikorsky SH-3H Sea King squadron at NAS Jacksonville, Florida, was disestablished on 30 April 1993 after almost 17 years of service. VS-

Below: The 23rd Wing at Pope AFB has recently added the 74th FS flying the F-16C/D. Its other two squadrons fly the A-10 and C-130.

38 'Red Griffins' at NAS North Island, California, began to convert to the Lockheed S-3B Viking from the S-3A model, with the first aircraft delivered in July 1993. Earlier, the squadron made the US Navy's final carrier deployment in the S-3A. VMFA(AW)-224 'Bengals' moved in March 1993 to MCAS Beaufort, South Carolina, from the squadron's former location at MCAS Cherry Point, North Carolina, in conjunction with transition to the F/A-18D. VMFA-323 'Death Rattlers' at MCAS El Toro, California, are completing transition to the McDonnell F/A-18C Hornet from the F/A-18A model, having received their first of the newer aircraft in April 1993.

The Marine Corps plans to consolidate CH-46E Sea Knight training at MCAS New River, North Carolina. HMT-204 will assume all of the training following deactivation of HMT-301 at MCAS El Toro, California, on 31 December 1993. HMH-772 'Flying Armadillos', a Marine Corps reserve squadron at NAS Willow Grove, Pennsylvania, has begun operating Sikorsky RH-53D Sea Stallion helicopters, replacing its CH-53D transport models. The RH-53D, which is being replaced by the MH-53E in the Navy's two reserve mine countermeasures (HM) squadrons, has an air refuelling capability.

VFC-12 'Fighting Omars', a Reserve adversary squadron at NAS Oceana, Virginia, flew its last mission in the Douglas A-4F ('Super Fox') Skyhawk on 16 July 1993. The squadron is transitioning to the

Above: One of the few remaining Phantoms in USAF service was chosen to celebrate the type's 35th birthday in spectacular style.

McDonnell F/A-18 Hornet.

VMO-1, the last active-duty Marine Corps operator of the North American OV-10D(Plus) Bronco, was disestablished at MCAS New River, North Carolina, on 31 July 1993 after 50 years of service. This leaves VMO-4, a Reserve OV-10D(Plus) squadron in Atlanta, Georgia, as the only remaining American operator of the Bronco. VMO-4 is scheduled to deactivate 31 March 1994. Though not all of its members agree, the Marine Corps claims that the forward air control mission can be taken over by F/A-18D Hornet strike fighters and AH-1W Super Cobra helicopter gunships.

AH-64D Longbow Apache

The McDonnell Douglas AH-64D Longbow Apache made its first flight with the Longbow fire-control radar installed on 20 August 1993 with Ed Wilson as pilot and Larry Proper as test engineer. The flight lasted 80 minutes. The radar is the key component of a system which will enable the Longbow Apache to scan a battlefield, identify and prioritise targets, and attack them from stand-off range. Two other aircraft are flying in the Longbow Apache configuration but without the actual radar installed. Following a 1 September 1993 roll-out ceremony, the Longbow Apache was scheduled to be transferred to Westinghouse in Baltimore, Maryland, for eight months of software evaluation and refinement. McDonnell Douglas has cancelled long-standing plans to sell its Mesa, Arizona, helicopter facility and will now remain in the helicopter business.

A-6 retirement

The US Marine Corps retired its last Grumman A-6 Intruder in an April 1993

ceremony at MCAS Cherry Point, North Carolina. An A-6E Intruder (BuNo. 161681, coded EA-500) of All-Weather Attack Squadron VMA(AW)-332 'Moonlighters' was the Marines' last example of the long-serving medium attack aircraft. The Marines gave up their Intruder fleet in an economy move aimed at fielding an all-Hornet force. The redesignated VMFA(AW)-332 is moving to MCAS Beaufort, South Carolina, where it is re-equipping with the F/A-18D.

Tanker and airlift reorganisation plans unveiled

Both Air Combat Command and Air Mobility Command have announced plans to restructure their airlift and tanker operations. Ahead of the plan, ACC inactivated its 2nd Air Force at Beale AFB, California, on 30 June, with the reconnaissance and airborne control assets being transferred to the 12th Air Force on 1 July. The 2nd Air Force reformed next day under Air Education and Training Command.

The Air Force announced on 27 May that ACC will receive an additional numbered Air Force by 1 October, as the Command will gain responsibility for the intra-theatre airlift role. The additional duty will see the transfer from AMC to ACC of the majority of active-duty C-130E and H models of the Hercules that are based within the continental USA. In addition, ACC will assume command of Little Rock AFB, Arkansas. The move follows recognition of the type's intra-theatre airlift role during combat, which will be co-ordinated more effectively by ACC.

The transfer will involve the C-130Es of the 314th AW at Little Rock AFB and 317th AW at Pope AFB, North Carolina, together with the C-130Hs of the 463rd AW at Dyess AFB, Texas. At Pope AFB the 317th AW inactivated on 16 July, along with the 40th ALS. The 40th's sister squadron, the 41st ALS, has been reassigned to the 23rd Wing, with C-130Es of the 40th ALS being redistributed between the 2nd and 41st ALSs. The 40th ALS will probably be resurrected to replace the 2nd ALS in due course, to preserve the former squadron as a flying unit.

Dyess AFB is making plans to amalgamate the C-130Hs of the 463rd AW into the resident 96th Wing by 1 October, enabling the 463rd to inactivate. The 96th Wing is likely to change identity also, as the Air Force has announced that the unit

Below: Two VC-25A aircraft undertake the Special Air Mission airlift task, carrying the President and his staff.

Regular US Navy squadrons are taking over more of the aggressor task from dedicated units. Above is a VFA-37 Hornet carrying ALQ-167 jamming pods, while below is a VFA-303 aircraft in aggressor scheme.

is to become the 7th Wing, which was formerly at Carswell AFB, Texas, until inactivated earlier in 1993. The change is yet another case of wishing to preserve units with a distinguished history. The composition of the 314th AW at Little Rock AFB will remain unchanged, but will report to the 8th Air Force within Air Combat Command. Hercules stationed at Pope and Dyess AFBs will adopt tailcodes 'FT' and 'DY' of the resident units, while those at Little Rock will apply 'LK', which was the unit identifier employed by the 314th AW until 1974.

The transfer involves 25,000 active-duty and reserve personnel and includes the 13 Air Force Reserve and 19 Air National Guard C-130 squadrons that will have ACC rather than AMC as their gaining command when mobilised. The move will see the return of tailcodes and tactical style serials to the vast majority of the airlift-dedicated C-130s. The three active-duty C-130 units were previously operated under tactical assignment, having been part of Tactical Air Command until December 1974 when they became part of Military Airlift Command and ultimately AMC.

Air Mobility Command inactivated one of its three numbered Air Forces on 1 July and reassigned its assets to the remaining two. The unit in question was the 22nd Air Force at Travis AFB, California, which controlled all AMC flying wings in the western half of the United States. In its place, the 15th Air Force has relocated north from March AFB. The reassignment is part of an overall reorganisation of tanker bases, and is in advance of the rundown of active-duty operations at March AFB.

The Command has already announced plans to form two airlift 'gateways' which will co-ordinate transatlantic and transpacific operations. The West Coast will be served by Travis AFB, which will add KC-10As from March AFB to the resident C-5s and C-141s. The East Coast gateway was to have been located at Plattsburgh AFB, New York, involving the transfer of C-141Bs from the 438th AW from McGuire AFB, New Jersey, enabling the

latter to close. The plan has run into problems as General H. T. Johnson, the former CinC MAC and now a member of the Base Closure and Realignment Commission, used his influence to reverse the Pentagon's decision to build up Plattsburgh AFB at the expense of McGuire AFB. President Clinton approved the decision, which was part of the revised base closure package, on 2 July. Provided Congress does not make amendments within the 45-day approval/rejection period, McGuire AFB will become the major gateway on the eastern seaboard at the expense of Plattsburgh AFB. Should this become a reality and Plattsburgh AFB close, the entire New England region will be devoid of an active air force base.

Despite the foregoing problem, AMC has taken its tanker reorganisation plan even further, as the Command wishes to create three KC-135R 'hubs' at Fairchild AFB, Washington, Grand Forks AFB, North Dakota, and McConnell AFB, Kansas. At present AMC has four squadrons flying the KC-10A and 15 operating the KC-135A/R at 13 bases (excluding the 305th ARW which relinquished its complement to the reserves during the summer of 1993). Under the new plan the three bases would expand their complement greatly, with in excess of 200 KC-135Rs being assigned.

The Air Force has begun preparations for this reorganisation with the announcement of its intention to relocate six B-1Bs from the 319th BW at Grand Forks AFB in mid-1994, with the remainder joining the 28th BW at Ellsworth AFB, South Dakota, later in the year. In their place will come KC-135Rs of the 509th ARS from Griffiss AFB, New York, and 906th ARS at Minot AFB, North Dakota, to join those already in residence with the 905th ARS. At McConnell AFB the B-1Bs of 384th BW will be redistributed, although some will remain for assignment

This CT-43A is assigned to the 58th Airlift Squadron for USAFE transport duties. The squadron is now assigned to the 86th Wing.

to the 184th FG (becoming the 184th BG) of the Kansas ANG. In their place, the KC-135Rs of the resident 384th ARS will be joined by others, including the 28th ARS from Ellsworth AFB. Fairchild AFB has already been earmarked as one of the major bomber bases of ACC, with the 92nd BW operating the B-52H. In addition, the 116th ARS Washington ANG is to become a bombardment squadron with the B-52H. This particular installation could become exceptionally overcrowded, with more than 100 bombers and tankers assigned.

Since its formation, ACC has operated three squadrons of KC-135A/Qs within the 2nd Wing at Barksdale AFB, Louisiana, the 9th Wing at Beale AFB and the 96th Wing at Dyess AFB. These aircraft will be transferred to AMC or retired from service on 1 October, enabling their air refuelling squadrons to inactivate. The only active-duty tankers resident in the USA that will not be assigned to AMC at that time will be the KC-10As operated by composite wings of the 4th Wing at Seymour Johnson AFB, North Carolina, and the KC-135Rs of the 366th Wing at Mountain Home AFB, Idaho. The concentration of KC-10/KC-135s at just five AMC bases will end tanker operations at Barksdale AFB, Ellsworth AFB, South Dakota, Griffiss AFB, New York, Grissom AFB, Indiana, K. I. Sawyer AFB, Michigan, Loring AFB, Maine, Malmstrom AFB, Montana, Minot AFB, North Dakota, and Robins AFB, Georgia. Some of these installations have already been earmarked for closure.

USAFE unit news

The Air Force announced its intention to close the two F-15 Eagle bases currently under 17th Air Force control. The 36th FW at Bitburg AB, Germany, will relocate its two squadrons, moving one the short distance to Spangdahlem, while the other will join the 48th FW at Lakenheath. The 53rd FS will be assigned to the 52nd FW, replacing one of the F-16 Falcon units that will relocate elsewhere. The 22nd FS will move to Lakenheath commencing November 1993, adopting the identity of the 493rd FS. The two F-15E squadrons currently in residence at Lakenheath are the 492nd and 494th FSs, so the reactivation of the 493rd FS is particularly appropriate due to its Gulf War record.

A total of 21 F-15C/Ds will be assigned to Lakenheath, although deliveries will be from the USA to ensure the squadron is equipped with FY 1986 aircraft to the highest modification state. The initial pair is due in November to enable maintenance personnel to familiarise themselves

with the new equipment and for operating procedures to be established. The remaining 19 will be delivered between January and May 1994. These aircraft will be drawn from the 59th FS, 33rd FW at Eglin AFB, Florida, which will in turn re-equip with those at present operated by the 22nd FS which are from FY 1979 and FY 1980 production. Once the squadrons have completed their move the 36th FW will inactivate and flying activities at Bitburg will cease.

The second USAFE Eagle base to close will be Soesterberg in the Netherlands, which currently houses the 32nd FS, 32nd FG operating the F-15A/B. The aircraft at Soesterberg have received the Multi-Stage Improvement Programme (MSIP) that includes upgrading the Hughes APG-63 radar to APG-70 standard, and provision for the AIM-120A AMRAAM, among a host of other enhancements. The F-15A/Bs of the 32nd FS will relocate to Otis ANGB, joining the 101st FS, Massachusetts ANG, commencing early 1994.

Air Force Chief of Staff had hoped to relocate the identity of the 20th FW and its three flying units – the 55th, 77th and 79th FSs – elsewhere in Europe following their inactivation at Upper Heyford by the end of 1993 (General McPeak had been a young lieutenant with the 79th TFS during the early 1960s and later occupied a more senior post with the 20th TFW). An announcement earlier in 1993 that the 20th FW would replace the 52nd FW at Spangdahlem AB, Germany, early in 1994 was met with howls of protest by personnel at the latter base; the objections were such that the plan was quickly rescinded. Undeterred, the general has announced that he wishes the 20th FW *et al* to assume the identity of the 363rd FW at Shaw AFB, South Carolina.

As stated, the 52nd FW will retain its wing number, although some squadron identities will change to retain some of the units displaced by the inactivation of the 36th FW. The 53rd FS will move from Bitburg with their F-15C/Ds and join the 23rd and 81st FSs equipped with the F-16C/D. The A-10A-equipped 510th FS will be redesignated as the 22nd FS, due to the latter squadron having a lengthy and illustrious history of operations within USAFE.

55th Wing expands role

The 55th Wing has begun to make preparations to perform photographic reconnaissance sorties of the former Soviet Union with the agreement of the latter nation. The sorties will be flown to implement the 1992 Open Skies Treaty by three OC-

The 'Bucaneros' of the Puerto Rico ANG fly the ADF version of the F-16A Block 15.

135Bs that are being modified from a trio of WC-135Bs formerly employed to conduct weather reconnaissance. The three aircraft will be fitted with photographic sensors including a KA-91B panoramic camera, two KS-87B oblique-mounted framing cameras and a KS-87B vertical-mounted framing camera along the underside of the fuselage. Internally, the weather-monitoring stations will be replaced by consoles for sensor operators and flight-following operatives. Improved navigation equipment is being installed, along with accommodation for 38 aircrew, sensor operators and observers.

The first aircraft to receive the modification is 61-2674, which commenced evaluation by the 4950th Test Wing at Wright-Patterson AFB, Ohio, at the end of May 1993. The aircraft is due for delivery to the 55th Wing by 1 October and will commence operations shortly afterwards. Mildenhall has been suggested as one of the forward operating bases, with the crew composed of US personnel with Russian officers aboard to act as interpreters and to oversee each sortie. In the meantime, the 55th Wing has received former 10th ACCS WC-135B 61-2667, which has been redesignated a TC-135B to conduct crew training for the specialised role. The TC-135B paid its first visit to Europe on 10 August. The OC-135B, together with other NATO and former Warsaw Pact aircraft, will be employed to overfly nations which are signatories of the Treaty.

USAF air training reorganised

The Air Force implemented its reorganised training system on 1 July with the activation of Air Education and Training Command (AETC) to replace Air Training Command. AETC has its headquarters at Randolph AFB, Texas, in the same building as the former ATC and retained ATC's commander General Henry Viccellio Jr. The Command has assumed a considerably expanded responsibility to encompass the entire spectrum of education, from the commencement of basic training by enlisted and officer new recruits to the time when the fully qualified serviceman is assigned to an opera-

An Army rarity is the Short C-23B. This example flies with the Connecticut AVCRAD, and sports Desert Storm artwork.

tional squadron. In addition, the Command undertakes all manner of education and retraining of existing Air Force personnel.

AETC established two numbered Air Forces on 1 July, with the 19th AF at Randolph AFB responsible for the six flying training wings that were joined by four additional units transferred from ACC and AMC. These latter four units are the 58th FW at Luke AFB, Arizona, with the F-16C/D, plus a small number of F-16A/Bs for training overseas pilots; the 325th Fighter Wing at Tyndall AFB, Florida, with the F-15A/B/C/D Eagles (with plans to replace the F-15A/B versions with additional C and D models); and the 542nd CTW at Kirtland AFB, New Mexico, operating various Special Forces and combat rescue helicopters together with examples of the HC-130P and MC-130E. The fourth unit to transfer is the 97th AMW at Altus AFB, Oklahoma, which trains C-5B and C-141B aircrew.

The wing also operated two squadrons of KC-135Rs until 1 July when the tankers were reassigned to the 457th Operations Group, which is subordinate to the 19th ARW, thereby remaining under AMC control. The 97th AMW was the KC-135 aircrew training unit, although the reassignment appears to have altered plans for AETC to conduct this duty at Altus AFB. The four additional units have been redesignated as flying training wings.

The 2nd Air Force was reactivated at Keesler AFB, Mississippi, on 1 July with responsibility for technical training at six locations. The technical training groups at Goodfellow AFB, Texas, and Keesler AFB have been upgraded to wing status with the reformation of the 17th and 81st Training Wings on 1 July. The 81st TW at Keesler became a flying unit on 1 July with the transfer of four C-21As of the 375th FTS from Scott AFB, Illinois, to train Learjet aircrew. The 4315th CCTS at Vandenberg AFB, California, which was the primary unit conducting ICBM training under SAC and latterly ACC, became

a part of AETC on 1 July and was redesignated the 392nd Space and Missile Training Squadron at the same time.

The expansion of the Specialized Undergraduate Pilot Training (SUPT) programme continues with the 12th FTW at Randolph AFB and the 64th FTW at Reese AFB, Texas, both having one squadron equipped with the Beech T-1A Jayhawk. The 47th FTW at Laughlin AFB, Texas, commenced receiving their complement of 39 T-1As in mid-1993, and will be followed by the 71st FTW at Vance AFB, Oklahoma, which is due to effect deliveries from mid-1994. Further equipment changes in the pipeline include the replacement of the T-41A/C Mescaleros of the 1st FSS at Hondo Airport, Texas, with 28 Slingsby T-3As in mid-1994, at the same time that the 557th FTS at the Air Force Academy replaces their 45 T-41As with the new Enhanced Flight Screener.

A/F-X and MRF cancelled

The Pentagon's Bottom-Up Review, released in September 1993, calls for cancellation of the A/F-X (originally AX) and MRF (multi-role fighter) aircraft projects. The A/F-X project began as a next-generation, carrier-based strike aircraft for the US Navy, which relies heavily on ageing Grumman A-6 Intruders. The MRF was to be the US Air Force's replacement for the Lockheed F-16 Fighting Falcon. Pentagon acquisition chief John M. Deutch ruled that future fighter/attack programmes must be jointly developed by the two services, and set 1 November 1993 as deadline for a Joint Advanced Strike Tech-

nology programme that would support meeting the two services' operational requirements for next-generation fighter/strike aircraft. Despite cancellation of the programme, plans survive for an A/F-X demonstrator aircraft to be built and evaluated by the Advanced Projects Research Agency (ARPA).

B-1B bombers circle globe

Two Rockwell B-1B Lancer bombers of the 28th Bombardment Wing, Ellsworth AFB, South Dakota, made an around-the-world flight 11-14 August 1993 to demonstrate long-distance projection of conventional bombing power. The two bombers changed crews at Diego Garcia in the Indian Ocean, their halfway point on the 47-hour flight.

Boeing B-52H modified for conventional role

In June 1993, the first Boeing B-52H Stratofortress to be modified for conventional bombing duties was delivered to Boeing's Wichita, Kansas, division for modification with conventional enhancement items. The programme calls for the transfer of the conventional capability of B-52Gs, which are being retired, to the B-52H, which until recently had been assigned a nuclear stand-off mission only. The modification will enable the B-52H to accommodate Have Nap and Harpoon and the universal bomb bay adapter.

This 'new' A-4M 'Mike' adversary flies with VF-126 at Miramar.

Right: Not the USAF's latest bomber, but a Cessna T-37 assigned to the 2nd Bomb Wing to provide additional flying time for bomber and tanker pilots.

Operation Deny Flight

In an attempt to contain the fighting in Bosnia, NATO implemented a 'No-Fly Zone' over the republic, policed by Europe-based fighters. This has at least made the beleaguered population safe from air attack, while a naval blockade has stemmed the flow of arms into the region. Here we review the NATO operations, and their successes.

"The skies over Bosnia are ours — Operation Deny Flight has been a great success," declared a NATO spokesman six weeks after the first USAF F-15C Eagle took off on the first combat air patrol over the civil-war-ravaged former Yugoslav republic.

To enforce the United Nations ban on flights by military aircraft in the air space of Bosnia-Herzegovina, NATO aircraft began flying round-the-clock combat air patrols (CAP) at noon GMT on 12 April 1993. The enforcement of the ban was prompted by a bombing raid by three Bosnian Serb An-2 aircraft on a Muslim village near

An F-15C launches from Aviano AB past a parked RAF Sentry. The AWACS contingent has been vital to the monitoring of Bosnian airspace throughout Operation Deny Flight.

the besieged Muslim town of Srebrenica on 15 March 1993. This attack, and further Bosnian-Serb helicopter activity near Maglaj on 4 April, finally snapped the patience of the UN after some 500 violations since the UN ordered the air space of Bosnia-Herzegovina to be closed to military aircraft on 9 October 1992. NATO Airborne Early Warning Force (NAEW) Boeing E-3 Sentry AWACS aircraft then began Operation Sky Monitor on 16 October to monitor air activity over Bosnia. The AWACS initially flew in an orbit over the Adriatic Sea, but two weeks later in an unprecedented show of East-West military co-operation the NATO aircraft established a second orbit over Hungarian air space to look deep into Bosnia and Serbia.

'No-Fly Zone'

With the AWACS now providing accurate information on air activity over Bosnia, NATO planners were able to begin developing contingency plans for enforcing the 'No-Fly Zone' (NFZ) should the UN decide to escalate its involvement. After much political debate the Serbian offensive against Srebrenica in March finally forced the UN to act. NATO was asked to enforce the NFZ, with the only aircraft allowed to fly over Bosnia being UN relief flights and other flights approved by the UN Protection Force (UNPROFOR).

NATO Supreme Allied Commander Europe (SACEUR) General John Shalikashvili ordered Admiral Mike Boorda, Commander-in-Chief

Adding a new dimension to the familiar multi-national peacekeeping operations of late is Turkey, which sent 18 F-16C/Ds to Ghedi. These operate with four AIM-9Ls.

AWACS support has come from NATO, France and the United Kingdom. The latter maintains a three-aircraft detachment at Aviano, and patrols both in the Adriatic and over Hungary.

Allied Forces Southern Europe (AFSOUTH), to execute Operation Deny Flight. Admiral Boorda was ideally placed for this mission because since late February he had been commanding the US Joint Task Force Provide Promise, which was air-dropping supplies to Muslim enclaves in eastern Bosnia, such as Srebrenica, Zepa and Gorazde.

Fighter contingent

A number of allied countries also offered to provide aircraft to enforce the ban and by 12 April the necessary forces were in place at Italian air bases or afloat in the Adriatic. Not surprisingly, the Americans provided a strong contingent, including 12 F-15C Eagles of the 53rd Fighter Squadron from Bitburg's 36th Fighter Wing, which deployed to Aviano in northern Italy. F-14A Tomcat and F/A-18C Hornet fighter aircraft based on the USS *Theodore Roosevelt* were also made available to NATO.

The Royal Netherlands air force (RNLAF) dispatched 12 F-16A/B Fighting Falcons air-superiority aircraft, of 315 Squadron from Twen-the, and six F-16A(R) photo-reconnais-sance aircraft, of 306 Squadron, to Verona-Villafranca. France completed the initial Deny Flight fighter

Above: In addition to its large AWACS commitment, the RAF sent Tornado F.Mk 3s to help man the CAP stations. They are based at Gioia del Colle.

Right: A Turkish F-16C approaches a USAF KC-135 for tanking. The Turkish pilots had little practice of long CAPs and inflight refuelling, so a short work-up was needed before they could begin operational sorties.

force by deploying 10 Mirage 2000C fighters, of EC 5 from Orange, and four Mirage F1CR photo-reconnaissance aircraft of 33 ER from Strasbourg, to Cervia near Rimini and Istrana near Venice respectively. A Mirage 2000C was lost on the first night of Deny Flight after a problem during air refuelling, but the pilot was recovered safely from the Adriatic by a French navy Lynx helicopter from the frigate *Cassard*.

Vital support for the operation was provided by the US naval air station at Sigonella, on Sicily, by a five-strong detachment of American KC-135R

Right: France was in the first round of nations to supply aircraft for Deny Flight. The sharp end of the detachment were 10 Mirage 2000Cs, supported by Mirage F1CRs, E-3F Sentry and C-135FR tankers.

Below: The F-15Cs carried a three-missile mix, comprising Sparrows, Sidewinders and AMRAAMs. In June they were replaced by 52nd FW F-16s.

Above: The Mirage 2000Cs are from EC 2/5 at Orange, deployed to Cervia. One of these aircraft was lost on the first night with technical problems.

AWACS operations are vital to Deny Flight, as many of the transgressions are made by light aircraft or helicopters. These controllers are on board an RAF Sentry.

Above: Alongside the US and France, it was the Netherlands which initiated fighter operations, flying from Villafranca. Both Twenthe squadrons are now involved, 313 and 315.

tanker aircraft from the 100th Air Refueling Wing, at RAF Mildenhall in Britain, to refuel US and Dutch fighters. The aircraft were Air Mobility Command machines from the 19th and 380th Air Refueling Wings and crews came from a number of units. All were on temporary duty (TDY) to the USAF's European Tanker Task Force. Some KC-135Rs were equipped with drogue refuelling attachments to allow them to refuel US Navy Hornets, Intruders and Tomcats. Whenever French aircraft required refuelling, a C-135FR tanker from ERV 93 would be tasked from the unit's detachment base at Istres on the Riviera.

Multinational AEW coverage

NATO's AWACS force continued to provide surveillance, command and control support over Bosnia. NAEW E-3A aircraft, supported by French E-3Fs and RAF E-3Ds plus US Navy E-2C Hawkeyes, set up a shift system to provide blanket coverage of the theatre of operations with two orbits in place around the clock. French aircraft of EDA 36 operated from either that unit's home base at Avord or Trapani in Sicily. The RAF's 8 Squadron machines set up a three-aircraft detachment at Aviano and also occasionally

operated from Trapani. At any one time six NATO AWACS were supporting Deny Flight from either their home base at Geilenkirken, Germany, or Aviano, Trapani and Preveza, Greece. Between 8 November 1992 and 21 May 1993, the RAF AWACS detachment at Aviano flew some 248 operational sorties in support of Operations Sky Monitor and Deny Flight. Normally the British AWACS crews spent three weeks in Italy before rotating back to the UK. Average sortie length was eight and a half hours.

Satellite communications equipment and personnel from the USAF's 603rd Mobile Command and Control Unit, normally based at Sembach, Germany, deployed to Aviano to help support the operation. The unit's equipment merged information from AWACS and other sources to provide NATO commanders at Vicenza with real-time information on air and surface activity in and near Bosnia.

CAP stations

To dominate the skies over Bosnia, two CAP stations were established, one in the north covering the Banja Luka/Tuzla area and the other over the Mostar/Sarajevo area. Pairs of fighters were on station round-the-clock with the aid of inflight refuelling from tanker aircraft which flew in a 24-hour track near the Croatian city of Split, on the Adriatic Coast.

Typical fighter missions usually lasted four to five hours. After take-off and an hour-long transit to their CAP station the fighters spent just over an hour on station before taking on fuel from a tanker. After a further hour on station the fighters needed to refuel again to allow them to make it back to their home base, after handing over to a new pair of fighters. A pair of fighters generally flew racetrack patterns waiting for the AWACS, using the callsign 'Magic' to report contacts. If these turned out to be UN flights they were left alone, but unauthorised aircraft were pursued with a vengeance.

Locating low-flying targets in the mountainous terrain over Bosnia proved difficult even for the 'all-powerful' AWACS. RAF E-3D crews admitted that they sometimes had problems tracking targets deep in valleys. US F-15C pilots even took to mounting telescopic sights, called 'Eagle Eye', in their cockpits to help them identify low-flying targets.

Rules of engagement

Great secrecy still surrounds the exact rules of engagement in force but it is understood that pilots first had to visually and then positively identify contacts. Radar-only contacts were termed 'Probable Air or Ground Detected Violations', but if the pilots were able to identify the contact as an illegal military flight it was termed an 'Air Detected Violation'. It is understood that armed combat aircraft could be attacked if they were a threat but unarmed transports or helicopters had to be forced to land. By 15 May some 22 probable violations had been detected and four positive identifications made. The first of these was made on the 19 April when a Bosnian-Serb Gazelle helicopter was forced to land by a USAF F-15C near Banja Luka. On 14 May the Eagles were in action when they spotted two more Bosnian-Serb Gazelles near Derventa but they landed as soon as the F-15Cs started to take an interest in them. A fourth Gazelle was forced down later in the day by the Eagles near Prnjavor. RAF Tornados reportedly forced a Croatian Mi-8 to land near Novi-Travnik on 13 May, and UNPROFOR troops found 20,000 rounds of ammunition on board. A previous attempt by RAF Tornados to intercept a contact near Doboj on 29 April was unsuccessful after the fighters could not make a visual identification.

The total violations had risen to 116 air detected, 25 probable and 10 positive ground violations by 2 August. NATO spokesman Major Steve Headley, USAF, said in June that the violations had involved helicopters in areas away from battle zones. "We've not seen any tactical jets," he said. During the first five months of Deny Flight the Serbian air force had made no attempt to interfere in NATO operations, according to US Navy pilots on board the USS *Theodore Roosevelt*. By 2 August some 5,265 fighter, tanker and AWACS sorties had been flown by NATO forces during Deny Flight, with some 3,800 personnel from nine alliance countries being involved.

By April 1993 UN and western air operations over Bosnia were becoming very intense, with more than 20 relief flights a day being flown into

Below: U-2Rs from the 9th Reconnaissance Wing have been highly active in the Bosnian theatre. This is a 'Senior Span' aircraft with satellite communications link.

the besieged capital Sarajevo and nightly airdrop flights by up to nine USAF C-130 Hercules, French and German C.160 Transalls to eastern Bosnia. US Navy E-2Cs, fighter and EW aircraft supported the airdrop missions. UNPROFOR was also using Ukrainian An-32 and Il-76 transport aircraft to move its commanders, personnel and equipment into Sarajevo from Zagreb in Croatia, Belgrade in Serbia, and Split. British Fleet Air Arm Sea King HC.Mk 4s of 845 Naval Air Squadron and French army aviation Pumas and Gazelles were operating from Tuzla to evacuate wounded Muslims from Srebrenica during March and April. The white-painted British and French helicopters were later involved in other casualty evacuation missions to other Muslim enclaves in central Bosnia, and in late July evacuated wounded Spanish UN soldiers from Mostar.

To co-ordinate these activities NATO,

Below: All fighter missions have required refuelling, and for US, Dutch and Turkish aircraft this has been supplied by KC-135Rs operating from Sigonella. The aircraft were initially provided by the 19th (illustrated) and 380th Wings.

Above: 53rd Fighter Squadron Eagles prepare to launch. Deny Flight has certainly driven jets away from the battle area, and several helicopters and light aircraft have been intercepted and forced to land.

Below: Electronic support has been provided by a variety of USAF special mission aircraft. This is an EC-130H Compass Call, which jams communications.

Operation Deny Flight

Above: A large maritime patrol effort is under way from Sigonella to enforce the naval blockade of former Yugoslavia. US Navy Orions lead the MPA force.

Above: Sigonella is one of the busiest bases, hosting elements of the maritime patrol force, USAF tankers and much of the transport support effort.

UNPROFOR and Western countries decided to concentrate the command and control of air operations over Bosnia at the Operation Deny Flight headquarters at Vicenza, in northern Italy. Day-to-day tasking of fighter missions was assigned to the commander of NATO's 5th Allied Tactical Air Force (5 ATAF), Lieutenant General Antonio Rossetti of the Italian air force, at Vicenza's Del Molina air base. UNPROFOR sent Brigadier Rody Cordy-Simpson to be their liaison officer at Vicenza and 5 ATAF sent liaison officers to the UNPROFOR HQ in Zagreb and its Bosnia-Herzegovina Command in Kiseljak, near Sarajevo. The Americans also moved the headquarters of JTF Provide Promise to Vicenza to ensure good co-ordination of UN airlift missions with Deny Flight fighters; the NATO aircraft took over from the US Navy much of the responsibility for protecting the nightly airdrops. Command of supporting tanker and AWACS missions, including those in support of the naval assets in the Adriatic enforcing the UN blockade of Serbia and Montenegro, was the responsibility of Lieutenant General Joseph W. Ashy, USAF, Commander Allied Air Forces Southern Europe in Naples, although close co-ordination took place with 5 ATAF at Vicenza.

Re-routing the airways

The Adriatic was a major civilian airway for holiday flights to Greece and the eastern Mediterranean area, so special measures had to be taken to prevent accidents. The Italian air traffic authorities closed off the eastern Adriatic to civilian traffic and, when not operating in this area, NATO aircraft had to follow civil routes. Air traffic consideration played a large part in deciding the basing of Deny Flight aircraft, with none being positioned near Rome in order to avoid the Italian capital's congested skies.

Within a week of the start of the operation, NATO commanders realised that more fighter aircraft were needed to maintain the CAP stations over Bosnia. Britain, Turkey and the Netherlands all agreed to send more fighters. Six more F-16A fighters from the RNLAF's 305 Squadron replaced the F-16A(R)s of 306 Squadron at Villafranca. This also smoothed logistic support because all the Dutch aircraft in Italy now came from the same home base. Regular flights by white-painted F27 Troopships, of 334 Squadron, brought in supplies and new personnel. In June, the Spanish air force sent a CASA C.212 liaison aircraft to Vicenza to support 5 ATAF command personnel.

RAF detachment

The first of six Tornado F.Mk 3s from 11 Squadron flew out to Gioia del Colle, near Brindisi, from RAF Leeming on 19 April. Two VC10 K.Mk 2/3 tankers from 101 Squadron deployed to Sigonella from RAF Brize Norton to support the British fighters. Two further Tornados deployed on 13 May and just over a week later the VC10s moved north to Milan-Malpensa because the Sicilian heat made it difficult to take off with heavy fuel loads. Plans were developed for the VC10s to be replaced by Tristars of 216 Squadron in early June.

A more controversial addition to Deny Flight was the deployment to Italy of the Turkish air force's 142 Air Unit from Murted air base on 20 April. The unit's 15 F-16Cs and three F-16Ds had to make a long ferry flight over the Mediterranean because the Greeks refused overflight rights. After a stop-over at Brindisi the Turkish fighters took up residence at Ghedi, to the west of Verona.

The four/five-hour length of typical Deny Flight sorties and the intensive use of air refuelling was a largely new experience for the Turks. Every pilot had to do a dry hook-up with a KC-135 before flying operational missions over Bosnia, and a 10-day work-up period was necessary before they could participate fully in maintaining CAP stations over Bosnia.

On 28 June, the 12 F-15Cs from the 53rd FS, 36th FW, returned home to Bitburg, their place on the Deny Flight detachment taken by the F-16Cs from Spangdahlem's 23rd FS, 52nd FW.

Secret support

Great secrecy still surrounds some western air operations over Bosnia. Persistent rumours concerned the participation of newly delivered MC-130H Combat Talon II in Operation Provide Promise airdrops. Electronic warfare support for air missions over Bosnia is reported to have come from USAF RC-135 Rivet Joint aircraft on TDY to RAF Mildenhall and British Nimrod R.Mk 1Ps of 51 Squadron at RAF Wyton. The RAF and USAF special mission aircraft are reported to maintain a continuous orbit over the Adriatic to support Deny Flight and Provide Promise.

Western air, ground and naval operations related to the Bosnia crisis require a great deal of logis-

USS Saipan is in the Mediterranean to bolster NATO forces in the area, carrying a Special Forces MEU. HMM-264 is the aviation unit, including UH-1Ns in its complement.

In addition to the Marine CH-46s of HMM-264, the Sea Knights of the US Navy are also active around Sigonella. This HC-8 aircraft is assigned to USS Seattle for utility transport purposes.

Saipan's air wing includes a number of AV-8B Harrier IIs, which would be used to cover any ground operations should the 26th MEU be called upon to land in Bosnia.

tic support, and Italy became the centre of such activities. Ancona-Fralcora became the main hub for UN relief flights into Sarajevo and Split in January 1993 with detachments of British and Canadian C-130s and French and German C.160s, while Rhein Main air base near Frankfurt remained the main base for USAF C-130s and French and German C.160s flying airdrop missions. The 37th Airlift Squadron from Rhein Main's 435th Airlift Wing bore the brunt of the airdrop effort augmented by reserve aircraft and personnel from the Kentucky Air National Guard and Air Force Reserve units. The German aircraft came from Air Transport Wings 61 and 63 at Penzing and Hohn respectively. C-9A Nightingales of Rhein Main's 55th Aeromedical Airlift Squadron also regularly flew mercy missions to the former Yugoslavia for UNPROFOR and other agencies. In June 1993 the USAF moved its forward operating base from Split to Zagreb because of fears that fighting between Croat and Muslim forces would endanger the base.

Naval Support base

Sigonella provided vital support for naval operations in the Adriatic. Its own CH-53E Sea Stallions of HC-4 were in great demand for logistic work, as were Sigonella's CT-39G Sabreliners. To provide logistic support to the US Navy and UNPROFOR in Croatia and Romania, US Navy Reservists from VR-57 were flying C-9B Skytrains and C-130T Hercules from Sigonella. Crews and aircraft rotated on a two-week basis. Two C-2A Greyhounds of VRC 40's Det. 2, responsible for COD flights to USS *Theodore Roosevelt* during its six-month deploy-ment in the Mediterranean, were shore-based at Sigonella. The base is the Mediterranean air head for Air Mobility Command, with C-141Bs and C-5A/Bs being regular visitors. During July, USAF C-130s, C-141Bs and C-5A/Bs moved elements of the US Army's Berlin Brigade to Skopji to join the UN Monitoring Force in Macedonia. Two C-141Bs landed the advance party on 5 July and a Galaxy flew in further elements of the US force the following day.

In May 1993 Sigonella also played host to the air group of the 26th Marine Expeditionary Unit (Special Operations Capable) from the USS *Saipan* which was making a port visit to nearby Augusta Bay. Centred on HMH-264 it included AH-1W Cobras, CH-46E Sea Knights, CH-53Es, UH-1N Hueys and AV-8B Harriers. UH-46s of HC-6 also made a visit at this time. The amphibious assault ship entered the Mediterranean for a

six-month deployment in early April 1993, supported by the USS *Pensacola* and USS *Ponce*.

The US Naval Support Activity at Naples' Capodichino Airport became a regular stop-off point of VIP aircraft carrying NATO, UN and western commanders to conferences with Admiral Boorda. On a typical day, aircraft seen at the base included Admiral Boorda's own VP-3A Orion VIP transport, UN C-12s, American CH-53Es, SH-60s, C-9Bs, C-12s and C-2As, British HS 748s and Sea Kings, Dutch SH-14B Lynx, assorted Italian and French executive jets and even East European military aircraft from countries involved in imposing sanctions on Serbia. Maritime patrol aircraft supporting the UN naval blockade of Serbia fly eight-hour patrols from Sigonella, looking for sanction-busting ships in the Adriatic. For six months up to April 1993 the US Navy's VP-24 deployed eight P-3C Orion Update IIIs to Sigonella from Jacksonville, Florida and they were replaced by Orions of VP-11 from Brunswick, Maine. Portuguese air force P-3s of 601 Squadron from Ovar, and Royal Netherlands navy Orions from Valkenburg, along with British Nimrods from RAF Kinloss, have also joined this effort. Half a dozen Italian air force Atlantics of 41° Stormo/88° Gruppo normally based at Sigonella have regularly patrolled

Right: A huge logistics effort has involved many support aircraft. The former VR-24 CT-39Gs have been busy from their base at Sigonella.

Below: Initially operating from Sigonella, RAF VC10s now fly from Milan/Malpensa to provide the RAF detachment with tanking support.

US Navy, Dutch and Portuguese (illustrated) Orions man the naval blockade, alongside RAF Nimrods, Italian and German Atlantics, and French Atlantiques.

the Adriatic, and French Aéronavale Atlantics have also supported the blockade effort from their home base at Nîmes/Garon and from Sigonella. German Marineflieger Atlantics of MFG 3 from Nordholz have operated from Elmas on Sardinia, along with more Italian Atlantics.

The maritime patrol aircraft were heavily involved in tracking the Serbian navy's six-strong diesel submarine fleet, as well as looking for blockade runners. NATO commanders were particularly worried about the threat to their ships in the Adriatic and mounted intense anti-submarine sweeps, involving ships, helicopters and fixed-wing aircraft, whenever the Serbian submarines put to sea.

Until 15 June 1993 both NATO and the Western European Union (WEU) ran rival naval operations in the Adriatic, codenamed Maritime Monitor/Guard and Sharp Fence. To increase co-ordination the two operations were combined

Operation Deny Flight

Britain's Tornado F.Mk 3 detachment was provided by No. 11 Squadron, normally based at Leeming. The detachment's home at Gioia del Colle houses Italian AF Tornados.

under the codename Operation Sharp Guard. Under command of an Italian Admiral, the naval forces enforcing the naval blockade were designated Combined Task Force 440 (CTF 440). It boasted some 17 surface warships from 11 NATO

Below: The Sikorsky CH-53Es of HC-4 at Sigonella have been active in supporting the vessels sailing on blockade duties in the Adriatic. The Marine Corps also have the CH-53 in-theatre as part of Saipan's air wing.

navies. Maritime patrol aircraft supporting Sharp Guard were grouped under CTF 431 commanded by US Rear Admiral Daniel Oliver. Eight Italian Tornado IDS aircraft based at Gioia del Colle were assigned to provide strike support for Sharp Guard.

A number of western countries have deployed naval forces into the Adriatic under purely national command to support their forces in Yugoslavia if they should come under direct attack. In July the Royal Navy replaced *Ark Royal* with the *Invincible* and the French rotated out the *Clemenceau*, bringing in the *Foch* to take over its duties in the Adriatic. The Italian carrier ITS

Guiseppe Garibaldi also operated in the Adriatic with its air group of AV-8B Harriers and Sea Kings, in co-operation with allied ships. For a few weeks in late June and early July the *Theodore Roosevelt* had to temporarily deploy to the Red Sea because of increased tension in the Middle East but the ship was back on station off Bosnia by the end of July.

By early August 1993 western governments had not developed a coherent policy for further action in Bosnia. Much speculation about US-led air strikes on Bosnian Serb positions or NATO plans to defend so-called safe havens have yet to be translated into action.

From the outset, the air wing of the **Theodore Roosevelt** *has been available for Deny Flight operations. F-14s from VF-84 have undertaken their fair share of* **CAP** *duties.*

Air Wing of USS *Theodore Roosevelt*

In late March 1993 the USS Theodore Roosevelt took over duty from the USS *John F. Kennedy* in the Mediterranean and was quickly involved in air operations over Bosnia. The ship's Carrier Air Wing Eight fielded some of the most modern aircraft in the US Navy inventory, including fully night strike-capable F/A-18C Lot 14 Hornets, F-14A 'Bombcat' strike fighters, A-6E (SWIP) attack aircraft, EA-6B Prowlers and E-2C Hawkeyes, plus SH-60F Ocean Hawk ASW and HH-60H Rescue Hawk helicopters. In a new development, the carrier boasted a Special Purpose Marine Air-Ground Task Force with CH-53D Sea Stallions, UH-1N Huey assault helicopters and 600 Marines embarked on the carrier.

Until 12 April the carrier played an important role supporting US-led airdrops over eastern Bosnia, flying early warning and probably fighter missions. An E-2C was lost with five crewmen returning from one of these missions on 26 March but it was not thought to be due to enemy action. While the US airdrop aircraft were over Bosnia the *Roosevelt* kept its Marines on alert, ready to fly combat search and rescue (CSAR) in case one of the C-130s went down.

Once Deny Flight began the carrier started to launch Hornets and Tomcats to fly CAPs. TARPS- F-14s also regularly flew photo-reconnaissance missions over Bosnia to provide information for NATO planners. Support for Provide Promise continued with the E-2C flying and the Marines standing ready for CSAR every night. Hornets and Intruders also began to fly surface CAPs (SUCAPS) over the Adriatic for allied warships armed with Paveway LGBs, Walleye EO-guided bombs and IR Maverick missiles. By June 1993 the carrier's aircraft had yet to fire a shot in anger.

CVW-8 - CAG Captain Willie Moore

VF-84 'Jolly Rogers'	10 x F-14A
VA-36 'Roadrunners'	14 x A-6E
VFA-15 'Valions'	10 x F/A-18C
VFA-87 'Golden Warriors'	10 x F/A-18C
VMFA-312 'Checkerboards'	10 x F/A-18C
VAW-124 'Bear Aces'	4 x E-2C
VAQ-141 'Shadowhawks'	4 x EA-6B
HS-3 'Tridents'	2 x SH-60F;
	4 x HH-60H

Special Purpose Marine Air-Ground Task Force

HMH-362 'Ugly Angels'	6 x CH-53D
HMLA-167	4 x UH-IN

Ashore: NAS Sigonella

VRC-40 'Rawhides' Det. 2	2 x C-2A

Above: A-6 Intruders of VA-36 stand ready to mount attacks if required. The EA-6Bs of VAQ-141 are carried for jamming support.

Below: The Special Purpose MAGTF on board 'TR' is equipped with CH-53Ds from HMH-362 for the rapid transport of Marine troops.

F/A-18s equip three squadrons aboard aboard 'TR', including VMFA-312 (above) provided by the Marines. The VFA-87 aircraft below carries an intake-mounted FLIR pod, and is fully night-attack capable.

Right: Central to any carrier air wing operation is the E-2 Hawkeye, which on Theodore Roosevelt is provided by VAW-124. These aircraft have been used on Deny Flight monitoring operations.

BRIEFING

New life for the Tiger

'More bangs for the buck' is an oft-heard phrase, but in the squeezed-budget 1990s it could be reinterpreted as 'the same bang for fewer bucks'. New fighter deals are rare events compared to past years, yet nations around the world have to maintain defence readiness on ever-shrinking finances. Consequently, the upgrade market is booming. Undisputed world masters at the rework game are Israel Aircraft Industries, offering a long tradition of transforming other manufacturers' designs into fully modern warplanes, combined with the considerable expertise in the avionics field offered by Elta and other electronic specialists.

Among the many upgrade programmes offered by IAI is a major avionics refit for the Northrop F-5E, responding to a requirement of the Fuerza Aérea de Chile. According to non-IAI sources, the FACh has 12 F-5E single-seaters, augmented by two F-5F two-seaters, serving with Grupo de Aviación 7 at Antofagasta-Cerro Moreno. All of the fleet is being upgraded to IAI's F-5 Plus standard.

The prototype for the F-5 Plus is an F-5E single-seater, dispatched to the Shaham Aircraft Maintenance and Upgrading Plant at Ben Gurion airport, part of Bedek Aviation Division, for integration of the new equipment. The project test pilot took the aircraft aloft for the first time in its new guise on 8 July 1992.

Producing a state-of-the-art

The IAI upgraded F-5 takes off from Ben Gurion during the test phase. The cannon barrels were replaced with telemetry equipment for the flight trials.

fighter within an existing airframe was the primary goal of the F-5 Plus programme. In fact, there are no airframe/engine modifications involved. However, the avionics have been completely revised to produce an aircraft which IAI claims to be 'a half-generation ahead' of current service fighters. The basis of the upgrade is a central computer with MIL STD 1553 databus, new multi-mode radar and modern cockpit displays. The radar is Elta's EL/M-2032B, offering air defence, air-to-ground and mapping modes. One of IAI's main achievements has been to maintain the radar's excellent performance while reducing the size of the scanner to fit the narrow confines of the F-5's radome.

Centralised computing allows data from all the aircraft's systems to be integrated and presented on a single Tactical Situation Display in the cockpit, something that few fighter pilots have available at the present time. The cockpit has a central up-front controller for rapid control of the avionics system, above which is an El-Op head-up display. This is cued by HOTAS controls, and features standard air-to-air, air-to-ground and navigation/approach modes. Computer-generated sights are provided for missile launch (with different symbology for different weapons), gun aiming and bombing. For the latter, the HUD presents a CCIP (continuously-computed impact point) as a cross at the end of a vertical line.

Either side of the up-front controller is a large multi-function display. In the FACh aircraft these are monochrome (in green) but colour MFDs are available if required.

These primarily present tactical data to the pilot at a glance, but can also display aircraft systems data and check lists. In the air-to-ground role, electro-optical imagery can be displayed for aiming/designation purposes. In the air-to-air role, the pilot would normally employ the left-hand MFD to provide the radar display on a grid system. The right-hand MFD is used for the tactical situation display. This represents the biggest advance offered by the F-5 Plus.

Combining data from the navigation suite, radar warning receivers and radar, the central computer presents all tactical data on one display. National borders and areas of water can be presented, overlaid with threat zones, active radars and aircraft returns. Whereas in current-generation fighters the pilot would have to check navigation display, radar return and radar warning receiver display, and then mentally process the gathered data, the F-5 Plus pilot is presented with everything on one display. The advantages of this immediate appraisal of the tactical situation are obvious: considerably reduced workload and 'head-down' time.

A further feature of the new avionics suite is a video debrief function, which works using INS/GPS data and computer returns. This allows, in effect, a function similar to an ACMI range, but without the need for expensive installations. In line with other modern fighters, the 'black boxes' of the avionics suite are LRUs (line-replaceable units) for ease of maintenance and rapid sortie generation.

Radar and new avionics were fitted from the first flight, presenting a challenging series of flight trials. Whereas most test programmes proceed at a leisurely pace, testing one

system at a time, each F-5 Plus flight involved the trial of many systems concurrently. IAI has a highly-instrumented telemetry range which was significant in the speed of the trials, for which the prototype was fitted with telemetry transmitters in the cannon ports. In less than 50 flights, the F-5 Plus went from first flight through specification testing to operational evaluation, all on a 'fly-fix-fly' basis.

Notwithstanding some difficulties in adapting the radar scanner to the F-5's airframe, flight trials showed the whole system to be well above specification. Both cockpit displays and navigation suite performed excellently throughout. Once the radar had been modified to work at full capability with its very small, oval scanner, it too proved to be well above spec. Various tests were undertaken against and with current fighter aircraft. In one set-piece, the F-5 Plus flew alongside an F-16A with APG-66 radar at 5,000 ft (1524 m), in a head-on intercept with a Kfir target flying at 500 ft (152 m). The F-5 detected the Kfir consistently some 1-2 miles (1.6-3.2 km) before the F-16. In another scenario the F-5 ran head-on against an F-16 at similar altitude, and proved able to detect the F-16 long before its adversary picked up the F-5. While this demonstrated the radar's capability, it also revealed the much lower frontal radar cross-section of the F-5 compared to the larger F-16.

In terms of weaponry, the F-5 retains the wingtip rails for AIM-9 Sidewinder/Rafael Shafrir missiles and twin 20-mm cannon, but adds greater missile capability in the form of the Rafael Python 3, mounted on new low-drag outboard pylons. The Python is a third-generation missile with all-aspect capability and seeker head slaved to the radar. A

very powerful warhead ensures a kill, whereas some targets may have survived a Sidewinder hit. In air-to-air engagements, the F-5's legendary manoeuvrability allows it to position advantageously against most opponents.

For air-to-ground missions, the accent is on precision-guided munitions. The F-5 is not well-suited to the carriage of large bombloads, relying on a 'slippery' aerodynamic shape for its performance rather than brute power. Hanging large draggy bombs under the aircraft erodes the performance considerably, so 'smart' weapons make a much better choice, trading explosive power for accuracy. An F-5 carrying three or four small, EO- or laser-guided weapons can wreak as much destruction as a larger aircraft carrying four times the number of 'dumb' weapons. In addition to fighter and air superiority missions, the F-5 Plus is also available for tactical reconnaissance work with a pod-mounted system.

The first reworked aircraft was due for redelivery to the FACh in July 1993, while the first F-5F was already undergoing rework in Israel for redelivery towards the end of the year. The remainder of the fleet will be upgraded by ENAER, where the second F-5E is starting its update process. IAI has received considerable interest from other customers, in the face of other companies offering F-5 upgrades. At present IAI is the only company with a fully upgraded aircraft flying, and it expects several more orders.

In IAI tradition, the company offers a virtually unlimited variety of options for the F-5, able to match the upgrade package precisely to the customer's requirements and purse. These include inflight refuelling, helmet-mounted sights, secure communications, new air data computer and new ejection seats. For 'a tenth the price of a new fighter', a customer can have a warplane offering avionics/pilot interface technology that is at present only found in new-generation fighters such as the Rafale, MiG-29M and EFA.

Radar
The F-5 Plus has an Elta EL/M-2032 radar, which offers full multi-mode operation. In the air-to-air mode it outranges the APG-66 as fitted to the F-16. The radar has an ultra-low sidelobe planar array antenna, which for the F-5 was specially tailored to fit the narrow oval-section nose of the Tiger.

Python missile
The hard-hitting Python 3 entered service in time to be used in the 1982 fighting over the Bekaa Valley, where it was credited with many kills. It has a launch weight of 264 lb (120 kg), is 9 ft 10 in (3.0 m) long and has a body diameter of 6.3 in (0.16 m). The warhead is an 24-lb (11-kg) HE fragmentation unit, fuzed by active radar. The missile is guided by infra-red, with radar-slaved, scan or boresight modes available.

Northrop F-5E Plus Tiger III

Blessed with good performance and excellent agility, the Northrop F-5E still serves in sufficient numbers to warrant the effort of producing a thorough upgrade package. IAI has not altered the airframe or powerplant as these were deemed to be adequate. However, the avionics and armament options have seen a major reworking, including a new and far more capable radar, completely revised state-of-the-art cockpit with twin MFDs displaying the complete tactical situation, and new missiles and provision for LGBs.

Sidewinder
Carried on the wingtip rail is an AIM-9P Sidewinder, although alternative missiles (such as the Rafael Shafrir 2) are available. The 'Papa' version is 10 ft 1 in (3.07 m) long.

Cockpit
Inside the F-5 Plus the pilot has one of the most up-to-date displays available to any combat pilot. There are two MFDs, one of which can be used to combine data from various sensors for a complete situation display.

Markings
The first F-5 Plus stayed in its basic FACh markings throughout the test programme, with various IAI-applied markings superimposed – principally for the type's appearance at the 1993 Paris air show. The aircraft wore IDF/AF insignia during the flight trials.

Cannon
The F-5E is fitted with two M39A2 20-mm cannon, each armed with 280 rounds.

RWR
The Chilean F-5s are fitted with a 360° radar warning receiver system, with antennas either side of the nose and tail. The system provides threat data for the tactical situation display.

Powerplant
Power comes from two General Electric J85-GE-21B turbojets, each rated at 5,000 lb (22.24 kN) thrust with afterburning.

BRIEFING

IAI/Elta Phalcon

New-generation AEW platform

Israel Aircraft Industries is no stranger to the Boeing 707. Over the last 20 years the company has maintained the type for the IDF/AF, and also been involved in many conversions for special purposes. These have included tankers with both hose/drogue and boom refuelling systems, signals intelligence platforms, command posts and other electronic specialists. For the last four years, IAI and its electronics subsidiary, Elta, have been developing an airborne early warning version, which made its public debut at the 1993 Paris air show. The new aircraft represents the culmination of much of the company's work in fitting 707s with advanced electronic sensors and systems.

The name Phalcon relates to the system, rather than the 707 which presently carries it. IAI stresses that it can be tailored for other large aircraft platforms, the C-130 being an obvious candidate. Phalcon is a complete package, which features many options to match customer requirements. The full system provides a 360° coverage in both passive and active AEW modes, with a central battle management system.

At the heart of the system is the Elta EL/2075 phased-array radar. For full coverage there are four antenna arrays – two either side of the forward fuselage housed in giant cheek fairings, one in the nose in a bulbous radome, and one under the

The prototype Phalcon 707 visited the Paris air show for just one day, but this was the public debut for the type. It is configured with three antenna arrays instead of the maximum four, but features full ESM/Elint fit, with antennas in bulged wingtip fairings and under the tail. The aircraft is believed to be the first for Chile.

rear fuselage. The radomes do add considerable drag, eroding speed performance, but the main concern is for long endurance, which is not dramatically affected. The nose radome has a flattened underside for ground clearance, and its fitment has necessitated the resiting of the two pitot probes to above the flight deck. The first customer is believed to be Chile, which has not specified the rear array. Coverage with three arrays is believed to be 260°.

Each array consists of hundreds of antennas, each with an individual transmit/receive module in the forward fuselage. They are electronically steered, and mounted on a floating bed so that flexing in the aircraft's structure does not affect their alignment. The radar works in L-band, and the electronic steering and power management computer allows it to be very flexible. Detection range is in the order of 250 miles (400 km) for fighter-sized targets, and around 100 can be processed at any one time.

Fast scanning is possible, so that area coverage can be maintained while concentrating on an important target. For extra range all power can be assigned in one direction. A sharp beam mode is incorporated to keep track of a fast or manoeuvring target, and the scan area can be limited to just the battle area, thereby increasing the scan rate in this region. Track initiation is in the region of two to four seconds, which is roughly a tenth that of rotodome-equipped platforms. This is one of the major advantages over the previous generation of AEW aircraft.

Backing up the radar is an advanced IFF (identification, friend or foe) system, which is incor-

porated in the main radar arrays. The IFF and radar are fully co-ordinated to avoid interference with each other, and use similar antenna elements and transmit/receive modules.

Passive sensors include an advanced tactical ESM/Elint suite with antennas mounted on the rear fuselage and wingtips. This uses narrow-band super-heterodyne receivers and wide-band IFM (instantaneous frequency measurement) techniques, combined with DTOA (differential time of arrival) direction finding to provide high accuracy and a high probability of intercepting airborne and surface emitters in a highly dense electronic environment. It is integrated with the IFF and radar to provide a rapid identification function of all targets.

Last of the sensor systems is an Elta EL/K-7031 CSM/Comint suite, which receives in HF, VHF and UHF. A search mechanism hunts through the frequency spectrum to find communications of interest, and a DF mechanism locates their source. Computers 'filter' much of the catch before assigning the more interesting communications to the operators.

All the data from the four sensor systems is processed and integrated by a central computer system. This consists of multiple computers connected by three databuses. Each computer has several signals proces-

The cheek fairings are much larger than those fitted to USAF RC-135s. The bottom of the fairings contain hatches for rapid access to the antenna arrays. The controlling modules are in the forward cabin.

sors, with a reserve processor. A back-up computer is also provided should the reserve processors not be adequate to handle any problems. The capability exists to change 'black boxes' in flight.

Internally, the Phalcon 707 has a forward and rear 'black box' area, central operator's cabin and crew rest facilities. On the first aircraft are 13 consoles, two for tests, two for system management, two for ESM/Elint, three for radar, one for CSM/Comint, two for communications and one for the mission commander. Most of the consoles feature two high-resolution colour screens, and are interchangeable.

IAI/Elta offer a command post option with the Phalcon system, using a large back-projected display screen in a rear cabin. This allows commanders to view and direct the air battle in comfort, and in real-time. Alternatively, a datalink allows the transfer of secure communications between the Phalcon and ground command posts.

As noted above, non-IAI sources quote Chile as the first customer, and the aircraft which made a fleeting appearance at Le Bourget in 1993 was believed to be the first for delivery, due before the year's end. No information has been released about further customers, although the IDF/AF seem likely to have the type on order. Singapore and South Africa have also been mentioned in connection with Phalcon, although this is strictly rumour.

As it stands, the Phalcon AEW system is just the first operational incarnation of an ever-developing technology. Elta is working on a maritime system, and is also believed to be working on a J-STARS-style ground target system. If these could be integrated into one airframe, then Phalcon or its derivatives could become complete battle management systems in one airborne platform.

Boeing 707

Tanker conversions

In recent years a number of additional nations have sought to acquire inflight refuelling capability and, with the cost of new airframes being prohibitive, have chosen the airline-surplus Boeing 707 as the platform for tanker conversions. A variety of configurations have been produced, according to the needs and purses of the customer.

Most 707 tankers have been fitted with a simple two-point probe and drogue system, with hose-drum units mounted under the wingtips. Three types of wing pod are in common use: the Flight Refuelling Mk 32, the Beech 1800 and the Sargent Fletcher 34-000. All have similar characteristics, with power provided by a ram air turbine on the front of the pod. These pods are plumbed into the aircraft's central fuel system, and the majority of tankers do not have additional fuel capacity, allowing them to remain fully effective in their original transport role.

In some cases, 707 tankers have been fitted with a flying boom for the refuelling of receptacle-equipped receivers, retaining the wing pods for probe-equipped aircraft. These conversions are more costly, as they involve reworking the lower rear fuselage to fit the boom and retain structural integrity.

Options for the tanker conversions include additional tankage (typically 5,030 US gal/19040 litres) in the underfloor compartment, boom or pod operator's station, underfuselage TV camera for monitoring refuelling, refuelling control panel at the flight engineer's station, strengthened wings and new wingtips for mounting the HDUs, and improved pump/hydraulic systems. With the optional tanks and a

three-point system, a 707 tanker can typically offload 123,200 lb (55885 kg) of fuel at a radius of 1,150 miles (1850 km) from base.

Conversion work is often undertaken by the local aircraft industry, with assistance from Boeing or IAI. The latter has developed its own tanker conversions following the refusal of the United States to supply surplus KC-135s or booms for refuelling the F-15/F-16 fleet which Israel had acquired. The IAI KC-707 boom tankers feature extra tankage in the lower fuselage compartment, and are fitted with a unique camera system. A stereo camera is mounted at the base of the boom, and a further camera on the boom itself. Further forward under the fuselage is a camera for initial acquisition of the receiver. The boom operator sits in a compartment in the rear of the aircraft, with the cameras displaying the refuelling scene through a stereoscopic sight. Flight deck crew monitor the refuelling on a TV screen.

Tanker 707s are now in service with 12 countries. Australia has four tankers in service with No. 34 Squadron at Fairbairn, converted by Hawker de Havilland with IAI kits and FRL Mk 32 wing pods. These support the Hornet force, and were to have been joined by two boom-equipped 707s for refuelling the F-111C fleet, but the latter were shelved due to budgetary constraints.

IAI has supplied single tankers to Peru (FRL pods) and Venezuela (possibly also to Argentina), and has supported the conversion of at least four for the South African Air Force's No. 60 Squadron. The latter have variously been reported as three-point HDU-equipped tank-

ers, or two-point dual role Sigint/tankers.

Israel itself operates at least six 707 tankers, and they have been noted in three different configurations. The first to be seen had a three-point HDU conversion, with the centre unit located in the rear fuselage. The flying-boom version appeared next (with Sargent Fletcher wingtip HDUs), followed by Sigint aircraft fitted with wing HDUs only. The flying-boom tanker can refuel F-15s and F-16s from the boom, and other IDF/AF types (Kfir, Phantom, Skyhawk) from the wing pods.

Further 707 tanker conversion operators have aircraft produced with Boeing assistance. Canada's two tanker CC-137s have Beech 1800 pods, but will be retired shortly. Brazil has four KC-137 tankers with 2/2 GT, again with Beech pods. Morocco has a single tanker, converted locally by AMIN with Beech pods, while Spain flies two Boeing-converted T.17 tankers with Sargent Fletcher equipment. Italy has recently produced four tankers with Sargent Fletcher wing pods, and a

*Boeing's original 707 **TT** demonstrator was fitted with a Sargent Fletcher wing pod (port) and fuselage **HDU**, and starboard pod by Beech. The latter has a hinged section so that the drogue is held below the wing out of the tip turbulence.*

single Flight Refuelling 480C HDU in the fuselage. These were converted by Alenia Officine Aeronavali.

In addition to the conversion operators, two nations fly 707 tankers which were built as such. Iran had four of its 14 707s completed as tankers with boom and Beech wingpods, and may have subsequently added more conversions. More recently, Saudi Arabia procured the KE-3A, a pod-and-boom-equipped tanker with CFM56 high bypass ratio turbofans. The eight aircraft serve with No. 18 Squadron, flying alongside E-3 AWACS platforms.

*Below: Italy's four tankers serve with 14° Stormo. In addition to the SFC 34-000 wing pods, it has an **FRL** centre HDU.*

Left: An Israeli air force KC-707 demonstrates its three-point capability. Note the boom monitoring camera in a fairing under the rear fuselage, and the KC-135-style receiver director lights.

Below: This Beech 1800 wing pod is fitted to one of Brazil's four Boeing KC-137s, which serve with 2° Esquadrão/2° Grupo de Transporte.

BAe Sea Harrier FRS.Mk 2

AMRAAM fires further progress

Previously described in Briefings and the Harrier main article in *World Air Power Journal* Volumes 1, 6 and 7, the BAe Sea Harrier FRS.Mk 2 is now drawing close to service entry. Here we review the programme, including recent progress. Despite the success of the Sea Harrier during the 1982 Falklands War, during which it destroyed some 22 enemy aircraft without suffering a single air-to-air loss itself, the conflict did underline several shortcomings in the aircraft, most notably a lack of lookdown/shootdown and beyond visual range missile capability.

In 1984, it was (inaccurately) reported that the MoD had decided to award BAe and Ferranti a £200 million contract for the mid-life upgrade of the entire RN fleet of 57 Sea Harriers. In fact it was not until February 1985 that a much smaller project definition contract was placed, for an upgrade of 30 of the Navy's Sea Harriers.

The upgrade was originally intended to cover installation of Blue Vixen radar and JTIDS, provision of AIM-120 AMRAAM missiles and installation of an enhanced RWR system (the Marconi Zeus was originally specified, although it was later decided to upgrade the existing ARI.18223 RWR to Marconi Sky Guardian standards), role change wingtip extensions, new vortex generators, and wingroot leading-edge extensions. The new equipment necessitated increased internal volume, and this was provided through a fuselage stretch using a 1-ft 2-in (0.35-m) fuselage plug aft of the wing. The original BAe proposal also covered the installation of new wingtip missile launch rails for AIM-9 or ASRAAM missiles.

The designation FRS.Mk 2 was assigned to the upgraded aircraft, and the programme was streamlined by deletion of most of the proposed aerodynamic changes (the role change wingtips being deleted later, when they were found to be unnecessary). A kinked wing leading edge, and a new fence were retained, however. A contract for the conversion of FRS.Mk 1s was finally signed on 7 December 1988, and was believed at the time to have covered all 42 surviving FRS.Mk 1s. Various reports suggest that contracts exist covering the conversion of some 29 or 31 existing Sea Harrier FRS.Mk 1s (in addition to the two development aircraft ZA195 and XZ439, which made their maiden flights on 19 September 1988 and 8 March 1989), and there is talk of funding a further five conversions. Aircraft undergoing conversion are stripped at Dunsfold, then delivered by road to Brough for structural work, before being shipped back to Dunsfold for completion. A contract for the manufacture of 10 new-build Sea Harrier FRS.Mk 2s was signed in March 1990, and this was increased to 15 in 1992, with manufacture of long-lead-time items already funded. It seems likely that between 18 and 21 new FRS.Mk 2s will eventually be procured. Additionally, five two-seat Harrier T.Mk 4Ns are being converted to T.Mk 8N standards, with FRS.Mk 2 standard cockpits, but still without radar.

With the aerodynamic characteristics fully explored, the Blue Vixen (A version) radar was flown in a

BAC One-Eleven in a 114-hour, 121-sortie programme which ended in November 1987, and from August 1988 in a BAe 125 (XW930). A second BAe 125-600B (ZF130) was fitted with an FRS.Mk 2 type cockpit in the co-pilot's position. B version radar was added in 1989 and was also flown in the second FRS.Mk 2 development aircraft, XZ439, on 24 May 1989.

Above: The Sea Harrier FRS.Mk 2 inside the hangar at Eglin, parked beneath the Union Jack, the Stars and Bars and a Royal Navy White Ensign.

The next step was to clear the aircraft to carry and fire the AIM-120 AMRAAM. Live firings of the AIM-120 were originally scheduled for mid-1991, but XZ439 was not shipped to the USA until January

Below: Cameras to record AIM-120 AMRAAM launches are fitted inside a modified practice bomb container, seen here mounted on the starboard outer pylon.

Below: A live AIM-120, identifiable by the broad yellow bands. Stripes on the tailfins are for calibration. On this sortie, AMRAAMs were carried below the starboard outer and port fuselage pylons.

Above: XZ439 lets fly with an AIM-120, shock-cones pulsing from the missile's rocket motor. The FRS.Mk 2's combination of Blue Vixen radar and AIM-120 makes it a very much more capable fighter.

1993. The aircraft was taken across the Atlantic aboard the new *Atlantic Conveyor*. On arrival at Norfolk, Virginia, the aircraft made a vertical take-off from the ship and flew ashore to be refuelled before flying on to Eglin AFB, Florida. The trials include 10 live AMRAAM firings, against sub-scale MQM-107 and full-size QF-106 target drones, the first on 29 March.

The first production FRS.Mk 2 (XZ497) was delivered to Boscombe Down for CA Release trials and for use by the new Sea Harrier OEU, while the second (ZE695) was handed over to the Royal Navy at Dunsfold on 2 April and flown to Yeovilton. It wears No. 899 Squadron markings.

Right: The test aircraft on the ramp at Eglin, armed with AMRAAMs.

Below: The instrumentation pod is packaged inside an AIM-9 Sidewinder airframe.

Above: A G-band transponder was mounted in the extended tailcone to allow accurate tracking and identification over the massive Eglin range.

Right: For its detachment to Eglin, XZ439 received a ferocious-looking sharksmouth aft of the radome. The significance of this is unknown.

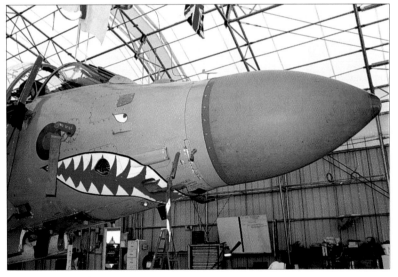

BRIEFING

Sikorsky UH-60Q 'Dust Off' Hawk

New medical Black Hawk variant

The Dust Off callsign (Dedicated Unhesitating Service To Our Fighting Forces) has been used by a wide variety of helicopters, usually standard transport machines pressed into service to fulfill a demanding and unglamorous but crucially important duty. Although US Army Sikorsky UH-60A and UH-60L Black Hawks have regularly been used for such air ambulance and casualty evacuation duties, seeing active service in these roles in Grenada, Panama, the Gulf and Somalia, it was felt that a dedicated aeromedical evacuation helicopter would be necessary to support the US Army's global mission in the 1990s. Impetus was added to the programme by the inadequacy of the 380+ UH-1V air ambulances in service during the Gulf War, and by the perceived need to improve patient care by comparison with the 120 or so existing medevac-configured UH-60As, which do not carry equipment to stabilise patient condition during the crucial first hour post-wound/injury. Combat experience showed the UH-1V to have inadequate speed and range to keep up with fast-moving armoured warfare, poor hot-and-high performance, and limited medical equipment. The UH-60A had adequate speed and range, but equipment was limited, and the use of an internal rescue hoist used up too much internal space.

The UH-60Q was designed to meet this requirement and was developed by a joint Army/National Guard/Army Surgeon General's office team, supported by Sikorsky, Serv-Air Inc. and the Air Methods Corporation. A single UH-60Q

prototype has been produced by conversion of an existing UH-60A as a proof-of-concept aircraft. This made its maiden flight from the Lexington-Blue Grass Army Depot in Richmond, Kentucky, in late January 1993, and was formally rolled out and handed over to its operator, the Tennessee National Guard MEDEVAC CECAT (Combat Enhanced Capability Aviation Team) Medical Aviation Detachment on 8 March 1993, at the Marilyn Lloyd Army Aviation Flight Facility at Lovell Field, Chattanooga. The ceremony was conducted in the presence of VIP guests, including local Congresswoman Marilyn Lloyd and senior National Guard Bureau, Surgeon General's Office and Army staff. Lloyd is described as the driving force behind getting the Tennessee National Guard selected as recipients of the first UH-60Q.

A prolonged test and evaluation period using the prototype will determine what equipment and modifications will be selected for the definitive 'production' UH-60Q. When fully equipped, the unit hopes to have four UH-60s assigned, which will give an enormously improved battlefield casualty evacuation capability and will give the state of Tennessee a new level of capability in responding to civilian medical emergencies.

The UH-60Q is not the first dedicated aeromedical evacuation version of the S-70 Black Hawk series, although it is the first dedicated version to be produced for the US Armed Forces. The eight S-70A-1L Desert Hawks built for Saudi Arabia (in addition to 13 basic

Above: The UH-60Q prototype, showing the nose radome, undernose FLIR pylon and pylon-mounted auxiliary fuel tanks. Prominent red cross markings are carried on the doors.

Below: The modern-looking cockpit of the UH-60Q, which has a similar digital avionics suite to the MH- and HH-60 variants. Multi-function displays show FLIR and radar pictures.

transport/VIP S-70A-1s) carry the Moslem red crescent (the Arab world's red cross equivalent) and are dedicated medevac aircraft, with an external rescue hoist, a high inten-

sity search light and provision for up to six litters. Several other versions have been produced for the search and rescue role, which often entails the medical evacuation of

The new interior of the UH-60Q, with the rail-mounted attendants' seats in the foreground and litters lining the cabin walls. The huge size of the UH-60's doors makes stretcher loading easy.

An excellent view of three litters. One has been raised to roof level, giving extra space around the other two. The box mounted against the rear bulkhead contains medical equipment and monitoring systems.

survivors. The UH-60Q, however, is considerably more advanced and more capable than any of these versions, and incorporates more improvements and refinements, some of which are aimed at offering an unparalleled night/adverse weather capability.

Two FLIRs are being evaluated, one a military Martin Marietta night vision sensor, the other made by FLIR systems and available off-the-shelf commercially. The evaluation will also compare the Bendix King RDR-1300C weather radar with the BF Goodrich WX-1000+ Stormscope. Both weather radar and FLIR imagery will be displayed on multi-function displays which are fully compatible with the use of night vision goggles (NVGs). NVGs made by Elbit and GEC Avionics will be competitively evaluated. The hard shell of the Aeromedical interior was designed and installed by Air Methods of Denver, Colorado, while other modifications (many of them designed by Sikorsky) were incorporated at Lexington-Blue Grass by Serv-Air. Sikorsky were consulted throughout the project.

While the basic UH-60A can carry a six-stretcher carousel in the centre of the cabin, the UH-60Q has nine litters in stacks of three on each side of the cabin and against the rear bulkhead. (These can be replaced by seats for ambulatory patients if required.) This arrangement gives much better inflight access to the litters, which have electrical lifts allowing them to be raised and lowered in flight. Three attendants can be carried, using seats mounted on fore-and-aft rails which run the full length of the cabin. An onboard oxygen generator filters engine bleed air to produce oxygen for patients and crew, eliminating the need for bulky and heavy oxygen bottles. Provision is also made for monitoring vital signs and for intravenously administering various fluids, which can be stored heated and cooled on board. Neonatal isolettes and intra-aoric balloon pumps can be facilitated, effectively making the aircraft an intensive care unit in its own right.

One of the problems experienced by the UH-60A in the Gulf War was actually finding casualties on the battlefield. To this end, the aircraft has Canadian Marconi CMA-2012B Doppler, Rockwell-Collins GPS, TACAN and inertial navigation systems for pinpoint navigation, as well as satellite, high frequency and multiband communications radios, and VHF/UHF homing and Cubic ASR-6 personnel locator beacon receivers. The com-

Above and right: Formal roll-out and hand-over of the UH-60Q was attended by Congresswoman Marilyn Lloyd, one of the project's most staunch supporters.

Below right: the UH-60Q in flight, emblazoned with red cross insignia. The aircraft has the same defensive systems as assault transport UH-60s.

munications suite includes Have Quick and SINCGARS military radios, and an In-Flight Phone commercial airborne telephone.

Baseline UH-60As have analog avionics, but the UH-60Q, like specialised combat rescue and special forces variants, has a digital system, with a Mil-Std 1553B dual digital databus. This brings a level of commonality with the OH-58D and AH-64C/D and allows the proof-of-concept UH-60Q to serve as an avionics testbed for a potential 'digital' Black Hawk upgrade.

Completing the avionics suite are an EDL altitude-hold auto-hover/hover stabilisation system and a Breeze-Eastern cargo hook loadmeter. Avionics integration is by Canadian Marconi, whose CMA-2082 avionics management system controls the databus.

Survivability is enhanced by the provision of HIRSS infra-red exhaust suppressors, of missile and laser (AVR-2) warning systems, and of chaff and flare dispensers.

Below: The proof-of-concept UH-60Q prototype, 86-24560, was converted from a stock UH-60A, but incorporates many modifications.

Above: The nose contours of the UH-60Q are strongly reminiscent of those of the MH-60K and UH-60J, with a centrally-mounted radome and underslung FLIR housing. It remains to be decided which radar and which FLIR will be selected.

Above: The cabin doors incorporate the domed observation windows previously seen on the UH-60J.

A-10

Fighting Warthog

Main picture: Big, ugly and awkward, the Warthog is far from blessed with outstanding performance, but it makes up for it by being able to carry a heavy load right into harm's way, deliver a deadly punch, and escape from the most dangerous situations.

Above: The A-10 has always been an fierce performer in both peacetime exercise and real combat situations. Its pilots are perhaps the last of the 'real' fighter pilots, flying aggressively to wring the most from their low-tech mount in a fashion more akin to World War II flying than to their contemporaries.

Seemingly destined for the scrap heap by 1991, the A-10 earned itself at least a few more years of front-line service when the 1991 Gulf War showed that it was not too old, too slow and too vulnerable to operate in a modern battlefield. Never a beauty queen, and the butt of many jokes to the effect that it was the 'only airplane vulnerable to rear hemisphere birdstrikes', it more than makes up for these shortcomings in rugged character and performance on the battlefield. During the Gulf War it quickly became a favourite of the press and public, much to the mortification of generals who desperately wanted to replace it with more F-16s.

Above: Gulf veteran 'Hogs' from the 706th TFS 'Cajuns' cavort for the camera. Despite their powerful contribution to the Gulf War, the A-10 is slowly on the way out. This New Orleans-based Reserve fighter unit has recently re-equipped with the Lockheed F-16.

Right: The A-10 was designed with virtually no relaxed stability. Until LASTE provided an autopilot, this meant that the aircraft had to be flown 'hands-on" the entire flight, but on the plus side it gave tremendous agility. To A-10 pilots, this attribute means the ability to survive on the battlefield, jinking and rapid turns remaining the A-10's foremost defence.

Right: A 355th FW A-10 peels away from the tanker. Inflight refuelling was not a major factor in the A-10's original tasking, as it was expected to operate mainly from forward bases. However, tanking is regularly practised as it is used regularly on deployments.

The genesis of the A-10 dates from before the Vietnam War, during which some of the Navy's ancient Douglas A-1 Skyraiders were pressed into service by the Air Force as close air support (CAS) and search and rescue (SAR) aircraft after the conventional solution of using retired fighters (in this case the F-100 Super Sabre) or dedicated interdictors (such as the F-4 or F-105) proved expensive, inaccurate and largely ineffective, while purpose-built lighter aircraft, from the U-10 to the brand-new OV-10, lacked punch and the speed necessary to survive in a high-threat environment.

Although the design dated from World War II and was thought to be too old and too slow to survive in the 'modern battlefield', the 'Spads' (as they were called) proved remarkably successful. Learning that speed can sometimes be a liability, and that ruggedness and reliability count for a lot in combat, the Air Force's Attack Experimental (AX) programme set out to develop a replacement which would have a similarly simple but strong airframe, many weapons pylons, great battle damage resistance and excellent low-speed agility. It was determined that during any war in Europe there would generally be 4,000 ft (1219 m) of runway left in operation after an anti-airfield strike. This distance was therefore written into the requirement as the maximum ground roll of a fully armed aircraft. A more lightly loaded aircraft would have to be able to take off in 1,000 ft (305 m). Today this seems ridiculously optimistic, and restrictive, but in the early 1960s it seemed to be a very stringent requirement. The new aircraft was also to be designed to survive in the 'anticipated ground fire environment of the 1970s and 1980s', which suggested a hitherto-unknown level of armour protection and systems redundancy.

Initially it seemed that a twin turboprop with a wing replete with high lift devices, and packed with cheap, reliable, combat-survivable and maintainable systems, would be the ideal solution, rather than accepting the carrier-optimised A-7 Corsair II, although this aircraft was procured for USAF service in the interdictor role. Politically the requirement for a dedicated CAS aircraft was important, since the Air Force wanted to secure the role as a USAF mission, to foil efforts by the US Army and Marine Corps to try to acquire their own CAS types.

The Attack Experimental programme was launched in June 1966 and a requirement was issued in that September. The Air Force issued the request for proposal (RFP) to 21 companies for AX design studies on 6 March 1967. Before

these could be submitted, follow-on study contracts were issued to General Dynamics, Grumman, Northrop and McDonnell on 2 May 1967, calling for detailed research on exactly how armour should be configured and located, how

fuel, hydraulics and other systems should best be protected and routed and, where necessary, duplicated. It was reasoned that these larger companies would have the resources and computer power to achieve this research, which would then be made available to all AX contenders.

Most studies were still of B-57 Canberra-sized twin turboprops of between 40,000 and 60,000 lb (18144 and 27216 kg) weight, and with a unit cost, including R&D, of about $1.5 million. By 1969, however, the target weight had been reduced to 35,000 lb (15876 kg) and the cost to $1 million, and twin fanjets had started to look like a sensible powerplant option, especially since studies were showing that very high bypass fans were likely to be more economical than turboprops. The use of turbofan engines also offered other advantages. The lack of propellers meant that such engines could be located closer to the aircraft centreline (with the attendant reduction of asymmetric handling problems) and were easier to install and maintain, with fewer complex components (e.g., propeller and reduction gear). The bypass air helped reduce IR signature, and the engine is also exceptionally quiet.

Performance requirement

The final draft requirement left engine choice to industry, but recommended the use of turbofans of between 7,000 and 10,000 lb (31.1 and 44.5 kN). Sufficient fuel was to be provided for a mission radius of 250 miles (402 km), with a loiter time of two hours while carrying a warload of 9,500 lb (4309 kg). Take-off distance was set at 4,000 ft (1219 m) or less. The requirement demanded a high level of agility, sufficient to manoeuvre below a 1,000-ft (305-m) cloud base. Another vital requirement was for 'ease of maintenance at austere forward bases', while the AX would have to embody all these attributes while remaining 'low-cost'. The requirement also reflected the process by which the AX had gone from being a general-purpose bomb-truck to a more specialised, cannon-armed tankbuster.

Melvin Laird, Robert MacNamara's eventual successor as Secretary for Defense, abandoned the former's use of fixed-price contracts in favour of a cost-plus (incentive) scheme, while also abandoning the concept of concurrence under which all new items required are developed simultaneously. The emphasis on a low-cost aircraft, together with the new Secretary's 'good housekeeping' measures, allowed serious consideration of a 'fly-before-buy' policy evaluating rival prototypes. It also imposed a requirement to use off-the-shelf hardware wherever possible and to abandon any thoughts of using the advanced composite materials then being developed.

Competitive prototype RFPs were issued to 12 companies on 7 May 1970, specifying an anticipated programme of 600 aircraft at a unit price of $1.4 million constant 1970 dollars, with a contingency inflation allowance of 15 per cent. Responses were received from Boeing, Cessna, Fairchild, General Dynamics, Lockheed and Northrop on 10 August 1970, the other companies approached (Beech, Bell, Grumman, LTV, McDonnell and North American Rockwell) declining to bid because of the very low price being offered. Northrop and Fairchild-Republic were declared the winners of this 'fly-before-buy' prototype competition on 18 December 1970, each winning the right to build two prototypes. The new aircraft received their official designations on 1 March 1971: the Northrop YA-9 and Fairchild-Republic YA-10. The first YA-10 flew from Edwards AFB on 10 May 1972, in the hands of Republic Division chief test pilot Howard 'Sam' Nelson, with the YA-9 flying on 30 May 1972, also from Edwards, in the hands of the unrelated Lew Nelson. The second YA-10 made its first flight on 21 July 1972.

Fly-off competition

The Air Force's formal evaluation of the prototypes lasted from 10 October until 9 December 1972, with the YA-9s logging 307.6 hours, and the YA-10s 328.1. Generally preferred by the evaluation pilots (three from AFSC and two from TAC, who each flew both types after role familiarisation in the A-37), the real advantage of the YA-10 was the ease of access to its underwing hardpoints. Other factors stated included the shorter, easier transition from prototype to production aircraft, the Fairchild aircraft having been built to what amounted almost to a production standard, at least structurally, The use of an existing engine (the TF34 being used by the Navy's S-3 Viking) was also

Warthog in its element: A-10 pilots feel happiest with their nose in the mud and trees, where the aircraft can use its agility to the full to keep hidden behind terrain. For Maverick attacks, the aircraft does have to pop up to acquire and lock-on the target.

Left: The main disadvantage of the high bypass ratio turbofans is not the lack of speed, but the lack of acceleration. However, with good energy management, the A-10 pilot can wring acceptable performance from his mount, and the tight turning radius can cause a nasty shock for opposing fighters.

Above: The prototype YA-10 lugs a heavy load of Mk 82 500-lb bombs during an early flight trial. The prototype was originally flown with an M61A1 20-mm Vulcan cannon in place of the intended GAU-8/A Avenger.

The two contenders for the AX competition showed considerably different approaches to a common set of solutions. The Northrop YA-9 (right) proved to be a good aircraft, but its low-set wing was more difficult to re-arm quickly, and overall the aircraft had far less redundancy than the YA-10 (far right). Interestingly, when the Soviets came to produce an aircraft in this general class (the Sukhoi Su-25 'Frogfoot'), they chose to 'copy' the layout of the YA-9 rather than the A-10.

vitally important. The A-10's superior MMH/FH figures and better redundancy were crucial factors.

As always, political considerations were very important, and awarding the AX contract to Fairchild meant much-needed employment for the company and the region, which was a less urgent need at Northrop or for southern California. The defeated YA-9 was not without advantages, the most notable being its unique side-force control system that linked the split airbrakes and the rudder and allowed the pilot to track a ground target without worrying about bank angle or fuselage direction. Both aircraft exceeded the specification, and while the Northrop aircraft was judged to have superior handling characteristics, with significantly less roll inertia, this was felt to be counterbalanced by the maintainability and survivability of the A-10. The decision, thus, was far from being a foregone conclusion.

Pre-production order

Fairchild-Republic was announced the winner on 18 January 1973, and set about building 10 pre-production YA-10As after signing the $159.2 million pre-production contract on 1 March 1973; simultaneously, General Electric received a $27.6 million contract for TF34 engines for these aircraft. This engine contract was not a foregone conclusion either, since there had been careful studies of a proposed Avco-Lycoming F102-powered A-10. The F102 was a significantly cheaper engine, and had greater growth potential. Eventually, as a result of the more advanced stage that the TF34 had reached, and a desire for commonality with a then-proposed eight TF34-engined AWACS, General Electric received the order.

This is perhaps not being entirely fair to the TF34.

Derived from the C-5 Galaxy's TF39, the new engine has a novel nickel alloy combustor which gives a long, maintenance-free life, while the fuel injection system uses a two-stage swirler which vaporises the fuel before ignition. The TF34 had a limited life, its use being confined to the A-10 and Viking and, in a civil form, the Canadair Challenger 601, but in many ways it formed the basis of the success of the later F404 and F110 fighter engines.

Modifications to the engine to suit it to the A-10 were very minor, being largely confined to modifications to meet the USAF's left/right interchangeability requirements, although jetpipes are angled upwards to reduce trim changes when the power is adjusted. The prototype A-10s flew with Navy-standard engines, but pre-production machines received the heavier, cheaper TF34-GE-100. Harder-than-anticipated use, dictated by more low-level hard-turning flight than had been envisioned, resulted in greater-than-expected hot section wear and tear. As a result, engines were upgraded in service to TF34-GE-100A standards with a modified combustor and high pressure turbine. This doubled hot section life to 2,000 hours, including 360 hours at maximum power. The Fairchild company took the contract very seriously, vice president and Farmingdale general manager Donald Strait, an experienced P-47, F-84 and F-105 pilot, setting up a 'Tiger Works' (modelled on the Lockheed 'Skunk Works').

In July 1973, when the Air Force was slow to act on a congressional recommendation that the new aircraft be evaluated against the A-7D, funding for four of the YA-10As was cut. From 16 April until 10 May 1974, the fly-off was held at McConnell AFB, in Wichita, Kansas. The second YA-10 and an A-7D were flown by four Air Force

pilots with combat experience in F-100s and F-4s. Because of its design, the YA-10 was found to be more survivable, more lethal because of its yet-to-be-fitted 30-mm cannon, and less expensive to operate. Perhaps its most remarkable coup over the venerable SLUF was when the YA-10 was able to spend two hours 'on station', 260 nm (299 miles/481 km) from base, with 18 500-lb (227-kg) bombs. The A-7D was only able to spend 11 minutes. This evaluation finally killed off the proposed A-7DER, a stretched, re-engined, rebuilt Corsair II incorporating the GAU-8 Avenger cannon. 1974 was not an entirely happy year for the A-10, a USAF committee expressing its concern with production progress forcing the acquisition of new numerically controlled machine tools, and the placing of contracts for some critical components with sub-contractors. This was hardly surprising, since Farmingdale had not run a major programme since the closure of the F-105 production line more than 10 years earlier.

The first prototype, 71-1369, was placed in flyable storage on 15 April 1975, after completing 467 sorties and 590.9 hours of flight time. The second YA-10, 71-1370, finished the 37-month prototype programme when it was placed in flyable storage on 13 June 1975, after completing 354 flights and 548.5 flying hours. It later became an Air Force recruiting display, before being turned over to the Air Force Museum.

Development

The pre-production YA-10As joined the test programme from February 1975. Although obviously similar to the YA-10s, a number of subtle external changes were incorporated in these aircraft, mostly around the wings. Fixed leading-edge slats and trailing-edge fairings, which were found to be necessary to avoid stalling the engines when the wing stalled, were standardised, although a moveable slat was later added to production aircraft. Ventral strakes that had been added to the YA-10s to smooth airflow around the underfuselage weapon pylons were also incorporated. The wingspan was increased slightly outboard of the ailerons, and maximum flap deflection was cut from 40° to 30° (and eventually just 20° on production aircraft). Finally, the vertical tails were reshaped, an air refuelling receptacle was added in the nose, as was an internal boarding ladder, and the gun was depressed 2°, while provision was made for an undernose pylon to carry the 'Pave Penny' laser spot tracker.

These six aircraft were each tasked with specific parts of the test programme. Aircraft No. 1, 73-1664, was the last A-10 to make its first flight from Edwards AFB, on 15 February 1975, and was used to test performance and handling. The second aircraft, 73-1665, was the first aircraft to make its first flight from Fairchild's Farmingdale, Long Island, facility, on 26 April 1975, and was tasked with armament and weapons certification. The third pre-production aircraft, 73-1666, made its maiden flight on 10 June 1975, and tested sub-systems and weapons delivery. The fourth aircraft, 73-1667, first flew on 17 July 1975, and conducted initial operational test and evaluation (IOT&E) and propulsion testing. The No. 5 aircraft, 73-1668, first flew on 9 August 1975 and assisted with IOT&E and stores certification testing. The final pre-production aircraft, 73-1669, made its first flight on 10 September 1975, and was the climatic test aircraft. Although these were their primary duties, the aircraft sometimes performed other testing. While it was testing a new gun propellant on 8 June 1978, both of 73-1669's engines flamed out and failed to restart. Its pilot had his ejection filmed by a chase plane and broadcast on the nightly news (both the prototype and pre-production aircraft used the Douglas ESCAPAC, while production aircraft switched to the standard McDonnell ACES II).

Since there were only six YA-10As, instead of the required 10, testing gradually fell behind schedule, although the test and evaluation programme was generally very successful. The first production aircraft, 75-0258, flew on 10 October 1975 and was delivered to the Air Force on 5

Above: This view of the prototype YA-10 reveals some important design features. The ability to survive in a hostile groundfire environment was partly due to the redundancy inherent in the design. It has oft been quoted that the A-10 could continue to fly with one of its tails or one of its engines shot away. The low-set tailplane and high-set engines meant that the exhaust fumes were largely shielded from the shoulder-launched heat-seeking missiles which proliferate on the modern battlefield.

Below: 71-1370 was the second YA-10 prototype, here seen at Edwards fitted with spin parachute in the tailcone, and painted in a charcoal grey with white surfaces.

Fairchild A-10

Above: 73-1665 was the first of the pre-production YA-10As to take to the air from the Farmingdale facility, and was used for weapons work. It was later fitted with these revised nose contours.

Right: This was the fourth pre-production airframe, and was assigned to operational evaluation. Like all the pre-production aircraft, it featured the GAU-8/A gun from the outset. The long nose boom was for test instrumentation.

November 1975. It and the next three production A-10As joined the testing effort. This shortage of aircraft delayed the delivery of the first operational A-10A to the 355th TFW until March of 1976, five months behind the original schedule. Apart from this delay, the only thing to mar the A-10's early success was the fatal crash of an aircraft at the 1977 Paris Air Salon at Le Bourget. Sam Nelson was killed when he hit the ground during a series of low-level loops on 3 June 1977, a grave loss to the programme.

The 355th TFTW conducted the final operational test and evaluation, flying a handful of their aircraft to Farnborough for the SBAC show and then on for a tour of Europe, which included compatibility checks with new-generation HASs. While in Europe, the aircraft took part in exercises. The wing also conducted Arctic tests (Operation Jack Frost) from Eielson in January 1977, and in April and May four aircraft from the wing's 333rd TFTS took part in Operation Red Flag at Nellis AFB, operating from an advanced strip on a dry lakebed. Later in 1977 the A-10 took part in a series of trials known as JAWS (Joint Attack Weapons System), which were critical in defining the role and tactics that would be followed by the new aircraft, in particular the ways in which it would operate in conjunction with Army attack helicopters.

A-10 nomenclature

The A-10 was christened the 'Thunderbolt II' by the Pentagon bureaucracy during the delivery of the 100th aircraft, 76-0553, on 3 April 1978, perpetuating a trend begun by McDonnell's very successful Phantom II. The ceremony was suitably grand, and was centred around a static display comprising the A-10 and its illustrious namesake. One can be excused for musing about the reasons for this now-maddening habit: maybe 'the brass' think tacking 'II' on a name will make a new design successful, or that reusing a previously-used name is safe and 'politically correct' (disguised as knowledge of a manufacture's past successes), or perhaps it is just a combination of laziness and lack of imagination. The truth of the matter is probably a combination of all of the above but, thankfully, this disease has not infected the lieutenants and captains who actually fly aeroplanes for a living.

As early as 1973, noting the new aircraft's not-so-smooth lines, and taking into account its not-so-high flying mission,

the Tactical Air Warfare Center, recalling the 'Groundhog' nickname of the F-84, the 'Superhog' of the F-84F and the F-105's 'Ultra-Hog', had proposed a far more appropriate name: 'Warthog'. However, hating the complexity of a word with two syllables, this was eventually shortened to simply 'Hog' (correctly pronounced 'Hawg'). No one closely associated with the A-10 calls it by that 'other name'. ('Hog' drivers' wives have observed that the best way to differentiate between a 'Hog' and its driver is that the former stops whining when the flight is over.) In one way, the official name is more appropriate than the brass intended. Like the original Thunderbolt, the A-10 is a rugged, dependable ground attack aircraft, and like its namesake its official name is virtually ignored in favour of an affectionate but more derogatory nickname.

The first pre-production aircraft, 73-1664, was bailed to Fairchild-Republic in 1978 for conversion into the two-seat YA-10B, commonly known as the Night/Adverse Weather (N/AW) A-10. Development was funded partly by the company, which put in $2 million, and partly by the DoD, which put in an amount variously reported as $5 million or $7.5 million. The possibility of conversion to two-seat configuration had been stipulated in the original concept. In addition to the second seat, the major change to this aircraft was the addition of 20 in (51 cm) to the top of the vertical tails. A pod-mounted ground-mapping radar was mounted on the left fuselage pylon, with a FLIR pod on the right fuselage pylon. Had the A-10B been produced, these sensors would have been installed in the front of the respective main landing gear pods. The aircraft was also fitted with an LN-39 INS and AN/APN-194 radar altimeter but, extraordinarily, armour was not extended to the rear seat.

In any event, the Air Force was not interested in either this night-attack version or a two-seat trainer (pilots usually

*Above: The first service unit to receive the A-10 was the 355th Tactical Fighter Wing, which was established as the training unit (and later redesignated as a TTW to reflect its primary role). The wing had previously been an A-7 operator, and it was this type which was the first to be displaced by the Warthog in **USAF** service.*

*Left: In operational service, it was the 354th TFW at Myrtle Beach AFB which became the first to swap its Corsair IIs for Warthogs. These were soon busy on deployments around the **US** outposts, this pair being seen over Hawaii.*

Fairchild A-10

Right: Fairchild bailed back the first pre-production YA-10A to produce the Night/Adverse Weather A-10 (designated YA-10B). This added a second seat for a weapon systems officer and night sensors.

Far right: The YA-10B remained a one-off as the USAF had no interest in its night capabilities (or in its potential as a conversion trainer). It has remained at Edwards AFB, and is now part of the base museum collection.

compare the A-10's flying qualities to the T-37 trainer, calling it a 'Big Tweet'), although Fairchild energetically marketed the aircraft as a combat-ready trainer, pointing out huge cost savings to be made by removing the need for an instructor's chase aircraft on many A-10 conversion and tactical training sorties. Fairchild also promoted the basic YA-10B as the basis for defence suppression, battlefield co-ordination and interdictor versions. Unfortunately, these relied on the LANTIRN system, which was also slated for the higher priority F-15E and F-16C. The YA-10B was evaluated during 1979, but night attack with the A-10 did not become reality until 12 years later.

As a final, desperate attempt to save the two-seater, Fairchild marketed it in the Pacific area as a maritime strike aircraft, carrying Harpoon or Exocet, but these attempts came to nothing. There have been other stillborn A-10 variants. In 1976, Fairchild showed a model of the A-10 with long, slim nacelles housing unreheated versions of the J101 or RB.199, trading endurance for higher speed in an attempt to win export orders. This would have given a speed increase in the order of 50 kt (57 mph; 92 km/h) in low-level flight with weapons, but was not sufficient to overcome the prejudices of the intended customers, who regarded a 450-kt (517-mph; 831-km/h) attack aircraft as little more than an obsolete anachronism.

Designed during the long war in Vietnam, the A-10 was always intended for use in Europe, and the first aircraft were delivered to the USAFE's 81st TFW during January 1979. The Connecticut ANG became the first Guard users of the

The YA-10B carried its FLIR and radar sensors in pods, but had a production order for the night version been ordered, the sensors would have been relocated into the 'kneecaps' of the main undercarriage fairings.

aircraft that April (and also the first Guard unit to receive a fighter not 'handed down' by the regulars), while the Reservists at Barksdale became the first AFRES recipients of the type in June. Never exclusively a CONUS/USAFE type, A-10As were also sent to PACAF and Alaska in November and December 1981.

One tough customer

The A-10 is an extremely unusual shape by comparison with other contemporary military aircraft, but its configuration is dictated by its role. The high aspect ratio unswept wing has a large thickness/chord ratio and is highly cambered for high lift, which allows great strength at relatively light weight. The outer panels incorporate some 7° of dihedral, but are tipped by anhedral Hoerner wingtips that reduce induced drag and reduce wingtip vortices, as well as improving aileron effectiveness at low speeds. The low wing loading gives good turn performance, and a single slotted Fowler flap can be used to further enhance agility. The cockpit is set high on the fuselage and is carried well forward, giving good visibility forward and down – a prerequisite for a successful ground attack aircraft. The cockpit itself is remarkably austere, a TV monitor for the EO Maverick being the only major feature that would not be immediately familiar to an F-84 pilot.

Realising that operations in direct support of ground forces in the Central European theatre of NATO would expose the A-10 to withering ground fire, keynotes of the new design became survivability in a combat environment,

Fairchild A-10

After many years training for an intense war in the Central European theatre, the A-10 eventually went to war in a wide open desert, with few terrain features to hide behind. However, the Warthog confounded its detractors by proving an exceptional weapon platform in this style of warfare. A change in operational procedures saw the 'Hogs' operating at a higher altitude than normal to avoid the intense groundfire, from where they could detect targets at long range and launch devastating attacks with cannon, Mavericks and cluster munitions.

Leading-edge slat
Inboard of the undercarriage fairings is a simple slat. This is closed at normal angles of attack but opens at high Alpha to prevent engine compressor blade stalls.

Defensive ordnance
The outer wing pylons of the A-10 are dedicated to the carriage of defensive ordnance. This aircraft carries the standard fit of AIM-9L/M Sidewinders on a dual rail adaptor on the port outer wing pylon, and an AN/ALQ-184 ECM pod on the outer starboard. Much use was made of mechanical countermeasures (more chaff than flares) during Desert Storm.

Ejection seat
The A-10 is fitted with an ACES II seat. This has two modes, one for low-altitude and one for high-altitude operation.

Markings
This A-10 was assigned to the 23rd Tactical Fighter Wing (Provisional) at King Fahd Airport, Damman, during Desert Shield/Storm. The wing featured two squadrons from the parent 23rd TFW, this aircraft wearing the blue fin-cap of the 74th TFS. No attempt was made to render the A-10s in a sand scheme, all aircraft flying in lizard throughout the conflict. Similarly, no attempt was made to tone down or remove the 23rd's traditional tiger's teeth.

Offensive stores
A typical general-purpose load for the A-10 in Desert Storm comprised single Mavericks on each main wing pylon, and six cluster bombs on the unoccupied pylons. The CBUs employ the SUU-30, SUU-64 or SUU-65 dispensers.

On Tactical Air Support Squadrons, the OA-10 replaced Cessna OA-37Bs. This pair illustrates the hand-over for the 103rd TASS, Pennsylvania ANG.

For several units in the ANG, the delivery of their new A-10s spelled goodbye to the venerable North American F-100 Super Sabre. The Warthog offered much greater persistence and accuracy in the close air support role.

remain controllable enough after sustaining damage to their flight controls to usually reach a relatively safe bail-out area; their new A-10 had a set of back-up flight controls designed in from the start, using cables rather than rods, which could jam more easily. Battle damage resistance was extensively trialled, tests including firing multiple 23-mm shells at representative structural units while also blasting these with a 400-kt airflow. The A-10's battle damage resistance and get-you-home abilities were designed not only to produce an aircraft which could be repaired and returned to the fray; an extensively damaged aircraft could serve as a spares source for other A-10As, such is the left/right and aircraft-aircraft interchangeability of parts and components.

To protect the 'Hog' drivers from anti-aircraft artillery (AAA), the A-10A's cockpit was surrounded with a 'bathtub' of titanium armour designed to withstand hits from 23-mm projectiles from the Soviet ZSU-23-4, and even to withstand some 57-mm shell strikes. The bathtub is not a casting, as the name might suggest, but consists of massive plates of titanium alloy bolted together and lined with a multi-layered nylon spall which prevents splinters from entering the cockpit even if the bathtub's integrity is compromised. Titanium was chosen after in-depth evaluation of ceramic and aluminium armour. This single unit represents 47 per cent of the weight of armour carried, with 37 per cent more protecting the fuel system.

The main fuel tanks form a cross in the centre-section, close to the centre of gravity, obviating the need for fuel transfers. The tanks, which are tear-resistant and self-sealing, can therefore be made into separate, independent units that can be isolated from one another. If all are holed, a pair of self-sealing sumps contains sufficient fuel for a 200-nm (230-mile/370-km) flight. The tanks are protected by rigid, reinforced fire-retardant foam, with a layer of reticulated flexible foam inside that. The foam is designed to minimise spillage of fuel, to prevent airflow through a holed tank and to inhibit fire. Tests which involved firing 300 rounds of high-explosive incendiary (HEI) ammunition into the tanks failed to cause an explosion.

Terrain masking

Agility makes a major contribution to survivability, since it allows the A-10 to make maximum use of terrain masking and to avoid exposing itself to hostile fire. At the A-10A's low speed, relatively low *g* turns produce a small turn radius and high turn rate. An A-10 making a 3.5 *g*, 180° turn at 320 kt will complete the turn in 16 seconds, and use a radius of 2,700 ft (823 m), while an F-16 travelling at 600 kt and pulling 6 *g* will take 17 seconds with a radius of 3,620 ft (1103 m).

Unlike its faster brethren, the A-10 has no tailhook or drag chute (virtual necessities on second-generation jet fighters). No provisions were made in the original design for an inertial navigation system (INS) or weapon delivery computer, a reflection of the miserable performance and reliability of the 'advanced avionics' used during the aircraft's design period.

Another aspect of a modern war is its incredibly high tempo of operations. To minimise its need for support equipment, the A-10 was designed with an auxiliary power unit (APU) to negate the need for externally assisted starting, and to allow systems to be run-up or checked without starting the engines. The APU's intake was located on the right side of the aircraft, underneath the engine, with the exhaust on the opposite side, where it leaves a stain on the bottom of the left engine nacelle. Reflecting a style of warfare where pilots fly several sorties without getting out of their cockpits, it was also fitted with a single point refuelling receptacle to allow it to be 'hot-pit' refuelled without shutting down its engines.

One of the most enduring qualities of Douglas's 'Spad' was its endurance. To replicate this feature in a jet designed

followed closely by maintainability. Single point failures were 'designed out' of the aircraft, accounting for its two engines and tails, and for the profusion of duplicated systems, hydraulic and fuel lines, etc. The dual hydraulic, electrical and pneumatic systems are widely separated and carried in protected ducts. The wings and horizontal tailplanes each have triple spars, giving an astonishing degree of structural redundancy. The main landing gear is housed in pods to avoid the need for a wheel well inside the wing, which would necessitate breaks in the wing structure. The engines are set high to avoid FOD ingestion during operation from semi-prepared strips, and are widely spaced to avoid a hit on one causing damage and debris which could 'take out' the second. Double curvature is avoided wherever possible, the bulk of the A-10A's skin consisting of flat plates, simple cylinders or cones which require no expensive and time-consuming stretch-forming during manufacture and which are easier to repair in the field.

Two-thirds of all battle damage was designed to be repairable in the field within 12 hours, and three-quarters within 24 hours. During the Vietnam War, Fairchild-Republic had been forced to make emergency modifications to its F-105 Thunderchiefs (a.k.a. 'Thuds') to allow them to

Left: One special capability of the A-10 is to use short, semi-prepared strips. The extending flaps and split wingtip airbrakes keep landing run short, and take-off distance is equally impressive.

Below: A pair of 138th TFS A-10As breaks for landing. The pair is the basic tactical formation, one aircraft providing cover while the other makes an attack. A-10 crews call it mutual support, and it allows maximum safety and the minimum of time between attacks.

for use at low altitude required the use of high-bypass turbofan engines. The 9,065-lb (40-kN) static thrust General Electric TF34 was chosen. Aside from endurance, the bypass air of this engine cooled the exhaust plume, reducing the A-10's vulnerability to IR-guided missiles. To further reduce the threat from surface-launched IR missiles (the SA-7 'Grail' had just been fielded), the engines were positioned high on the aft fuselage, just in front of and above the tail. This configuration formed a 'box' which hid the exhaust gases for several more feet, allowing them additional time to cool before becoming clearly visible from the ground. The combination of large frontal area (i.e. drag) and slow spool-up time of the engines resulted in the A-10 having poor acceleration characteristics. This lack of acceleration in a combat scenario was what really concerned crews, although higher speed was always seen as 'nice to have', especially on ferry flights. In the late 1970s, some consideration was given to replacing the turbofans with turbojets to cure this problem, but modification costs were determined to be too expensive.

Long endurance

Internal fuel capacity was about 1,650 US gal (7958 litres), which weighed about 10,700 lb (4853 kg). The combination of fuel-efficient engines and relatively generous fuel supply allowed the A-10 to spend one hour on station, 150 miles (241 km) from base – 10 times longer than any other aircraft. This could be supplemented for ferry flights only by up to three 600-US gal (2536-litre) external fuel tanks, holding about 3,900 lb (1773 kg) of fuel. The external

fuel tanks were the same as those used by the F-111; because they were not used frequently, their reliability was always suspect, and it was not uncommon to have tanks function on test flights prior to a deployment only to have them balk 'on the day'. Only three pylons were plumbed for fuel tanks, with a single tank carried on the centreline being the most common ferry configuration.

The AAS-35 Pave Penny target identification set, laser (TISL) is carried by the A-10A from a special pylon on the front right portion of the fuselage. TISL is not a laser designator, but instead senses coded energy pulses reflected from targets designated with lasers by ground troops. It then projects a symbol on the HUD to help the pilot locate his target more quickly, so he can then attack it with a Maverick, 'dumb' bombs, or cannon.

A design originated for work in the steamy jungles of South East Asia, the A-10 has operated with equal success in many different climates. At far left CONUS-based Warthogs arrive in Egypt for a Bright Star exercise, while at left an Alaska-based A-10 from the 18th TFS land at Kotzebue to practise operations in an austere Arctic climate. The latter has a soluble white paint applied for operations over snow.

Fairchild A-10

Right: The front end of the A-10 is dominated by the GAU-8/A. The seven barrels are rotated so that only the barrel facing to the direct starboard is firing at any given time. The barrel uses the rest of the rotation to cool down before firing its next round.

The YA-10 prototypes were initially fitted with the 20-mm M61A1 Vulcan cannon because the definitive production cannon was not ready. The RFP for this weapon had been issued six months after the AX RFP, and resulted in two new gun designs and four types of ammunition. General Electric (inventors of the modern Gatling-type cannon) and Philco Ford developed separate prototypes under $12.1 million development contracts, while Hughes licensed the Oerlikon 304RF-30 as an 'insurance policy'. Test firings began in 1972 and the General Electric cannon was selected in June 1973.

Seven-barrelled Gatling

The first prototype was retrofitted with the production model's seven-barrelled GAU-8 Avenger 30-mm cannon in February 1974 (the losing Philco Ford cannon had been a six-barrelled weapon). Test firings were conducted against 15 tanks, including US M48s and Soviet T-62s acquired from Israel. The use of seven barrels allowed a very high rate of fire to be achieved without exceeding the temperature limits of the barrels, since each barrel actually

Nose detail of a 103rd FS A-10A reveals the cooling sleeve around the rotary cannon. Several attempts have been made to divert gun gases away from the aircraft, including a vaned collar which was fitted to most A-10s for some time. However, this was not ideal, and the plain barrel end has been retained.

fires at a relatively slow rate. Each barrel is effectively a simple non-repeating 30-mm rifle, with its own breech and bolt, joined together into a single rotor revolving on a common axis, with firing mechanisms outside the moving rotor.

Proving the value of prototyping, this test programme, which ran through July, pronounced the cannon/aeroplane combination compatible, but not before discovering that the cannon's 10,000-lb (45-kN) recoil would force the production nose to be redesigned. This required moving the nose gear slightly to the right of the aircraft's centreline, which allowed the cannon's recoil to be directed down the centreline. Because only one barrel fires at a time (while the other six 'cool' as they rotate), the gun still appears to be offset slightly to the left. Even with any asymmetric recoil force cancelled out, firing the gun has a very noticeable effect. The muzzle horsepower of 17,700 compares with MHP figures of less than 100 for wartime aircraft cannons, and reduces the air speed by several knots. MHP is a factor of muzzle velocity, projectile mass and rate of fire, and gives an excellent idea of the power being generated.

The development of the GAU-8 was not always trouble-free. Much effort had to be expended in trying to eradicate the build-up of explosive gases during firing, and one aircraft was actually lost when both engines flamed out after ingesting such gases, as related above. Fortunately, the pilot was able to eject safely, while being filmed by his photo-chase wingman. An early solution was to weld onto the nose massive square-section vents but, while this allowed firing trials to continue, it clearly would not be an acceptable fix for production aircraft. A double flame-out is still extremely serious in an A-10, since the

engine relight speed of the TF34 is higher than the aircraft's maximum level speed. At high altitudes, the aircraft can be dived to achieve relight speed, but at low level the pilot has no option but to eject.

The GAU-8 is actually the gun part of the A/A 49E-6 gun system which, with a gross weight of 4,200 lb (1910 kg), includes a drum normally containing 1,174 rounds of ammunition. The whole unit is about the same size and

weight as a Cadillac.

Although there are different types of ammunition available, the most common load is called 'combat mix' (CM) and consists of a single 1.5-lb (0.68-kg) PGU-13 HEI round mixed in with five 1.65-lb (0.75-kg) PGU-14 armour-piercing incendiary (API) rounds. The depleted uranium (DU) projectile from the PGU-14 weighs 0.94 lb (0.43 kg) and leaves the gun travelling at 3,240 ft (988 m)

Fairchild A-10

Right: Warthogs were soon installed in Europe, where the biggest armour threat to the West lay in the plains and valleys of Germany. Based in England, the A-10s soon established a network of operations in the intended killing ground.

Below: The refuelling receptacle's position immediately in front of the pilot allowed easy alignment for rendezvous, but could lead to a momentary white-out when breaking contact.

per second, and can kill a main battle tank from as far away as 21,600 ft (6584 m), depending on the tank. The kill mechanism of this projectile is interesting: it is specifically designed to have enough energy to penetrate tank armour - once. Once inside the tank, it stays there; the reader is left to imagine the consequences. The use of depleted uranium led to predictable (and groundless) howls of anguish from the USSR, which described the shell as an atomic weapon. In fact, the radioactivity of the shells is negligible, and they can be safely handled. Their use did put the gun into a special export category, and this is understood to be one of the major factors which prevented a purchase of the A-10 by Thailand. All projectiles use an aluminium cartridge case for lightness and have plastic instead of copper bands on the shell itself. These save weight and cost, and save wear on the barrel, extending life and acting as crude barrel cleaners.

The Avenger system is capable of firing either 2,100 (normally) or 4,200 nearly 1-ft (31-cm) long 30-mm cannon shells per minute, powered by dual hydraulic motors. About 1987 the rate was fixed at 3,900 rpm in preparation for a gun gas deflector modification (which was later cancelled). The USAF specified a minimum barrel life of 21,000 rounds per gun. Rounds are stored radially, pointing in towards the axis of the ammunition drum, their bases slotted into lengthways grooves in the inside of the drum. This system requires a specialised piece of ground support equipment for loading (the only such equipment needed by the A-10) and can simultaneously unload spent cases and reload new ones, changing a full load in 13 minutes. Since most bursts are only a few seconds long, it is more practical to think in terms of 35 and 65 rounds per second (although in the first second, 'only' 50 bullets exit the cannon since it takes a half second for it to reach maximum speed). During Desert Storm, 940,254 rounds of combat mix (CM) were fired (an average of 119 per sortie, just a 2-second burst). An

Right: So important was the A-10 in Europe that the 81st TFW rapidly became the largest wing in the USAF, with six operational squadrons split over two closely-located bases (Bentwaters and Woodbridge). Their task was to cover the whole of Germany, and to augment other forces in Norway and the Mediterranean.

Warthog paint schemes

Few aircraft have had such a variety of paint schemes applied, or been so associated with just one, as the A-10A. The YA-10s were initially overall federal standard number (FSN) 36473 Aircraft Grey, and later repainted FSN 36118 Gunship Grey. The first YA-10A, 73-1664, was also Gunship Grey. Pre-production aircraft two, five and six (73-1665, -1668, and -1669) had a mottled pattern of white sprayed over a black base coat. Aircraft three (73-1666) was overall FSN 36320 Dark Compass Ghost Grey. Aircraft four (73-1667) was the first to have a paint similar to the first production scheme applied. It was overall 40 per cent MASK-10A, a light greenish-grey which reflected 40 per cent of the light hitting it. (The MASK-10A paints were never assigned FSN numbers.)

The seventh aircraft, which was the first production A-10A (75-0258), was overall FSN 36375 Light Compass Ghost Grey with a gloss overcoat, while the eighth and ninth (75-0259 and -0260) were the same colour but lacked the overcoat. Aircraft number 10 (75-0261) had its top painted like 75-0259, but had its underside painted 50 per cent MASK-10A. The 11th aircraft (75-0262) had 40 per cent MASK-10A on the upper surfaces, with a Dark Compass Ghost Grey underside. Aircraft 12 through 30 (75-0263 through 75-0281) had what became known as the 'Intermediate MASK-10A' scheme, with an asymmetric pattern of 30 per cent MASK-10A and the lighter 50 per cent MASK-10A. From aircraft 31 through 145 (75-0282 through 77-0230), a symmetrical pattern of improved-quality 30 per cent and 50 per cent MASK-10A, along with a 'false canopy' on the belly in Gunship Grey, was applied.

After the Joint Attack Weapons System (JAWS) exercise in 1977, which tested tactics for the use of A-10As with

The early A-10s exhibited a bewildering array of colours. This was the 'Intermediate Mask 10-A'.

Army attack and scout helicopters, it was discovered that the MASK-10A scheme was very visible to Aggressor F-5Es. To counter this prior to the follow-on JAWS II in November 1977, at least four aircraft assigned to Nellis in late 1977 (75-0258, -0259, -0260, and -0262) were painted in mottled camouflage patterns, which became collectively known as the JAWS schemes. Although effective, these schemes were difficult to maintain. However, the point had been made that the air-to-air threat in a 'NATO' war would outweigh the surface-to-air threat for the 'Warthog'.

In September 1978, a prototype 'Charcoal Lizard' scheme was applied in a wraparound pattern to 75-0266 of the 422nd FWS using FSN 34092 Dark Green, 34102 Medium Green and 36231 Medium Grey. Its evaluation proved successful and, after darkening the grey to FSN 36081, was selected to replace the two-tone 'MASK-10A' grey scheme, beginning with the 148th production airframe, 77-0223. These aircraft began to show up in Europe in April 1979, after about 30 grey aircraft had been delivered to the 81st TFW. A small factor in this decision may have been a tiff between the Air Force and aviation artist Keith Ferris over the legal rights to the false canopy painted on the belly of the grey aircraft, a feature not seen on Air Force aircraft since. The 917th TFW at Barksdale painted at least one A-10A (78-0552) in an experimental sand, tan and light green camouflage pattern, and another (76-0530) in a similar camouflage of medium, dark and extra dark greys. Neither scheme was adopted for the fleet.

In 1992, after evaluating the lessons of Desert Storm and in light of the demise

of the Warsaw Pact, it was decided that the surface-to-air threat was again predominant for any foreseeable operation in which the A-10 might be involved. A scheme using Dark Compass Ghost Grey upper surfaces and Light Compass Ghost Grey under surfaces was devised and applied. The first aircraft to be painted in this scheme was 81-0956, which first flew from RAF Bentwaters, UK, on 12 June 1992.

*Above: One of the most striking schemes was this **JAWS II** scheme to counter air-to-air threats.*

Below: Three pre-production aircraft had this scheme of mottled white over base black.

*Above: Both prototypes were repainted in this **Gunship Grey** to reduce conspicuity.*

During 1991 the 917th TFW applied two experimental camouflage schemes, a grey concoction (above) and a desert scheme (below).

Left: Most associated with the A-10 is the Charcoal Lizard scheme.

Below: Compass Ghost is the current standard A-10 scheme.

additional 16,360 rounds of HEI were fired by 23rd TASS OA-10As, which did not use combat mix (an average of only 18 per sortie).

European operations

The A-10 was designed during Vietnam, but intended for combat in Europe. It did not take long to discover that flying in Germany by the seat of one's pants at low altitude was not easy, that relying on line-of-sight TACAN was impractical at very low level and to realise that combat would not make the task easier (something just about anyone who had ever flown there could have attested to). The stability augmentation system ('Hog' drivers have nothing as sophisticated as an autopilot) helps reduce workload, and has been upgraded in service, but its function is to ensure consistent control responses and warn of

excessive angles of attack or an impending stall.

Bowing to reality, the Air Force finally began production installation of an AN/ASN-141 inertial navigation system (INS) with the 391st aircraft (79-0127). This also required the installation of a modified HUD with a new, more powerful symbology generator. To get INS-equipped aircraft to Europe as quickly as possible, a swap of all 81st TFW aircraft was conducted. Aircraft at RAF Woodbridge and Bentwaters were flown to Sacramento Air Logistics Center (SM-ALC), at McClellan AFB in California, and dropped off for programmed depot maintenance (PDM) where modification to install the INSs were made. Meanwhile, the pilots flew to Fairchild-Republic's A-10A production facility in Hagerstown, Maryland, picking up factory-fresh INS-equipped aircraft, and returned them to England. Once that process was complete, PDM for European A-10As was shifted to RAF Kemble.

The A-10A's European operations were built around the main operating bases (MOBs) at RAF Bentwaters and RAF Woodbridge in England, supporting several forward operating locations (FOLs) in Germany. (Although the focus was Germany, Europe-based A-10As were also prepared to deploy in support of other NATO allies, such as Norway or Italy.) The FOL concept allowed the A-10As to be responsive to the CAS requirements of NATO ground forces. Small detachments rotated through the FOLs on a continual basis, allowing pilots to be intimately familiar with the people they might have to defend, as well as their territory, including probable avenues of Soviet attack plus the friendly units along them. Over time, experienced crews actually became able to work their 75/100-nm long and 20-nm deep sectors of responsibility without referencing maps.

There were six FOLs, three under the control of each Allied Tactical Air Force (ATAF) in Germany. Only Sembach, Norvenich, Ahlhorn and Leipheim actually hosted squadron detachments; the other two FOLs would have only been activated had war broken out. Although the FOLs were capable of minor maintenance and emergency repairs, aircraft would have had to return to the MOBs for major maintenance. Had an FOL's runway been bombed, the A-10s, capable of taking off in three-quarters of a mile, could have used part of the runway or a taxiway, or even deployed to emergency airstrips using straight sections of autobahn (A-10As were sometimes allowed to practise this technique on new stretches of the roadway before they were opened to the public).

Each squadron was assigned its own FOL, with two squadrons assigned to the inactive detachments that were stationed at two other squadrons' FOLs one week out of three. This arrangement resulted in each squadron having eight of its aircraft deployed two weeks out of three, keeping 32 A-10As in Germany. In late 1988, when the

509th and 511th TFSs transferred to the 10th TFW, the number of 81st TFW aircraft in Germany at any given time dropped to 24, with the other eight belonging to the 10th TFW. From an individual pilot's perspective, a normal rotation was composed of two weeks at the FOL, flying about twice a day, followed by four weeks at home, flying about twice a week.

FOLs were split into 2nd ATAF (northern half of Germany) and 4th ATAF (southern half). In the former were Det 3 at Ahlhorn (activated 1 July·1979, assigned to 91st TFS pre-1989, 509th after), Norvenich (activated 1 October 1979, deactivated 19 March 1992, assigned to 78th TFS pre-1989, 510th TFS after) and Jever, which was only a planned FOL (509th TFS assigned pre-1989 and 511th after). In 4th ATAF, there was Sembach (activated 1 September 1978, deactivated 3 May 1991, assigned to 510th TFS pre-1989, 78th TFS after), Leipheim (activated 1 April 1979, deactivated 25 September 1992, assigned to 92nd TFS pre-1989, 91st TFS after) and the planned FOL at Wiesbaden (assigned to 511th TFS pre-1989 and 92nd TFS after).

If the Cold War had ever turned hot, 18 aircraft would have deployed to each FOL. During combat operations, three two-ship formations from each FOL would have been

in contact with Warsaw Pact forces, with three more en route to the battle, while the remaining six aircraft would have been on the ground being rearmed. Co-ordination between ground forces and the A-10As would have been provided by OV-10A Bronco forward air controllers operating just behind the battlefield. A FAC could have remained 'on station', just behind the forward edge of the battle area, for up to four hours, maintaining the 'corporate memory' which would allow him to co-ordinate the air-to-ground battle to maximum effect.

Top: Not particularly effective over snow, the Charcoal Lizard scheme nevertheless was highly effective in hiding the A-10 from the attentions of MiGs over the forest and fields of Central Europe.

Above: Today the A-10 is deployed in several composite wings. The 23rd Wing is dedicated to support of the army at Fort Bragg, and a squadron of A-10s provides close air support.

Like the F-111, the A-10 has long been a subject for hot debate. Its vulnerability on the battlefield has been called into question since it was first procured, yet its results in combat and exercises maintain it as a force to be reckoned with.

Above: Long considered a day attack platform, the A-10 picked up some night capability with the LASTE mod, which added an NVG-compatible cockpit and radar altimeter.

Far right: The rocket pods under the wing denoted the adoption of the forward air control mission under the guise of the OA-10A. In fact the OA-10A does not differ in the slightest from a standard A-10. However, the aircraft is not normally used in direct action as it is classified a command and control asset by the USAF, and is accorded a high value.

Below: A sight more associated with maritime patrol aircraft, an A-10 gets a wash-down at Myrtle Beach. The aircraft is a 354th TFW(P) Gulf veteran, displaying its kill scoreboard on the starboard side below the cockpit.

Air liaison officers, pilots operating with Army ground units, would have translated their needs into 'pilot speak', relaying this information to the FACs, who would have passed it on to the 'Hogs' and Army helicopters for 'appropriate action'. The transfer of information would have occurred by means of a technique called the 'nine-line brief'. These pieces of information would tell the pilot everything he needed to know to attack the target. They included the: initial point (IP), the place from which to begin the attack, usually a visual landmark; magnetic heading from the IP to the target; distance from the IP to the target; elevation of the target area; description of the target; geographical co-ordinates of the target; position of friendly forces; direction to egress the target area, should the aircraft be damaged during the attack; and any other significant information.

Tactics developed during the JAWS exercises were refined and renamed joint air attack team (JAAT). The A-10As would have initially attacked an armoured column from just above 100 ft (31 m), hitting its AAA and SAM defences with Mavericks, before dropping behind terrain cover. With these defences suppressed, the attack helicopters would have attacked the tanks from less than 100 ft (31 m) with BGM-71 TOWs and cannon fire, taking turns with the reattacking A-10As. As the 'Hogs' cleared the area, the helicopters would have risen from their cover to continue the battle and cover the A-10As' departure. In this complimentary team, the A-10As had the speed, survivability and firepower, while the helicopters could remain on station, co-ordinate artillery, and land, if necessary, to co-ordinate with ground commanders.

Obviously, any war in Central Europe would have

involved serious losses. NATO planning depended heavily on reinforcements arriving from the US to sustain the war effort. To improve their knowledge of European flying conditions, terrain and procedures, without the time and expense of deploying entire squadrons, Continental US A-10 units would conduct periodic exchanges of a few pilots with the 81st TFW in England. This operation, called Boar Swap, also allowed UK-based crews to visit US units, reinforcing the cohesion of the 'Warthog' community.

By the late 1980s, the Vietnam-vintage OA-37Bs and OV-10As were reaching the end of their useful lives. In the eyes of the Air Force, so was the A-10, as far as front-line combat operations were concerned. Beginning in 1987, selected 'Hogs' were redesignated as OA-10As, the firtst serving with the 23rd TASS. In keeping with the increasingly politicised and bizarre way in which American combat aircraft are designated, F-16s with different engine/inlet combinations and primary missions (day versus night attack with LANTIRN) are all called F-16C/Ds, while the lowly A-10A got a whole new designation because of a mission change. There is no physical difference between an A-10A and a 'fast FAC' OA-10A. Because they only employ rockets for target marking and do not use most of the rest of the A-10A's arsenal, the OA-10A costs about $45 (£30) less per hour to operate than an A-10A. In these days of ever-decreasing defence budgets, every penny counts.

Desert Shield/Storm

The 23rd TFW(P) and 354th TFW(P) formed the two halves of the 144-aircraft A-10A/OA-10A force (informally known as the 'Fahd Squad') which operated from King Fahd International Airport, near the city of Damman in north-eastern Saudi Arabia. Readers interested in a fascinating account of the A-10A's role in the Gulf War are encouraged to read William Smallwood's book, *Warthog*.

During Desert Storm the OA/A-10A force flew 19,545.6 hours in 8,755 sorties (16.5 per cent of the 53,000 sorties flown by the coalition), of which 7,445 delivered weapons (85 per cent of A-10 sorties flown, 18 per cent of the coalition's 41,000 strike sorties). Overall A-10 weapon system reliability during Desert Storm was 98.67 per cent (this was the percentage of times weapons were successfully expended when the trigger was squeezed or the 'pickle' button depressed). Targets listed as 'confirmed kills' included 1,106 trucks, 987 tanks (25 per cent of all destroyed, plus perhaps as many more hit, but not claimed), 926 artillery pieces (again, about 25 per cent of the war's total, with perhaps twice this number believed actually hit, but not claimed), 501 armoured personnel carriers (about 30 per cent of the total destroyed during the war), 249 command vehicles, 112 military structures, 96 radars, 72 bunkers, 51 'Scud' missile launchers (revisionist arguments about the number of those actually destroyed aside), 50 AAA sites, 28 command posts, 11 'FROG' missile launchers, 10 parked fighters, nine surface-to-air missile (SAM) sites, eight fuel tanks and two air-to-air helicopter kills.

Three sorties a day

Combat operations of both wings were very similar. Typical operations from King Fahd involved flying a sortie, landing at the King Khalid Military City (KKMC) FOL to re-arm, flying another sortie back to KKMC, then flying one last sortie to recover back at King Fahd. This resulted in about eight hours of flying time during a 12-hour duty day. However, if the missions involved 'Scud' hunting, the flying time would increase to about 10 hours. Search and rescue strip alert was another A-10A mission at KKMC. Each wing had a squadron designated for night combat. For the 354th, this was the 355th TFS, which developed most of the night tactics used by A-10As during the war. The 'Falcons' flew only about a dozen daytime missions against GCI sites during the first two days of the air war, and then flew exclusively at night for the rest of the war. After the first

two weeks of the air war, the 74th TFS became the dedicated night squadron for the 23rd TFW(P).

A second FOL was operated by the 917th TFW for the 23rd TFW(P) at Al Jouf, in far northern Saudi Arabia. Known as 'Cajun West', 10 aircraft at a time were deployed there for five days before rotating back to King Fahd. Despite very primitive living conditions, the flying there was relatively low threat and target rich. While their primary missions focused on 'Scud' hunting and support of special operations, other targets of opportunity soon presented themselves. These included 'Home Depot' (a massive complex of munition storage bunkers and warehouses just north of the Baghdad-to-Amman highway in south-western Iraq), 'Hicksville' (another munitions storage area, even larger than 'Home Depot', just south of the Euphrates River between Ramadi and the Syrian border, and named after Captain Al 'Gator' Hicks, who discovered it), 'The Villas' (yet another munitions storage area just north of 'Home Depot'), and 'East and West Tac' (named after two bombing ranges at Nellis AFB, Nevada, these were concentrations of armour from the 55th Infantry Brigade guarding a strategic road intersection near the town

Above: Ground troops sweated blood to keep the A-10 sorties generated during Desert Storm. Armourers loaded CBUs, 30-mm ammunition and, as here, Mavericks at a phenomenal rate. A-10 pilots expended them as rapidly, amassing a huge kill tally.

Below: A 'Combat Hogdriver' on the tanker. KC-135s extended the ability to range over much of Iraq.

Warthog nose art

During their time in Saudi Arabia, most of the 144 A-10s picked up nose art. Much of it was applied after the end of the war, along with kill tally scoreboards.

Even the tails of some aircraft received decoration, this being 77-0205 of the 706th TFS, part of the 23rd TFW(P).

Stephanie Ann/Bayou Babe 76-0531/23rd TFW(P)

Randi Lauren/Brenda Beth 77-0240/23rd TFW(P)

Fightin' Irish 80-0157/354th TFW(P)

Giv'em Hell 81-0953/354th TFW(P)

New Orleans Lady 77-0274/23rd TFW(P)

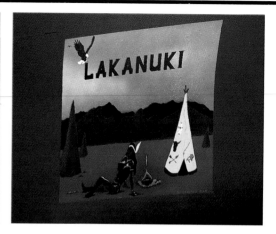

Lakanuki 80-0170/354th TFW(P)

Have Sun Will Travel 79-0224/354th TFW(P)

Poo! 80-0144/354th TFW(P)

of Nukhayb). Early in the war, pilots would hit one of these area targets on their way home from 'Scud' hunting; later, as 'Scuds' became more difficult to find, they would expend most of their bombs on the area targets, reducing weight and drag so they could spend more time hunting for 'Scuds' with their Mavericks. All these targets, combined with Colonel Bob Efferson's leadership style, made tours at Al Jouf a sought-after and rewarding experience.

Both of the A-10A's air-to-air kills during Desert Storm were made using the GAU-8. The first was scored by the 706th TFS 'Cajuns' Captain Bob Swain over what may have been a BO 105 (there really was not much left to identify) on 6 February 1991 in 77-0205, later named 'Chopper Popper' and now displayed at the USAF Armament Museum at Eglin AFB, Florida. The other was by the 511th TFS 'Vultures' Captain Todd 'Shanghai' Sheehy, who shot down an Mi-8 on 15 February 1991 in 81-0964. (On another occasion two 23rd TFW(P) aircraft were the only aircraft available to AWACS to confront an Iraqi 'Flogger'. When

they turned towards the MiG, it used its speed advantage over its opponents and ran.) Unfortunately, also on 15 February when Captain Sheehy scored his kill, two A-10As were shot down by IR SAMs and another badly damaged. As part of the tactical changes implemented the next day to help prevent similar losses, gun use was suspended until 23 February, when the ground war began.

A-10 ordnance

Like the A-1 Skyraider that was its inspiration, the A-10 employs a fascinating and varied array of air-to-ground ordnance. Most of these weapons were used with devastating effect during Operation Desert Storm in early 1991. There are 11 stores pylons on the aircraft, with number one at the left wingtip and number 11 on the right. Stations five, six and seven are on the fuselage, with stations four and eight inboard of the main landing gear sponsons. The other stations are outboard of these sponsons. The pylons on stations 2/10 and 5/7 can be removed in high threat areas to

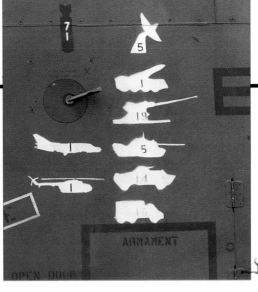

Kill marks were displayed on the starboard side on 23rd aircraft (left), and on the port for 354th (above). The machine above (81-0964) wears a helicopter for an air-to-air kill, and a 'Fitter' silhouette for an Su-22 destroyed on the ground. The other symbols are for radar sites, 'Scuds', artillery pieces, tanks, APCs and other vehicles.

Iraqi Nightmare *77-0266/23rd TFW(P)*

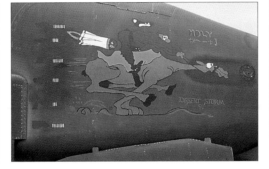

Camel Jockey *77-0255/23rd TFW(P)*

Holy *~...+! *77-0271/23rd TFW(P)*

Crawfish logo for 706th TFS *77-0260/23rd*

Desert Rose *77-0273/23rd TFW(P)*

Yankee Express *79-0220/354th TFW(P)*

Desert Belle *81-0947/354th TFW(P)*

improve manoeuvrability. During Desert Storm, this appears to have been done on all aircraft during the early stages of the air campaign. The centreline pylon (station 6) is not loaded for combat operations, and is most often used to mount a 600-US gal (2271-litre) fuel tank (P/N 7540863-10) for ferry operations (the same tank used by the F-111). While two more of these tanks can be carried from stations 4/8, this is not often done.

The primary defensive armament of the A-10 is composed of two AIM-9L/M Sidewinders. These are mounted to LAU-105 or LAU-114 launcher rails mounted on an Air National Guard-developed dual rail adapter (DRA). This assembly is usually mounted on the left outboard wing station (number one), unless there is a wiring problem on that particular aircraft, in which case it can be mounted on the opposing station. A-10s inadvertently fired three AIM-9s during Desert Storm, two by the 23rd TASS and one by the 74th TFS. Also, 23rd TASS 'Nail FACs' were only noted to have carried one AIM-9 during Desert Storm.

Of more practical, if less apparent, importance are the defensive avionics. An ECM pod is mounted on the wing station opposite the AIM-9s (usually number 11). During the time frame of Desert Storm, US-based aircraft normally carried an ALQ-119(V)-15 pods, while Shallow ALQ-131s were carried on overseas-based aircraft. The ALQ-184(V)-1 and Deep ALQ-131 are also authorised, although they do not appear to have been used during the war. In addition to ECM pods, A-10As carry ALE-40 chaff and flare countermeasures dispensers under their wingtips and at the back of the main landing gear sponsons. During Desert Storm, OA/A-10As expended 355,381 bundles of chaff and 108,654 flares in self-defence (an average of over 40 bundles of chaff and 12 flares per sortie).

During Desert Storm, A-10As launched 5,013 AGM-65 Mavericks – 90 per cent of the Air Force total (it is ironic that, following the war, the Air Force immediately moved to replace the Mavericks, while making plans to retire the only aircraft that used them effectively). These missiles are only

Fairchild A-10

Above: A-10s from the 23rd TFW seen soon after their arrival at King Fahd. The ferry tanks are used only for deployment flights, being stressed for too light a load for combat operations. They are the same type as used by the F-111.

Right: Dark green A-10s look somewhat incongruous in the searing light of Saudi Arabia. Among the important missions was 'Scud'-hunting.

Below: During the latter stages of the conflict, the A-10s worked closely with the Army. This 511th TFS aircraft lands at King Khalid past a row of OV-1 Mohawk battlefield surveillance platforms, which occasionally spotted targets for A-10s.

carried on stations 3/9, just outboard of the landing gear sponsons. The primary method of carriage is from single rail LAU-117 launchers, although triple-rail LAU-88s can also be used. When LAU-88s were used during Desert Storm, it was only with slant-loads of two missiles, even though virtually any symmetrical combination was authorised. (Some reliability problems were experienced with LAU-88s, causing them to be used less frequently than they might have been otherwise.) Typically, a mix of $22,000 AGM-65B 'Scene Magnification' electro-optical (EO) and $141,000 AGM-65D imaging infra-red (IIR) missiles were carried (if LAU-88s were used, EO missiles were loaded on one wing, with IIRs on the other). Both missiles were equipped with 125-lb (57-kg) shaped charge warheads, ideal for use against armour. AGM-65Bs were used exclusively for daytime missions, with 1,682 being fired during the war. IIR versions used included 3,128 of the AGM-65Ds, and 203 of the $150,000 AGM-65Gs, which were fitted with 300-lb (136-kg) blast warheads, and used against targets such as GCI and SAM sites (the latter could only be used from LAU-117). Lacking any night vision equipment, the two night squadrons improvised by using their IIR Mavericks to hunt for targets.

Bomb loads

Gravity bombs of less than 1,000 lb (454 kg) can be parent-loaded on any station except the centreline, but only one type of bomb is carried per mission. Generally though, they are only loaded on stations 5/7, 4/8 and 2/10. During Desert Storm, A-10As delivered 14,184 Mk 82 LDGP 500-lb (227-kg) bombs while flying missions from Fahd and the KKMC FOL. Cluster bomb usage included 2,278 Mk 20 Rockeye IIs, three versions of the SUU-30H dispenser (including 1,852 CBU-52 fragmentation cluster bombs, 2,326 CBU-58, and 278 CBU-71 frag/incendiary cluster mines). Other Mk 82-based weapons include the Mk 82 SE, Mk 82 AIR, Mk 36 Destructor mines, and BDU-50 inert practice bombs.

Triple ejector racks (TERs) have been used with all of the weapons in the previous paragraph. Although cleared for use on stations 3/9, since those are always occupied by Mavericks the only stations TERs are usually carried on with live bombs are 4/8, just inboard of the landing gear sponsons. (Stations 5/7 are also authorised for TERs, but in practice they are only used when BDU-33 practice bombs are being dropped.) While they can carry three bombs, the normal combat load during Desert Storm was two, usually flat-loaded, although a few slant-loads were also seen. Only the 354th TFW(P) used TERs, while the 23rd TFW(P) preferred pylon-mounted weapons.

Current-generation cluster bombs can also be used. During Desert Storm 1,033 CBU-87 combined effects munitions (CEMs), which use the SUU-65 version of the tactical munitions dispenser (TMD), were used from the Al Jouf and KKMC FOLs. The A-10 is also authorised to employ a second TMD weapon, the CBU-89 'Gator' mine, which uses the SUU-64 dispenser. In mid-1993 it was reported that it would also be qualified to deliver loads of four of another TMD weapon, the SUU-65-based CBU-97 sensor fused weapon (SFW). Again, while authorised from Maverick stations, these cluster bombs are normally only parent-mounted to stations 4/8 and 5/7.

Just prior to the Desert Storm ground campaign, 1,976 Mk 84 LDGP 2,000-lb (907-kg) bombs were used to cut lines intended to feed oil-filled trenches the Iraqis planned to use as a defensive measure. This weapon is carried on the

81st TFW inactivation process

Inactivation of the 81st TFW was announced in late May 1991. Indicative of how quickly events had overtaken the best laid of Cold War plans, the announcement was made at the opening ceremonies of the wing's brand new community centre. It, along with several other major new buildings and nearly 300 new houses, had been started as part of a much-needed facelift for a facility that would be needed indefinitely. Less than two years from the closure announcement, the last A-10As left RAF Bentwaters, and what had been the largest wing in the US Air Force only a couple of years earlier had ceased to exist. The 81st TFW did not go out with a whimper, however. It supported operational missions until less than four months before the final transfers took place; on 17 December 1992, it simultaneously put 20 A-10As

into the air for the final time in what was called 'Hog Joust 92'.

'Harvesting' a major flying operation is a complex task, especially when the unit is still supporting operational missions and upgrading aircraft. The process can be a confusing one; while each of these increasingly common inactivations is unique, most involve retiring some aircraft and transferring the rest to other units. Flying time must be carefully controlled so that gaining units do not receive a group of aircraft requiring major maintenance inspections at the same time. The need to transfer aircraft of similar ages leads to the need to rearrange the wing's aircraft assignment among its squadrons, since old and new aircraft are normally mixed so all the new ones do not belong to one squadron. A look at what happened with the 81st TFW makes similar events

One of the first aircraft to be repainted grey, 81-0964 took part in Provide Comfort. It is one of the few Bentwaters 'Hogs' to remain in Europe with the 52nd Fighter Wing at Spangdahlem.

easier to understand.

On 5 February 1992, the 81st TFW reassigned its aircraft so that squadron inactivations and aircraft transfers would mesh. Aircraft designated to undergo the LASTE modification process had been selected sometime before, and that modification programme was half-completed when the realignment took place. All aircraft sent to the 52nd FW not destined to be aircraft battle damage repair (ABDR) training aircraft were modified at RAF Bentwaters.

As the time to transfer an aircraft

approached, it was placed in 'transfer dock' where all necessary inspections were accomplished. Transfers to the US happened when groups of about six aircraft had gone through this process. All transfers were planned to avoid transatlantic flights during the winter, partly because of the generally inclement weather at that time of year but especially because of the strong headwinds. A-10As do not fly very fast in the best of weather, and none of the aircraft transferring had autopilots (aircraft not going to AMARC were to be modified with LASTE in the US). A long-planned February participation in an 'Air Warrior' exercise at Nellis AFB, Nevada, resulted in the first eight aircraft transferring about a month early. The final transatlantic transfer occurred in November 1992, with the final deliveries to Spangdahlem AB, Germany, beginning on 12 January and finishing on 23 March 1993.

No attempt was made to repaint aircraft with their new squadron colours; if an aircraft remained in the squadron it belonged to prior to 5 February, it retained its colours. However, if it changed units, the old colours were usually painted over with camouflage 'touch up' paint. The wing commander's aircraft was changed from 80-181 to 82-655 when the former went into transfer dock in June 1992. Based on lessons learned during Desert Storm, all aircraft used in Operation Provide Comfort were repainted in a new grey scheme during the late summer of 1992. It was later decided to repaint all aircraft being transferred to Spangdahlem, which were also the aircraft which had been LASTE-modified. The last aircraft to be painted was the commander's 'flagship', in late January 1993.

Right: Mavericks are easily transported in crates, ready for immediate use with the minimum of attention. Note the tiger's teeth on this 23rd TFW aircraft's ECM pod.

Below: Jinking violently, an A-10 releases a flare as it escapes from the target area. The use of flares and chaff is mandatory in most combat scenarios when an aircraft operates close to enemy defences.

same stations used by TMDs.

The two night squadrons, the 74th and 355th TFSs, were the exclusive users of SUU-25 dispensers during Desert Storm. Noted with unusual hemispherical nose caps, these dispensers were used to drop 5,488 flares and target markers, with eight loaded in each of these modified LAU-10 rocket pods. Allowable flares include Mk 24 or LUU-2 (which burn at 2 million candlepower for three and five minutes respectively), and the MJU-3 (modified LUU-2) IRCM flare. Target markers are the LUU-1 (red), LUU-5 (green), or LUU-6 (fuchsia). They differ from flares in that they burn for 30 minutes at 1,000 candlepower. SUU-25s are parent-mounted from stations 2/10, although they are also authorised on the Maverick stations.

Target marking

White phosphorous (WP), or 'Willy Pete', 2.75-in rockets were primarily used by the 23rd TASS OA-10As during Desert Storm, which used 2,748 for target marking. While official records indicate the OA-10As carried no other weapons (save their GAU-8 and AIM-9L/Ms), photographs from the war show them also carrying Mk 82s. An additional 138 rockets were used just prior to the beginning of the ground war during unsuccessful attempts by the 353rd TFS to ignite the oil already in Iraqi defensive trenches. The rocket configuration was M156 warheads mounted on Mk 66 wrap-around fin aircraft rockets (WAFARs). They were carried in either LAU-68 or similar LAU-131 seven-tube pods. Although TER carriage was authorised, primary carriage was to parent-mount the pods from stations 2/10, 3/9 and 4/8.

Records from Desert Storm show an unexplained entry, labelled '69', which may have been an additional FOL or an operation unrelated to OA/A-10As. The only munitions

81st TFW Warthogs in happier days. The wing flew F-84s, F-101s and F-4s prior to A-10s.

Aircraft	Before Feb 92	After Feb 92	Transferred	New Unit
76-514	510 TFS	510 TFS	23 Nov 92	AMARC
76-522	78 TFS	510 TFS	23 Nov 92	AMARC
76-550	91 TFS	510 TFS	9 Nov 92	52 FW ABDR
76-553	92 TFS	510 TFS	14 Sep 92	52 FW ABDR
79-217	78 TFS	510 TFS	23 Nov 92	AMARC
79-218	92 TFS	510 TFS	23 Nov 92	AMARC
79-221	510 TFS	510 TFS	23 Nov 92	AMARC
79-225	91 TFS	510 TFS	30 Oct 92	355 FW
80-143	78 TFS	78 TFS	28 Apr 92	355 FW
80-145	92 TFS	78 TFS	25 May 92	355 FW
80-147	510 TFS	78 TFS	24 Feb 92	602 ACW
80-155	510 TFS	510 TFS	20 Sep 92	355 FW
80-158	91 TFS	91 TFS	1 Aug 92	442 TFW
80-159	92 TFS	78 TFS	25 May 92	355 FW
80-160	510 TFS	510 TFS	30 Oct 92	355 FW
80-167	78 TFS	78 TFS	24 Feb 92	602 ACW
80-168	92 TFS	78 TFS	25 May 92	355 FW
80-169	510 TFS	78 TFS	24 Feb 92	355 FW
80-171	91 TFS	91 TFS	23 Jul 92	442 TFW
80-179	78 TFS	78 TFS	24 Feb 92	355 FW
80-180	91 TFS	91 TFS	8 Sep 92	442 TFW
80-181	92 TFS	91 TFS	23 Jul 92	442 TFW
80-192	92 TFS	91 TFS	15 Aug 92	442 TFW
80-195	510 TFS	510 TFS	30 Oct 92	355 FW
80-203	78 TFS	78 TFS	28 Apr 92	355 FW
80-204	91 TFS	91 TFS	25 May 92	355 FW
80-205	91 TFS	91 TFS	13 Sep 92	442 TFW
80-206	78 TFS	78 TFS	24 Feb 92	602 ACW
80-207	92 TFS	78 TFS	24 Feb 92	355 FW
80-215	510 TFS	91 TFS	22 Jul 92	442 TFW
80-216	510 TFS	510 TFS	10 Sep 92	355 FW
80-217	92 TFS	91 TFS	15 Aug 92	442 TFW
80-220	91 TFS	91 TFS	14 Sep 92	355 FW
80-228	510 TFS	91 TFS	15 Aug 92	442 TFW
80-233	78 TFS	78 TFS	28 Apr 92	355 FW
80-234	91 TFS	91 TFS	25 May 92	355 FW
80-235	78 TFS	78 TFS	24 Feb 92	355 FW
80-236	78 TFS	78 TFS	28 Apr 92	355 FW
80-270	78 TFS	78 TFS	28 Apr 92	355 FW

Aircraft	Before Feb 92	After Feb 92	Transferred	New Unit
80-271	91 TFS	91 TFS	21 Nov 92	355 FW
80-272	92 TFS	91 TFS	1 Aug 92	442 TFW
80-274	510 TFS	91 TFS	1 Aug 92	442 TFW
80-276	92 TFS	91 TFS	1 Aug 92	442 TFW
80-278	78 TFS	78 TFS	26 Sep 92	355 FW
80-279	510 TFS	91 TFS	22 Jul 92	442 TFW
80-280	91 TFS	91 TFS	28 Apr 92	355 FW
80-281	92 TFS	78 TFS	25 May 92	355 FW
81-941	78 TFS	78 TFS	24 Feb 92	602 ACW
81-942	91 TFS	91 TFS	30 Oct 92	355 FW
81-943	92 TFS	78 TFS	25 May 92	355 FW
81-944	91 TFS	91 TFS	15 Aug 92	442 TFW
81-950	78 TFS	78 TFS	25 May 92	355 FW
81-951	91 TFS	92 TFS	10 Feb 93	52 FW
81-952 *	510 TFS	510 TFS	5 Mar 93	52 FW
81-954 *	92 TFS	92 TFS	13 Jan 93	52 FW
81-956	91 TFS	92 TFS	29 Jan 93	52 FW
81-960 *	78 TFS	92 TFS	12 Mar 93	52 FW
81-961	92 TFS	92 TFS	5 Mar 93	52 FW
81-962 *	91 TFS	92 TFS	18 Feb 93	52 FW
81-963	92 TFS	92 TFS	22 Jan 93	52 FW
81-965	510 TFS	510 TFS	19 Mar 93	52 FW
81-966 *	510 TFS	510 TFS	10 Feb 93	52 FW
81-976	91 TFS	92 TFS	13 Jan 93	52 FW
81-977 *	92 TFS	92 TFS	18 Feb 93	52 FW
81-978	78 TFS	92 TFS	1 Mar 93	52 FW
81-980	510 TFS	510 TFS	9 Oct 92	52 FW
81-982 *	78 TFS	92 TFS	23 Mar 93	52 FW
81-983 *	91 TFS	92 TFS	22 Jan 93	52 FW
81-984 *	78 TFS	92 TFS	12 Mar 93	52 FW
81-985	92 TFS	92 TFS	19 Mar 93	52 FW

Aircraft	Before Feb 92	After Feb 92	Transferred	New Unit
81-988	510 TFS	510 TFS	13 Jan 93	52 FW
81-991	91 TFS	92 TFS	21 Dec 93	52 FW
81-992 *	92 TFS	92 TFS	19 Feb 93	52 FW
82-646 *	510 TFS	510 TFS	9 Oct 92	52 FW
82-649 *	91 TFS	510 TFS	29 Jan 93	52 FW
82-650	510 TFS	510 TFS	13 Jan 93	52 FW
82-654 *	78 TFS	92 TFS	1 Mar 93	52 FW
82-655 *	91 TFS	92 TFS	23 Mar 93	52 FW
82-656	92 TFS	92 TFS	21 Dec 93	52 FW
82-658	78 TFS	92 TFS	19 Feb 93	52 FW

(*If asterisked, LASTE modification occurred before the realignment.)

Above: 80-0147 lands at Nellis during an exercise. It stayed in the US afterwards, with the 602nd ACW.

Below: 76-0550 is one of two ex-81st aircraft used for battle damage repair training at Spangdahlem.

loaded at '69' were 3,071 Mk 82s, 653 Mk 84s, 298 CBU-58, 713 CBU-87, 87 CBU-89 and 6,959 bundles of chaff (these numbers are omitted in the previously mentioned totals). Significantly, no 30-mm ammunition, Mavericks or flares were loaded at this location.

Other weapons certified for carriage, but seldom, if ever, seen on operational aircraft include all versions of the GBU-10 and GBU-12 laser-guided bombs (LGBs) based on the Mk 84 and Mk 82 warheads (and carried on the same stations), BLU-52 tear gas bombs (all stations but 1/6/11), CTU-2 resupply containers (stations 3/9), BL755 cluster bombs (all stations but 6), and M117 LDGPs (all stations but 6). MXU-648 travel pods can be carried on stations 3/9, 4/8 and the centreline.

Although it was qualified on the A-10 (stations 3/9 and 4/8), the GBU-8 electro-optical guided bomb (EOGB) was never used operationally. Also, despite numerous publicity photos showing the aeroplane carrying 'everything but the kitchen sink', the need for maximum manoeuvrability over the battlefield resulted in much more modest combat loads. For the Central European scenario, tactics were to attack armoured column defensive vehicles with AGM-65 Mavericks, then to attack the offensive vehicles with bombs and the massive GAU-8/A 'Avenger' cannon.

LASTE

In the late 1980s the low-altitude safety and targeting enhancement (LASTE) programme was initiated to install several high-technology improvements into the rather basic A-10 avionics suite. The first addition was a radar altimeter (coupled with a voice warning system) to improve the pilot's situational awareness at low altitude. If the pilot descended beneath a preselected altitude or at too steep an angle to recover, the system would warn him in time to avoid hitting

the ground,. The second major change was the installation of the same weapons delivery computer used by the F-16. Even though the 'Warthog' lacks the radar ranging of the F-16, the computer dramatically improved bombing accuracy. In addition to displaying a continuously computed impact point (CCIP) bombing solution on the head-up display (HUD), it also provided a projection of the bullet trajectory to the A-10 pilots for the first time. Competing against other fighters with the help of these improvements for the

A pair of LASTE-equipped A-10s from the evaluation unit, the 57th Fighter Wing. Grumman has taken over as the product support contractor for the A-10 in its final years.

Fairchild A-10

Above: Following the end of the Gulf War, A-10s were sent from Bentwaters to Incirlik in Turkey to take their place on the Provide Comfort detachment protecting the Kurds in northern Iraq. Operations mostly consisted of armed reconnaissance and attack cover for helicopters and transports.

Right: The new-look A-10 sports the light grey camouflage it was born with. With the addition of LASTE and much experience behind it, it is now a far more effective warplane.

first time in the 1991 Gunsmoke bombing competition, the 'Warthogs' of the 175th Tactical Fighter Group (ANG) from Baltimore, Maryland, won the semi-annual contest. Although the victory was extremely satisfying for all 'Hog' drivers, it garnered only grudging recognition from Air Force officials.

LASTE added more than the two improvements from which it got its name; the 'Hog' finally got an autopilot. For the first time ever, the 'call of nature' ceased to be an emergency procedure in the A-10, and pilots were no longer required to hand-fly the airplane all of the time. In addition to making 'necessary chores' easier, this would also allow an OA-10A FAC to take his hands off the controls for a few moments to jot down vital notes for his nine-line briefs while directing CAS operations.

In recognition of the growing importance of night combat, LASTE also installed vastly improved cockpit

lighting that made the A-10 compatible with night-vision goggles (NVGs). Finally, to improve the safety of flying formation at night, strip lighting was added which, along with some 'warts' on the tail, provides the only external evidence of the modification. Fleet modification to the LASTE standard did not begin in earnest until mid-1991, after Desert Storm. While most of the LASTE modifications were installed at the SM-ALC, some aircraft were modified by 'speed lines' set up at overseas bases.

Future prospects

With the almost incomprehensible state of flux in the American military, it is difficult to predict how much longer the 'Warthog' will continue to serve. The Air Force seems to be keeping it more because the Army wants them to rather than for any real appreciation of the aircraft's attributes. But, to their credit, the USAF is investing in it to make it more compatible with night combat. New 'paper aeroplanes' intended to replace the A-10 have ended up in the waste basket almost as quickly as the paper on which they are printed can be crumpled, making coherent discussion of 'replacement programmes' useless. Its a safe bet that 'Hogs' will be answering the call of duty in whatever Iraqi- or Bosnian-type situation the US finds itself involved in for some time to come. With their acquisition by Turkey and rumoured sale to Korea, the A-10 will certainly be flying well into the next century.

Opposite page: 'Slime' lights glowing, a pair of A-10s flies into the sunset. Once considered as totally obsolete, the change in world conflicts has ensured a limited place for the Warthog for some years yet.

Right: Defence against groundfire was the driving concern for putting the 'Hogs' back into grey, although the false cockpit is intended to deceive opposing fighters. Proven against helicopters, just quite how the A-10 would fare in air-to-air combat has never been put to the test in combat.

Specification
Fairchild A-10A

Powerplant: two General Electric
TF34-GE-100 turbofans, rated at 9,065 lb
(40.3 kN) each

Wing span: 57 ft 6 in (17.53 m)
Length: 53 ft 4 in (16.26 m)
Height: 14 ft 8 in (4.47 m)
Wing area: 506 sq ft (47.01 m2)
Tailplane span: 18 ft 10 in (5.74 m)
Wheel track: 17 ft 2 ½ in (5.25 m)
Wheelbase: 17 ft 8 ¾ in (5.40 m)

Empty weight: 21,541 lb (9771 kg)
Operating empty weight: 24,959 lb
(11321 kg)
Forward airstrip weight: 32,771 lb
(14865 kg)
Maximum take-off weight:
50,000 lb (22680 kg)
Internal fuel: 10,700 lb (4853 kg)
Maximum ordnance: 16,000 lb
(7258 kg)
**Maximum ordnance with full
internal fuel:** 14,341 lb (6505 kg)

Maximum speed at sea level:
439 mph (706 km/h)
Cruising speed: 387 mph (623 km/h)
at 5,000 ft (1525 m)
Rate of climb: 6,000 ft (1828 m) per
minute at sea level
Take-off distance: 4,000 ft (1220 m)
at MTOW, 1,450 ft (442 m) at forward
airstrip weight
Landing distance: 2,000 ft (610 m) at
MTOW, 1,300 ft (396 m) at forward
airstrip weight
Ferry range: 2,454 miles (3950 km)
Combat radius: 288 miles (463 km)
with 20-minute reserve and 1.7-hour
loiter, 620 miles (1000 km) with 20-
minute reserves and no loiter

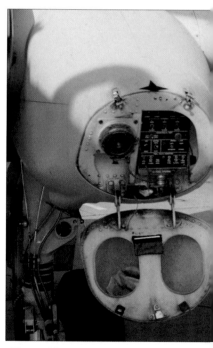

*Above: The tasked mission of the
A-10 dictates rapid turn-rounds
between sorties. Ground troops
regularly practise the art of
refuelling and rearming 'Hogs' in a
matter of minutes. To aid the
former task, the A-10 has a single-
point refuelling point in the port
'kneecap' of the undercarriage
fairing, and a control panel.*

*Above and left: The 'office' of the
'Warthog' is quite simple compared
to other fighters. The head-up
display provides standard combat
data, aiming cues provided by the
Pave Penny laser spot tracker and
CCIP information. The central
panel is dominated by the attitude
indicator and navigation display.
On the right, at top, is the display
screen for Maverick imagery,
below which are engine
instruments. On the left at top is
the RWR display, below which is
the armament panel. The right-
hand panel is mainly for
communications, while the left
panel (left) has system controls.*

Markings

After having spent most of its career in a 'Charcoal Lizard' scheme to foil interception from aircraft above, the A-10s began reverting to a grey scheme to protect against surface threats. There are two shades of grey, and the scheme is known as 'Compass Ghost'. All other markings are in black, and consist of 'SP' tailcode for the 52nd Wing, serial number, stencilling, national insignia and squadron fin-tip markings for the 510th FS 'Buzzards'.

Ammunition

Three types of ammunition are provided for the GAU-8/A. The PGU-13/B is an HEI (high explosive, incendiary) round, and is mostly suitable against soft targets and non- or lightly-armoured vehicles. It has a jacket of naturally fragmenting material and standard explosive filling. The PGU-14/B is the API (armour piercing, incendiary) round, and is of greatest effect against armour. A lightweight aluminium body surrounds a depleted uranium core which penetrates through armour. Although radioactivity is minimal, the uranium is nevertheless incendiary, and creates heat once inside the tank shell. Finally the PGU-15/B is a TP (training practice) round, and has no explosive filling. It matches the ballistics of the HEI round for aerial marksmanship. For normal combat sorties, the HEI and API are carried in a ratio of 1:5, or Combat Mix. The rounds are fed from the drum on to a continuous belt, and taken to the gun. Spent cartridge cases or unfired rounds are returned via the belt to the drum.

Lights

The A-10 has standard daytime formation lights on the extreme tailcone, lower fins, wingtips, spine and belly. The LASTE mod adds LVF 'slime' lights to the wingtips, fin, and spine (just aft of the cockpit). Floodlights are incorporated in the inner face of the outer pylons to light the nose area for night refuelling.

Keith Fretwell

Above: A front-view shows detail of the aerial refuelling slipway (which is covered by a door) and its accompanying cueing marks, head-up display, forward-hemisphere antennas for the radar warning receiver and the offset position of the GAU-8/A cannon.

Above: The cambered flaps increase wing area when deployed. Take-off setting is 7° and landing setting 20°.

Above: Mavericks are usually carried on an LAU-117 single rail, with aft connector for the motor. The LAU-88 triple rail can also be used.

Mike Bodrocke

93 Twin missile carrier/launcher
94 AIM-9L Sidewinder air-to-air 'self-defence' missiles
95 Rockeye II cluster bomb
96 Port wing stores pylons

97 Port mainwheel
98 AGM-65 Maverick air-to-surface missile
99 Missile launch rail
100 Pressure refuelling connection
101 Mainwheel semi-recessed housing
102 Mainwheel leg strut and pivot mounting
103 Hydraulic retraction jack
104 Outer wing panel joint rib
105 Inner wing panel integral fuel tank
106 Wing panel/fuselage frame pin joint
107 Inboard leading-edge slat
108 Slat hydraulic actuators
109 Rockeye II cluster bombs on inboard pylons

Operating in an intense battlefield scenario, the A-10 needs all the defences it can carry. An important deterrence against shoulder-launched SAMs are infra-red decoy flares. These are carried in ALE-40 dispensers (which can also eject radar-defeating chaff) mounted under the turned-down wingtips (above) and in the rear of the undercarriage fairings (left).

Above: Minor maintenance can be performed on the TF34 engine with the large side-access panel hinged down. However, for more work the engine is very easily removed.

Left: A close-up of the AAS-35 Pave Penny laser spot tracker. This is mounted on a special pylon below the aircraft's nose, giving it an excellent 'look' ahead of the aircraft. The sensor can be programmed to pick up coded laser 'sparkles'.

Above: The A-10 has the capability to operate from austere locations. The most basic of needs is for the pilot to be able to access the aircraft without any support equipment. A door on the port side covers a sturdy telescopic entry pole, with attached steps. Ground crew quickly found the step door as the ideal place to carry on their art.

Fairchild A-10A Thunderbolt II

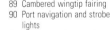

1 Cannon muzzles
2 Radar warning antennas
3 Flight refuelling receptacle, open
4 Nosewheel bay offset to starboard
5 Gun bay venting intake
6 Cannon barrels
7 Electrical equipment compartment
8 Battery
9 UHF aerial
10 Nosewheel hydraulic steering unit
11 Forward-retracting nose undercarriage
12 Nosewheel hydraulic steering unit
13 Shock absorber leg strut
14 Ammunition feed chutes
15 Titanium armour cockpit 'bathtub' enclosure
16 Instrument panel shroud
17 Pilot's head-up display
18 Armoured windscreen panels
19 Upward-hinged canopy cover
20 McDonnell Douglas ACES 2 ejection seat
21 Engine throttle lever
22 Side console panel
23 Ladder stowage compartment
24 Retractable boarding ladder
25 Emergency canopy release
26 Ammunition feed hydraulic drive
27 VHF homing aerial
28 Ammunition magazine, 1,174 rounds

29 Incidence vane
30 Ammunition magazine armour plating
31 Electrical system test and servicing panel
32 Ventral strake
33 Cartridge case return chute
34 Avionics equipment bays
35 Aerial selector switches
36 IFF aerial
37 Fuselage top longeron
38 Lateral control and cable ducts
39 Fuselage bag-type fuel tanks
40 Tank access panel
41 Anti-collision light
42 UHF/TACAN aerial
43 Integral wing tank fire suppressant foam filling
44 Gravity filler cap
45 Starboard wing stores pylons
46 Mk 20 Rockeye II cluster bomb
47 AN/ALQ-119 ECM pod
48 Pitot head
49 Starboard navigation and strobe lights
50 Split aileron/deceleron
51 Aileron tab
52 Two-segment Fowler-type flaps
53 Starboard engine nacelle
54 Fan face
55 General Electric TF34-GE-100 turbofan engine
56 Engine oil tank
57 Cantilevered engine mounting beams
58 By-pass (fan air) duct

59 Core engine exhaust nozzle
60 One-piece horizontal tailplane
61 Endplate tailfin
62 Starboard rudder
63 Starboard elevator
64 Elevator hydraulic actuators
65 Tail navigation light
66 Radar warning antennas
67 Rudder and elevator honeycomb composite construction
68 Three-spar fin construction
69 Rudder hydraulic actuator
70 Formation light
71 Radar warning antennas
72 VHF/AM aerial
73 Port engine nacelle exhaust ducts
74 Engine mounting bulkhead
75 APU exhaust
76 APU bay, fireproof container
77 Air conditioning equipment
78 Conditioned air delivery duct
79 Wingroot fillet
80 Trailing-edge flap shroud ribs
81 Flap track and guide rail
82 Flap hydraulic jacks
83 Synchronising linkage
84 Port single-slotted Fowler-type flaps
85 Flap and aileron honeycomb construction
86 Aileron hydraulic actuator
87 Split aileron/deceleration hydraulic jack
88 Port split aileron/deceleron, open

89 Cambered wingtip fairing
90 Port navigation and strobe lights
91 Three-spar wing panel construction
92 Honeycomb leading edge panels

Airbrakes
The large hydraulically-powered ailerons bestow an excellent roll rate on the 'Warthog', but also split above and below the wing to act as airbrakes. These are deployed on landing to reduce the roll, and can also be used to stabilise the aircraft for aiming in a dive.

Fairchild A-10A Thunderbolt II
510th Fighter Squadron,
52nd Fighter Wing
Spangdahlem AB, Germany

Once the mainstay of NATO's anti-armour force ranged against the massed tanks of the Warsaw Pact, the A-10 now serves with only one squadron in Europe, part of a composite wing alongside 'Wild Weasel' F-4s and F-16s. In 1993 its most likely combat scenario was not in a high-tech tank battle on Europe's Central Front, but in the hills and forests of former Yugoslavia, rooting out isolated artillery positions. Like other A-10 units, the 510th Fighter Squadron also has OA-10As on strength, and would use these in a fast-FAC role in support of the regular A-10s and attack aircraft from other units. The regular A-10s would be used in a traditional anti-armour role, as ResCAP aircraft to cover combat rescue attempts and on non-fragged close air support missions. The latter is the modern version of the old 'cab-rank' tactic, heavily armed A-10s loitering in or near the battle area waiting for ground commanders to call on their talents.

LASTE

A major alteration to the A-10, the Low-Altitude Safety and Target Enhancement programme added an autopilot to the A-10, among other improvements. These include a radar altimeter and a continually-computed impact point for high accuracy in bombing and gun aiming, NVG-compatible cockpit and night formation lights.

RESCUE

1. PUSH LATCH TO OPEN DOOR
2. PULL HANDLE OUT 6 FEET
   TO JETTISON CANOPY

Above: An A-10 lays down retarded bombs at low level. This option is only used in a relatively threat-free environment.

Right and below: For destroying area targets, the cluster bomb is highly effective, but the need to directly overfly puts the A-10 at great risk from groundfire. These are **CBU-87s**.

Above: During its development, the A-10 was tested with precision weapons, such as the Paveway **LGB** and Hobos **EOB**.

The AGM-65 Maverick (below) is the principal ordnance carried by the A-10, used for stand-off precision attacks. Shown above are the two seeker heads for the imaging infra-red version (upper) and **TV** scene magnification (lower).

Above and left: For self-defence, the A-10 usually carries an **ECM** pod on one outer pylon (AN/ALQ-131 illustrated above) and twin **AIM-9Ls** on the opposite.

Above: Standard ordnance for the **OA-10A** is the **LAU-68** rocket pod, each pod containing seven rockets for marking targets. The rockets are Mk 66 motors, usually with white phosphorus warheads.

A-10 weapons

As successor to the legendary Skyraider, the A-10 was provided with an excellent range of weapons, and 11 hardpoints from which to carry it. The stations are numbered from port outer to starboard outer, with Station 6 being the centreline. Stations 2 and 10 are often removed to save weight and drag.

A-10A ORDNANCE LOADS

Sta 1	Sta 11	Sta 2/10	Sta 3/9	Sta 4/8	Sta 5/7	Sta 6	Remarks
2 AIM-9	ECM pod	removed	1 AGM-65	2 Mk 82	removed	empty	flat-TER
2 AIM-9	ECM pod	1 Mk 82	1 AGM-65	1 Mk 82	1 Mk 82	empty	
2 AIM-9	ECM pod	removed	1 AGM-65	3 Mk 82	removed	empty	
2 AIM-9	ECM pod	empty	2 AGM-65	1 Mk 82	1 Mk 82	empty	slant-LAU-88
2 AIM-9	ECM pod	1 Mk 82	3 AGM-65	1 Mk 82	1 Mk 82	empty	
2 AIM-9	ECM pod	1 SUU-25	1 AGM-65	3 Mk 82	empty	empty	(night)
2 AIM-9	ECM pod	1 SUU-25	2 AGM-65	3 Mk 82	empty	empty	(night)
2 AIM-9	ECM pod	empty	1 AGM-65	1 Mk 84	empty	empty	oil feeder lines
2 AIM-9	ECM pod	1 LAU-68	1 LAU-68	3 Mk 82	empty	empty	oil trenches
2 AIM-9	ECM pod	empty	2 AGM-65	empty	empty	empty	ground war
2 AIM-9	ECM pod	removed	1 AGM-65	2 SUU-30	removed	empty	flat-TER
2 AIM-9	ECM pod	empty	1 SUU-30	1 SUU-30	1 SUU-30	empty	
2 AIM-9	ECM pod	empty	1 AGM-65	3 SUU-30	empty	empty	
2 AIM-9	ECM pod	1 SUU-30	1 AGM-65	1 SUU-30	1 SUU-30	empty	
2 AIM-9	ECM pod	1 SUU-25	1 AGM-65	3 SUU-30	empty	empty	(night)
2 AIM-9	ECM pod	1 SUU-25	2 AGM-65	1 SUU-30	1 SUU-30	empty	(night)
2 AIM-9	ECM pod	empty	1 AGM-65	1 SUU-64	1 SUU-64	empty	Gator
2 AIM-9	ECM pod	empty	1 AGM-65	1 SUU-65	1 SUU-65	empty	CEM & SFW
2 AIM-9	ECM pod	removed	1 AGM-65	2 Mk 20	removed	empty	slant-TER
2 AIM-9	ECM pod	removed	1 AGM-65	2 Mk 20	removed	empty	flat-TER
2 AIM-9	ECM pod	empty	1 Mk 20	1 Mk 20	1 Mk 20	empty	
2 AIM-9	ECM pod	1 Mk 20	1 AGM-65	2 Mk 20	1 Mk 20	empty	flat-TER
2 AIM-9	ECM pod	1 SUU-25	1 AGM-65	3 Mk 20	empty	empty	(night)
2 AIM-9	ECM pod	1 SUU-25	2 AGM-65	3 Mk 20	empty	empty	(night)

OA-10A ORDNANCE LOADS

Sta 1	Sta 11	Sta 2/10	Sta 3/9	Sta 4/8	Sta 5/7	Sta 6	Remarks
1 AIM-9	ECM pod	1 LAU-68	1 LAU-68	empty	empty	empty	
1 AIM-9	ECM pod	1 LAU-68	empty	1 Mk 82	empty	empty	
1 AIM-9	ECM pod	1 LAU-68	1 LAU-68	1 Mk 82	1 Mk 82	empty	

Above and below: The massive gun takes up a considerable amount of space in the forward fuselage. A special trolley loads the ammunition automatically into the large armoured drum tank.

Right: A long firing pass from an 81st TFW A-10. The kinetic energy released by firing the gun slows the aircraft appreciably.

Left: A short muzzle blast signals a round leaving the cannon. Several different blast deflectors have been applied to the cannon, but the A-10 has reverted to a standard open barrel arrangement.

Above: An A-10 fires its GAU-8/A Avenger cannon in a shallow dive. With the right elevation fixed, the pilot can 'walk' the gunfire along a line of, say, trucks, using the rudders.

Pave Penny

On the pylon under the starboard side of the nose is the AAS-35 Pave Penny laser seeker. This is a marked target seeker, which spots targets that have been designated by other sources (usually ground or heliborne FACs). Aiming cues are then provided on the HUD.

GAU-8/A Avenger

The massive Avenger is a seven-barrelled rotary cannon driven by two hydraulic motors. It is spun up to its full firing rate of 4,200 rounds per minute in 0.55 seconds, and has a maximum capacity of 1,350 rounds of 30-mm ammunition on a linkless feed system. The ammunition is held in a drum that is 6 ft 1 in (1.85 m) long and 2 ft 9 in (0.85 m) in diameter. The feed system weighs in at 3,412 lb (1548 kg) when loaded, to which can be added 620 lb (281 kg) for the gun itself. The gun and feed system is over 13 ft (4 m) long, of which 7 ft 6 in (2.30 m) is barrel.

Maverick missile

Although the gun is the most powerful such weapon ever fitted to a tactical aircraft, it is the Maverick that is the weapon of choice for the anti-armour mission to which the A-10 is so well adapted. The missile is 8 ft 2 in (2.49 m) long, and has a wing span of 2 ft 4 in (0.72 m). Two versions are in general use on the A-10 for anti-armour work: the AGM-65B with TV scene magnification seeker, and the AGM-65D with an imaging infra-red seeker. The former has a launch weight of 463 lb (210 kg) and the latter weighs 485 lb (220 kg). Both of these versions have a 57-kg (125-lb) shaped-charge high explosive warhead, which penetrates armour easily. One further Maverick variant is used by the A-10: the AGM-65G. This is an IIR weapon with revised seeker so that the pilot can designate a specific point within a larger heat source. It is used principally against radar or SAM sites, and incorporates a 136-kg (300-lb) blast penetration warhead. To launch a Maverick, the pilot must climb to get a good view of the target, select a missile and then use the image supplied by the seeker head to acquire and designate. The image is presented on a screen in the cockpit. Once the target is designated, using cross-hairs on the screen, the missile can be launched. It holds the designated image in its own memory, guiding itself to impact and allowing the launch aircraft to escape immediately.

ECM pod

The AN/ALQ-131 is the standard ECM pod for USAFE tactical aircraft, and is carried by the A-10 on one of the outboard pylons. The pod is a modular system, allowing it to be adapted to various scenarios. Each module can slot into the pod structure without complete disassembly. A digibus connects the various modules, which are controlled by a digital computer. Cooling is provided by a self-contained freon/ram air system, which has no moving parts and requires no power.

Gun position
The gun is mounted in the forward fuselage so that the firing barrel is on the centreline. In order to accommodate the massive weapon, the nosewheel is offset to starboard.

Formation lights
The only external identifier of LASTE-equipped 'Warthogs' is the addition of LVF (low-voltage formation) lights on the fin, wingtip and rear fuselage.

ECM pod
A development of the ALQ-119, the ALQ-184 is the standard pod for US- and Pacific-based USAF aircraft. It is a multi-purpose pod which is effective against SAM, AAA-laying and airborne interceptor radars.

Fairchild OA-10A

OA-10As differ only in role and designation from the standard A-10, and several units have both variants assigned. In a battlefield scenario, the OA-10 would be used to spot targets and direct attack aircraft. Other tasks involve close co-ordination with ground commanders, monitoring of the land battle and warning of threats. As it is regarded as a command and control asset, the OA-10 is not expected to undertake any direct action itself unless in emergency.

Markings
This OA-10A wears the markings of the 103rd Fighter Squadron, 111th Fighter Group, Pennsylvania ANG, flying from NAS Willow Grove. This unit previously flew the Cessna OA-37B in the FAC role, and fully converted to the OA-10A on 31 December 1989.

RWR
Antennas for the AN/ALR-69 radar warning receiver are located either side of the nose and tailcone, combining to provide 360° coverage.

Rockets
This OA-10 is depicted with an overload configuration of 12 LAU-68 rocket pods, in addition to the standard twin 'Winder installation and ALQ-184 ECM pod. In wartime each pod carries seven marker rockets, but for peacetime training missions they only carry six.

A-10 Operators

United States Air Force

Procurement of the A-10A for the USAF totalled two prototype and 713 production aircraft, although initial plans called for the procurement of 750 aircraft. Two YA-10s (71-1369/70) won the AX competition against the Northrop YA-9A prototypes. These were followed by six YA-10A pre-production aircraft, 71-1664/69 (production sequence numbers 1-6); 71-1664 was modified into the only two-seat A-10, the Night/Adverse Weather YA-10B. Production A-10A aircraft included 75-0258/0309 (52 aircraft, numbers 7-58), 76-0512/0554 (43 aircraft, numbers 59-101), 77-0177/0276 (100 aircraft, numbers 102-201), 78-0582/0725 (144 aircraft, numbers 202-345), 79-0082/0225 (144 aircraft, numbers 346-489), 80-0140/0283 (144 aircraft, numbers 490-633), 81-0939/0998 (60 aircraft, numbers 634-693), and 82-0646/0665 (20 aircraft, numbers 694-713).

The dates in this section reflect official USAF activation/inactivation dates as much as possible. In some cases, inactivation dates are considerably later than when the last aircraft departed. Wherever possible, the actual dates of aircraft movements are also given.

An A-10 closes on the tanker during a training sortie. The A-10 at its peak formed the backbone of the USAF's close air support force, a position it has now lost to the ubiquitous F-16. Nevertheless, the type continues to provide excellent service, notably in the forward air control role. Reduced numbers of aircraft remain in service with active-duty, National Guard and Reserve units.

5th Tactical Air Control Group

On 1 January 1984, the 25th TFS 'Assam Dragons' transferred from the 51st COMPW(T) to the 5th Tactical Air Control Group (TAIRCG), remaining at Suwon AB, Republic of Korea (RoK). At this time, they recoded their aircraft from 'OS' to 'SU', and added a green background to their red lightning bolt fin-flashes. The 25th remained at Suwon until inactivating on 31 July 1990. From about September 1989, the 19th TASS, which was also part of the 5th TAIRCG, began to divest itself of its OV-10As which it had been operating in the FAC role, and transition to OA-10As from the inactivating 25th TFS. On 1 October 1990, the 19th TASS moved from Suwon to Osan AB, and transferred to the 51st FW.

In the late 1980s, the 25th TFS flew regular A-10s from Suwon. These were in the front line of the Korean stand-off.

10th Tactical Fighter Wing

The 10th Tactical Reconnaissance Wing (TRW), based at RAF Alconbury, UK, was redesignated as the 10th TFW, in August 1987, in anticipation of gaining two squadrons of A-10As from the 81st TFW at RAF Bentwaters to ease overcrowding at the 81st's twin bases. This process began with the arrival of aircraft 81-0979 on 26 April 1988. The 509th TFS 'Pirates' formally activated on 1 June 1988, followed by the 511th TFS 'Vultures' on 1 September 1988. Both squadrons used the 'AR' tailcode, with the 509th having a grey fin stripe, and the 511th a black one. The squadrons continued to support the same FOLs in Germany as they had when attached to the 81st TFW. The 511th TFS was detached to

The 'Pirates' of the 509th TFS were one of two squadrons which moved out of crowded Bentwaters to occupy empty shelters at Alconbury.

the 354th TFW (Provisional) for participation in Operation Desert Shield/Storm on 27 December 1990, flying over 1,700 sorties without loss. Seven aircraft returned to 10th TFW on 12 May 91: 79-0218; 80-0170, 0194, 0277; 81-0939, 0967, and 0987 (79-0218 was then returned to 81st TFW on 15 May). The remaining 12 aircraft returned on 8 June 1991: 79-0220, 0224; 80-0144, 0157, 0172, 0209, 0229; 81-0947, 0948, 0953, 0964; and 82-0657. Almost immediately thereafter the process of inactivating began, with 511th aircraft transferring to the 507th ACW between 29 October and 18 December 1991, although the squadron did not formally inactivate until 18 December 1992. This was followed by 509th TFS aircraft being sent to AMARC, at Davis-Monthan AFB, AZ, between late January and March 1992, with the squadron also officially inactivating on 18 December 1992. The wing became the 10th Air Base Wing on 31 March 1993.

Above: The 10th TFW 'boss-bird' featured both grey and black fin-stripes.

Above: The nose of the CO's aircraft, 81-0979, was given a bright nose art featuring a bald eagle.

Below: The 511th TFS 'Vultures' was the second Alconbury squadron, and the unit which went to the Gulf.

20th Fighter Wing

With the end of its long association with F-111Es at RAF Upper Heyford, the 20th FW designation may supersede that of the 363rd Fighter Wing at Shaw AFB. If this is the case then some of the 20th's former squadron numbers may also be assigned. The 20th number was originally to have been applied to the 52nd FW, but the German-based unit protested.

23rd Wing 'Flying Tigers'

The 23rd TFW, based at England AFB, near Alexandria, LA, began its transition from A-7Ds on 23 September 1980, when the 74th TFS 'Flying Tigers' received its first A-10A (believed to have been 79-0137). The 74th completed its transition on 6 March 1981; its aircraft received a blue tail band with a white lightning bolt, and the wing's unique shark mouth, dating its lineage back to the 'Flying Tigers' of World War II. The 75th TFS 'Sharks' completed their transition during the summer of 1981, applying the squadron's black-and-white checked fin-flash. On 30 October 1981, the 76th TFS 'Vanguards' became the last squadron to complete the transition to the 'Warthog', marking their jets with a red tail band with white stars. The wing's pre-existing 'EL' tailcode was retained.

The 76th TFS deployed as part of the 23rd TFW(P) in support of Desert Shield/Storm between 31 August 1990 and 25 March 1991. The 74th TFS also deployed, between 2 September 1990 and 21 March 1991. The process of transferring the wing and closing the base began immediately after their units returned from Desert Storm. The wing dropped 'tactical' from its designation on 1 October 1991, becoming the 23rd FW, although the squadrons remained TFSs until 1 November 1991, when they became Fighter Squadrons. The 75th FS formally inactivated on 2 December 1991, followed by the 74th FS in 15 February 1992 and the 76th FS on 29 May 1992. The 75th FS 'Sharks' reactivated at Pope AFB, NC, on 1 April 1992 (still part of the 23rd FW), with a new 'FT' tailcode. The squadron retained its black-and-white fin-flash and changed its composition to 18 A-10As and six OA-10As.

The 23rd FW inactivated at England AFB and activated at Pope AFB on 1 June 1992 as the 23rd Wg, gaining a C-130E squadron (2nd ALS), and reactivating the 74th FS 'Flying Tigers' as a Block 40 F-16C/D squadron on 15 June 1992. The unit is ideally placed to provide support to the US Army at Fort Bragg.

Above: The 76th TFS marked its aircraft with a red fin-stripe with white stars.

One incarnation of the 74th TFS tail-stripe was the blue band, with white stars and '74th' in white.

Above: The most notable feature of the 23rd's aircraft are the tiger's teeth nose markings.

Left: The 75th TFS wore black/white checkers as a fin-band. These marks were carried forward to Pope, where the unit is now the 75th FS.

A variation on the fin-stripe is the lightning bolt (above) with the unit designation. The 74th FS (above left) now flies F-16C/Ds.

Right: The 75th Fighter Squadron 'Tiger Sharks' is now part of the 23rd Wing, which encompasses a C-130 and an F-16 squadron. Even the Hercules wear the wing's tiger teeth. The A-10s are all in the grey scheme: note the false canopy painted underneath.

A-10 Operators

23rd Tactical Fighter Wing (Provisional)

Two 24-aircraft squadrons from the 23rd TFW deployed to King Fahd Airport in Damman, Saudi Arabia, as the 23rd TFW(P) in support of Operation Desert Shield. The 76th TFS 'Vanguards', arriving on 31 August 1990, followed by the 74th TFS 'Flying Tigers' on 2 September 1990 (a red 'Hell's Angel' was applied to the left side only of all 74th TFS aircraft). They then absorbed the 12-plane 23rd TASS 'Nail FACs' OA-10As from the 601st TACW on 21 November 1990, and the 18-strong 706th TFS 'Cajuns' A-10As from the 434th TFW on 1 January 1991 to complete the 23rd TFW(P). All units used gun-related callsigns (such as Buckshot, Hitman, Derringer, Mauser, Glock, etc.) and were augmented by people and aircraft from other squadrons. The aircraft continued to carry their home unit markings (e.g., A-10A 78-0582 from 46th TFTS at Barksdale AFB used by 706th TFS, and several 75th TFS aircraft used by deployed 23rd TFW units).

Rows of A-10s line the extensive ramp area at King Fahd Airport, Damman. The 23rd TFW(P) was based mainly on the 74th (illustrated) and 76th TFS.

Aircraft marked their 'kills' on the right side of the aircraft, with 'purple hearts' awarded for battle damage.

Four combat losses were suffered by the 23rd TFW(P): A-10A 80-0248 on 2 February 1991 with the pilot taken POW; OA-10A 76-0543 on 19 February 1991 from 23rd TASS with pilot taken POW; and OA-10A 77-0197 on 27 February 1991 from 23rd TASS, with the pilot killed while attempting to land at the FOL at King Khalid Military City (KKMC). In addition, 79-0181 from 76th TFS was

destroyed while making an emergency landing on 22 February 1991, and the wreck was buried at KKMC along with that of an F-4G.

The 74th TFS departed for home on 21 March 1991, followed by the 76th TFS on 25 March 1991, the 706th TFS on 17 May 1991, and the 23rd TASS sometime in May as well.

A squadron of FAC OA-10s and a unit from the Reserve made up the 23rd TFW(P). The latter was the 706th TFS from New Orleans, one of whose aircraft is seen here after its return from the theatre.

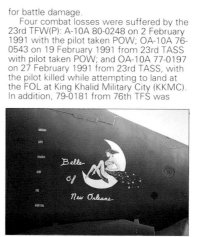

Above: Freed from peacetime constraints, nose art blossomed in the Gulf. All the A-10s wore kill marks, those of the 23rd TFW(P) displaying them on the starboard.

Above: The 706th TFS aircraft featured nose arts based on the crawfish. 'Chopper Popper' was the aircraft (77-0275) which shot down a helicopter on 6 February 1991.

51st Wing

The 25th TFS 'Assam Dragons' transferred from the 18th TFW at Kadena AB, Okinawa, to the 51st Composite Wing (Tactical) on 1 February 1981. Although the wing was headquartered at Osan AB, RoK, the 25th was detached to Suwon AB and began receiving A-10As in January 1982, coding them 'OS', and featuring a red lightning bolt on their tails. On 1 January 1984, the 51st became a TFW, while the 25th TFS came under the 5th TAIRCG. On 1 October 1990, the 19th TASS moved from Suwon to Osan AB, transferring from the 5th TAIRCG to the 51st FW (which changed its designation from the 51st TFW the same day), applying a blue fin-flash and the 'OS' tailcode. Aircraft wear a black racehorse on the side of the upper fuselage. On 7 February 1992, the 51st became the 51st Wing.

Right: A-10s remain in Korea with the 19th TASS, undertaking the FAC mission. CAS is now assigned to the co-located F-16Cs of the 36th Fighter Squadron.

Left: Between 1982 and 1984, the 25th TFS was part of the 51st TFW, flying regular A-10s with a red lightning flash mark. The wing's HQ was at Osan (hence the 'OS' tailcode), but the 25th flew from Suwon.

19th TASS OA-10As wear the wing badge (above) and a racehorse silhouette (above left) on the aircraft's spine.

52nd Fighter Wing

The 510th FS 'Buzzards' reactivated as part of the 52nd FW at Spangdahlem AB, Germany, on 4 January 1993, receiving 24 aircraft from its former sister squadron, the 92nd TFS at RAF Bentwaters (nine of them being redesignated as OA-10As). Carrying 'SP' tailcodes and flying only grey aircraft, its purple squadron colours were not applied to the aircraft for several months because it was 'the only A-10A squadron at Spangdahlem'. However, by the time they deployed to Italy in mid-1993 as part of potential UN operations against Bosnian Serbs, colours had been applied to the fin-caps (but not rudders) of some aircraft. In 1994 the wing is to gain the 53rd FS with F-15Cs from the deactivating 36th FW, and the 510th FS will assume the 22nd FS number from the other Bitburg Eagle squadron. The former 22nd FS is going to Lakenheath, where it will become the 493rd FS.

Right: The last vestige of a once massive presence in Europe, the 510th Fighter Squadron has moved from Bentwaters to Spangdahlem, to become part of a composite fighter wing. The squadron currently wears black fin-stripes (instead of the unit's previous purple) with a white lightning bolt.

Above: Old soldiers leading the new: examples from each of the 52nd Fighter Wing's four squadrons fly over a typical German landmark. The A-10 fulfils both CAS and FAC roles with the wing, some nine aircraft being designated as OA-10As. The F-4Gs of the 81st FS are backed up by F-16C/Ds in two squadrons in the defence suppression role, with Block 50s now on strength. The wing is heavily involved in contingency operations in the Balkans, having deployed some aircraft to Italy to cover the situation in Bosnia.

57th Wing

Headquartered at Nellis AFB, NV, the USAF Weapons and Tactics Center (USAF WTC) is the USAF's main tactical evaluation and trials unit, tasked with assessing aircraft modifications (OT&E) as well as developing and teaching new tactics to experienced fliers so they can pass them on to their squadrons. The centre evaluates the lessons of combat so they can continue to evolve better tactics. Therefore, small numbers of each tactical aircraft are assigned to the wing throughout the front-line careers of the type.

The flying organisation at Nellis has been known by a number of designations during its history, and when one of its fighter weapons squadrons, the 66th FWS 'Fighting Cocks', began flying as a 'Hog' unit on 1 October 1977, the wing was called the 57th Tactical Training Wing (TTW). Nellis A-10s have always been coded 'WA' and had the traditional parent unit's yellow/black check fin-band. On 1 March 1980, the 57th reverted to its previously used Fighter Weapons Wing designation. On 30 December 1981, the 66th became A-10 Division, USAF Fighter Weapons School (A-10 FWS). A separate fighter weapons squadron, the '422 FWS', was formed in the late 1970s to operationally evaluate new weapons and tactics. On 30 December 1981 the 422nd became a TES. Its mission has remained separate from that of the fighter weapons school, which teaches these new tactics to top crews from throughout the A-10A community. The wing became the 57th Fighter Wing on 1 October 1991. On 15 June 1993, the wing became the 57th Wing and the A-10 FWS the A-10 Division, USAF Weapons School (A-10 USAF WS).

Above: A-10s were assigned from an early stage to the 57th TTW for trials and evaluation work.

Above and below: All 57th aircraft wear the yellow/black fin-stripe of the wing.

Above: The initial A-10 operating unit was the 66th FWS, this becoming the A-10 FWS in 1981.

Below: Turning full circle, the current 57th FW A-10s look little different from the original aircraft.

81st Tactical Fighter Wing 'Blue Dragons'

The 81st TFW began its transition from F-4Ds to A-10As in the July 1978 Operation Ready Thunder when the 92nd TFS 'Skulls' (also known as 'Avengers') received their first aircraft on 26 January 1979, becoming the first Europe-based A-10A squadron to be declared operational. The squadron immediately redeployed several aircraft to the FOL at Sembach to participate in Operation Certain Sentinel. Based at RAF Bentwaters, the squadron colour was yellow. As would all the other squadrons based at Bentwaters and RAF Woodbridge, the southern of the twin bases operated by the 81st, these aircraft carried the wing's traditional 'WR' tailcode throughout their tenure in England.

On 1 October 1978, the 510th TFS 'Buzzards' formed, using purple as their squadron colour. The 91st TFS 'Blue Streaks' became the first A-10A squadron to form at RAF Woodbridge in July 1979, using blue as their squadron colour. They were followed in May 1979 by the 78th TFS 'Bushmasters' (locally known as the 'Snakes') at the same base, using red as their squadron colour. On 1 October 1979, the 509th TFS 'Pirates' activated at RAF Bentwaters, with a squadron colour of grey. The 511th TFS 'Vultures', with their squadron colour of black, rounded out the complement of six squadrons and 108 A-10As when they activated on 1 January 1980 at RAF Bentwaters.

At first, all aircraft had a stylised white (American) Indian head motif superimposed over their squadron's coloured fin stripe. By 1985, this had given way to squadron-unique markings over the squadron colours. For the 78th it was a simple red band outlined in white, for the 91st a white lightning bolt on a white-outlined blue band, for the 92nd a skull with lightning bolts emanating from its eye sockets on a yellow band, for the 509th it was the name 'Pirates' in black over a grey band, for the 510th a white buzzard head on a purple band, and for the 511th the word 'Vultures' on a black band.

With the addition of an F-16 aggressor squadron in 1988, RAF Bentwaters became intolerably crowded and the 509th TFS was transferred to the 10th TFW at RAF Alconbury on 1 June 1988. It was followed by the 511th TFS on 1 September 1988.

By the early 1990s, the markings on the remaining squadrons had evolved into fin-caps in the squadron colours, although an occasional 91st aircraft maintained a white lightning bolt. In February 1992, all aircraft were shuffled into different squadrons in preparation for inactivating the wing. Unless an aircraft happened to remain in its original squadron, its fin colours were overpainted in camouflage green. From that time on, the only aircraft formally marked was the wing commander's flag ship (80-181 until June 1992, when it became 82-655).

Operation Provide Comfort started on 5 April 1991 and was supported by rotating contingents of 81st TFW squadrons at Incirlik AB, Turkey, from 6 April 1991 until 4 December 1992, when tasking was transferred to the 52nd FW. These

Badge of the 81st TFW, worn on the fuselage side.

deployments included the 78th TFS from July to September 1991; the 91st TFS from January to March 1992; the 92nd TFS from October to December 1991, June to August 1992, and October to December 1992; and the 510th TFS from April to June 1992 and August to October 1992.

While the majority of aircraft used during a particular period would be from the given squadron, it was quite normal to have aircraft from other squadrons involved. During their initial deployment, several 92nd TFS aircraft received markings similar to the 'kill' markings applied to Desert Storm A-10s to annotate the number and type of Provide Comfort missions they had flown. These markings were soon removed from most aircraft and were not applied to any others in following rotations. Also, the 510th TFS supported Desert Storm operations between October and December 1991 at Dhahran RSAFB.

With the end of the Cold War, the 81st TFW was slated for inactivation and never converted to Fighter Wing status. The squadrons generally inactivated in reverse of the sequence in which they had activated. The 78th TFS officially inactivated on 4 May 1992, the 91st TFS on 14 August 1992, the 510th TFS transferred to the 52nd FW as the 510th FS on 4 January 1993 (having ceremonially closed its doors at Bentwaters on 1 December 1992), and the 92nd TFS on 31 March 1993 (although all meaningful flying had ended in January, and the final two aircraft had departed on 23 March).

Above: Early 81st TFW aircraft wore the original grey scheme.

Below: The 91st TFS 'Blue Streaks' had, naturally, a blue fin-stripe.

Above: Although their official name was the 'Bushmasters', the 78th TFS was known as the 'Snakes', the reptile featuring prominently on their unit insignia.

Left: Various squadron colour presentations were carried through the 81st's history. Often the squadron colour (here the yellow of the 92nd TFS) was repeated on the cockpit rail.

The 510th TFS were the 'Buzzards' and their aircraft sported a stylised bird of prey's head on the purple fin-band. This is the only squadron to have survived the force run-down in Europe.

Several of the A-10s which remained at Bentwaters during the wing's draw-down received the Compass Ghost Grey scheme. The last major contribution of the 81st was support of the Provide Comfort detachment.

103rd Fighter Group (ANG)

In May of 1979, the 118th TFS 'Flying Yankees' of the 103rd TFG (ANG) became the first Air National Guard unit to convert to the A-10A, having previously flown the F-100D. In doing so, it became the first ANG unit to ever receive new aircraft directly from the manufacturer. Wearing a 'CT' tailcode and based at Bradley Field in Windsor Locks, CT, the 103rd became a Fighter Group (and the 118th a Fighter Squadron) on 16 March 1992. Originally scheduled to convert to F-16C/Ds in mid-1993, they will now remain in A-10As indefinitely as part of an Air Force commitment to the Army to keep two 'wing equivalents' of A-10s for CAS.

One would expect the 'Flying Yankees' of the 118th FS to feature colourful unit markings, but this is not the case.

104th Fighter Group (ANG)

Based at Barnes Airfield in Westfield, MA, the 131st TFS 'Death Vipers' of the 104th FG (ANG) converted from the F-100D to the A-10A in July 1979. Aircraft are marked with an 'MA' tailcode, a red fin-flash with white stars, and the state silhouette on the side of the engine nacelles. On 16 March 1992, the 104th became a Fighter Group and the 131st a Fighter Squadron. In addition to their 12 A-10As, they gained six OA-10As in late 1992.

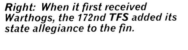

Left: The Massachusetts ANG A-10s are more brightly marked, featuring a stylish fin-stripe (far left) and a prominent state silhouette (left) on the engine cowling.

Above: This 131st TFS A-10 wears the tell-tale codes of AMARC at Davis-Monthan. As newer aircraft are released by the deactivation of front-line units, they are cascaded to reservist squadrons, allowing the retirement of the earlier FY machines.

110th Fighter Group (ANG)

Based at W. K. Kellogg Airport in Battle Creek, MI, the 172nd TFS of the 110th TFG (ANG) converted from the OA-37B to the A-10A in mid-1991. Aircraft are marked with a 'BC' tailcode. On 16 March 1992, the 110th became a Fighter Group and the 172nd a Fighter Squadron. They maintain nine OA-10As and 15 A-10As as part of the Air Force commitment to the Army to keep two 'wing equivalents' of A-10s for close air support duties.

Right: When it first received Warthogs, the 172nd TFS added its state allegiance to the fin.

Below: The 172nd FS was previously an OA-37 unit, dedicated to the FAC mission. Although OA-10s are included in the present inventory, the squadron is also tasked with regular CAS, using standard A-10s. Surviving A-10s are slowly being repainted in Compass Ghost Grey.

A-10 Operators

111th Fighter Group (ANG)

Based at NAS Willow Grove, PA, the 103rd TASS 'Black Hogs' of the 111th FG (ANG) converted from the OA-37B to the A-10 in June 1990. Aircraft are marked with a 'PA' tailcode, with red, yellow, or blue fin-caps (depending on flight), and a red 'keystone' (the state symbol) on the engine nacelles. On 16 March 1992, the 111th became an FG and the 103rd an FS, and all their aircraft were redesignated as OA-10As.

Right: Carrying a red keystone motif on its engine cowling, this was one of the first OA-10As assigned to the 103rd TASS at Willow Grove. It is posing alongside the unit's then Operational Support Aircraft, a C-131. Today the unit flies a C-26A.

Above: The 103rd TASS was the first ANG unit to receive OA-10As for the FAC mission, and the whole squadron is dedicated to the task.

Right: The 103rd FS is arranged in three flights, with either blue, red or yellow fin-stripes. This quartet contains examples of each.

128th Fighter Wing (ANG)

Based at Dane County Regional Airport (formerly known as Truax Field) in Madison, WI, the 176th TFS 'Badger Militia' of the 128th TFW (ANG) converted from the OA-

37B to the A-10A on 9 June 1981. Aircraft were marked with a 'WI' tailcode. On 16 March 1992, the 128th became a Fighter Wing and the 176th a Fighter Squadron.

The A-10As left between June and December 1992, and the 128th converted to the Block 30 F-16C/Ds between November 1992 and March 1993.

Wisconsin A-10s are no more, the 176th FS having converted to the widespread F-16 Fighting Falcon.

176th FS aircraft carried the Minutemen insignia of the ANG.

174th Tactical Fighter Wing (ANG)

Based at Hancock Field in Syracuse, NY, the 138th TFS of the 174th TFW (ANG) upgraded to Wing status when they

converted from the A-37B to the A-10A in mid-1979. Their aircraft were marked with an 'NY' tailcode and had their traditional

inscription, 'The Boys from Syracuse', carried in black on the engine nacelles. They converted to the F-16A/B in late 1988 and, because of their extensive CAS experience with the A-37B and A-10A, became the first F-16 unit dedicated to this mission.

Below: The 'Boys from Syracuse' showed references to Bavaria, carrying that region's markings.

The Bavaria theme has been continued on the 174th FW's current aircraft: the CAS-optimised F-16C/D.

175th Fighter Group (ANG)

Based at Glenn L. Martin State Airport, near Baltimore, MD, the 104th TFS of the 175th TFG (ANG) converted from the A-37B to the A-10A on 3 October 1980, marking its aircraft with the 'MD' tailcode. Fin markings have evolved over the years from the initial application of flight colours (blue, yellow or red) outlined in white with five blue stars and the state name in black, to a green stripe outlined in white with the state name in black, to the current pennant in the flight colours (again blue, yellow or red) with five white stars superimposed on a white stripe with the state name in black. Currently, the group patch is also carried on the engine nacelles. On 16 March 1992, the 175th became a Fighter Group and the 104th a Fighter Squadron. After modification of their jets to LASTE standard, the 104th won the 'Gunsmoke 91' bombing competition at Nellis AFB, NV. They gained six aircraft in late 1992 and, although they were supposed to be OA-10As, the unit continues to refer to all of its 24 aircraft as A-10As.

Above: For a while all 104th aircraft had a green fin-stripe.

Right: Victorious Maryland aircraft at Gunsmoke '91.

Above: The original fin-stripe presentation had white stars on the flight colour. The group badge (above left) was carried prominently on the engine cowling.

Left: Today the 104th **FS** features a simpler version of the fin-stripe, without the stars. The squadron's patch is carried on the engine.

343rd Wing

The 18th TFS 'Blue Foxes' of the 343rd Composite Wing from Eielson AFB, AK, acquired 26 A-10As beginning on 1 October 1981, coding them 'AK', and giving them blue fin-flashes. On 8 June 1984, the 343rd became a TFW. The 18th gained four OA-10As in October 1989. The 343rd became a Wing in March 1991, and the 18th TFS began converting to F-16C/Ds. The 11th TASS activated with the 18th's remaining aircraft (redesignating them as OA-10As) on 1 October 1991. By January 1992, the 11th TASS had seven OA-10As. On 1 August 1993 the renumbered as the 354th Wing.

Below: The Warthogs currently assigned to the 343rd Wing (badge, above right) are OA-10As, operated by the 11th TASS. The wing is well placed to rapidly deploy to Korea if required.

Right: Standard A-10s served the 343rd for many years, flying with the 18th TFS 'Blue Foxes'.

Right: Basing A-10s in Alaska deterred any aggression across the Bering Strait.

A-10 Operators

354th Fighter Wing

Based at Myrtle Beach AFB, SC, the 354th TFW began its transition from A-7Ds to A-10As in late 1976 when the 353rd TFS 'Panthers' began giving up its SLUFs for 'Warthogs' to become the first operational A-10A squadron. It retained the wing's 'MB' tailcode and the squadron's black panther on a red fin-stripe. The next squadron to transition was the 356th TFS 'Green Demons', which was declared operational on 15 October 1977. This unit was the first A-10 outfit to undergo an Operational Readiness Inspection, deploying to Travis Field for a four-day ORI in January 1978. Their squadron marking was initially a green and white checkerboard, which was later changed to four white arrows on a green stripe.

The final squadron to transition was the 355th TFS 'Falcons', which activated on 15 February 1978 and decorated their tails with six blue stars in a white band. The 354th

*The 353rd **TFS** carried a panther on its red fin-stripe.*

TFW became the first operational A-10A wing in October 1978. In November 1979 the 353rd TFS deployed to Guantanamo Bay, Cuba, for Exercise Coronet Loop, a show of force designed to demonstrate US displeasure at the continued presence of a Soviet combat brigade on the island.

During 1982-83, the 355th changed their tail markings to seven blue stars in a white band. During the 1983-84 timeframe, all three squadrons began marking their tails with fin-caps painted in the basic squadron colours: 353rd, red; 355th, blue; 356th, green. The 353rd and 355th participated in Desert Shield/Desert Storm as part of the 354th TFW(P) from mid-August 1990 through mid-March 1991. The 354th became a Fighter Wing on 1 October 1991, with the squadrons dropping their 'tactical' prefixes on 1 November 1991. The 355th FS officially inactivated on 31 March 1992, the 356th FS on 30 June 1992, the 353rd FS on 15 December 1992, and the 354th FW on 31 March 1993. On 1 August 1993, the 354th Wing was reactivated at Eielson AFB, AK, replacing the 343rd.

*Above: As the first operational wing, the 354th **TFW** (badge, left) received its Hogs in the original grey scheme.*

*Below: A change to lizard camouflage introduced a revised fin-stripe for the 355th **TFS**, with staggered blue stars.*

*Left: The green/white checkerboard signified the 356th **TFS** 'Green Demons', which also added four green arrows. From Myrtle Beach the 354th **TFW** could deploy to Europe or face threats to the south.*

*Above: The 353rd **TFS** 'Panthers' were the first operational Warthog unit.*

*Below: Seen at Gunsmoke '91, the 354th **TFW** commander's aircraft wears a four-colour fin-stripe.*

354th Tactical Fighter Wing (Provisional)

Two 24-aircraft squadrons from the 354th TFW deployed to King Fahd Airport in Damman, Saudi Arabia, as the 354th TFW(P) in support of Operation Desert Shield. Both the 353rd TFS 'Panthers' and 355th TFS 'Falcons' arrived on 16 August 1990. They then absorbed the 24-plane 511th TFS 'Vultures' from the 10th TFW on 27 December 1990. As with the co-located 23rd TFW(P), all units used gun-related callsigns and were augmented by people and aircraft from other squadrons. The aircraft continued to carry their home unit markings (e.g., A-10A 79-0218 from the 92nd TFS, 81st TFW at RAF Bentwaters used by 511th TFS). Nose art was prevalent on A-10As from all these squadrons, with 'kill' markings located on the port side.

Only two combat losses were suffered by the 354th TFW(P): A-10As 78-0722 and 79-0130 from the 353rd TFS were both lost during the same mission on 14 February 1991. After weeks of apparently unstoppable success, the seeming loss of two pilots over the Medina Division of the RepublicanGuard, far into Iraq, resulted in restrictions being placed on the use of A-10s to reduce the chance of further losses. Thankfully, it was discovered after the war that only one of the crew had been killed; the other became a POW and was freed after the ceasefire.The 353rd TFS departed for home on 19 March 1991, followed by the 355th TFS on 23 March 1991, and the 511th TFS on 12 May and 8 June 1991.

Above: 353rd TFS Gulf patch.

Above: 354th TFW(P) A-10s at King Fahd. The parent wing supplied two squadrons for Desert Storm.

Right: Armourers prepare an A-10 for battle at King Fahd. The ground troops worked hard to generate sorties at an impressive rate.

Above: The 354th TFW(P)'s helicopter kill was supplied by Todd Sheehy, flying 81-0964.

355th Wing

The 355th TFW, based at Davis-Monthan AFB, AZ, began transitioning from the A-7D to the A-10A in March 1976 for the purpose of training new 'Warthog' drivers. The first squadron to transition was the 333rd TFTS 'Lancers' in March 1976, with aircraft painted in the original light grey paint scheme but with versions of the wing's 'DM' tailcode, eventually applying red and white checks to the fin-cap. The 358th TFTS 'Lobos' followed suit, transitioning on 1 July 1976, with a green fin-cap.

Aircraft from Davis-Monthan toured PACAF in June/July 1977, paving the way for the eventual stationing of A-10s in the area full-time. The final squadron to transition was the 357th TFTS 'Dragons' on 31 March 1979, with a yellow fin-cap and black lightning bolt. On 1 September 1979, the wing became the 355th Tactical Training Wing (TTW), with the squadrons remaining TFTSs. The 358th adopted black for their fin stripe in the late 1980s. The wing became the 355th FW on 1 October 1991, and the squadrons the 333rd FS, 357th FS and 358th FS. The 333rd FS inactivated on 15 February 1991, reactivating in the 602nd ACW on 1 November

Below: The 355th TFW 'boss-bird' wore markings for the 832nd Air Division.

1991. The 333rd FS 'Lancers' and 354th FS 'Bulldogs' transferred from the co-located 602nd TAIRCW on 1 May 1992 with OA-10As. At the same time, the wing became the 355th FW.The 354th FS moved from Davis-Monthan AFB to McChord AFB, WA, on 5 January 1993, having transferred its operation between January and September 1992. It remained part of the 355th FW, with a mix of 20 OA-10A and A-10A aircraft and a new tailcode, 'TC'. On 1 May 1993, the wing gained two EC-130H squadrons and became the 355th Wing.

Above: The 355th TFW became the first regular USAF unit to get A-10s in early 1976, undertaking the training effort. Initially aircraft featured over-sized tailcodes over the light grey camouflage.

Above: A variation on the grey theme, this 355th TFW A-10 shows much patching.

Below: The 358th TFTS wore a yellow fin-stripe with black lightning bolt.

Above: The 333rd **FS** is back with the 355th Wing after a spell with the 602nd **ACW**.
Left: Tail of the 357th **FS**.

The 354th **FS** was absorbed by the 355th Wing from the 602nd **TACW**, having previously been known as the 23rd **TASS**. The squadron flew the FAC mission with OA-10As but has since gained A-10s as well.

Still under 355th Wing control, the 354th **FS** has moved to McChord AFB, Washington, and adopted the 'TC' (for Tacoma) tailcode. It supports army operations at the nearby Fort Ord.

363rd Fighter Wing

On 1 April 1992, the 21st FS 'Black Panthers' transferred from the 507th ACW to the co-located 363rd FW at Shaw AFB, SC. With a mix of six OA-10As and 12 A-10As, the squadron changed their tailcode from 'SF' to 'SW', but retained their fin-flash of black. The wing is expected to renumber as the 20th FW.

The 21st FS changed only its tailcode when it switched from 507th ACW to 363rd FW control. The landing aircraft carries an AIS pod for an ACMI range.

412th Test Wing

The AX Joint Test Force (JTF) formed in 1972 under the 6510th Test Wing (TW) at Edwards AFB, CA. This wing conducted flying operations for the Air Force Flight Test Center (AFFTC), the USAF's primary test facility for new aircraft, ongoing modification programmes, and many other operational and experimental trials. The YA-10s were turned over from Fairchild-Republic to the USAF on 24 October 1972 and participated in a fly-off against the Northrop YA-9s until 31 December 1972. After the YA-10 was declared the winner of the competition, the organisation became

Below: The sixth pre-production YA-10A served for several years on the 6512th TW's test force. The red tips were for conspicuity on the ranges.

the A-10A JTF on 18 January 1972 and continued to fly the YA-10s until 13 June 1975. The first pre-production YA-10A arrived at Edwards on 15 February 1975, and these aircraft and the first four A-10As were used to conduct developmental test

The single YA-10B was operated from Edwards, although it was technically bailed to Fairchild as a company-funded demonstrator.

and evaluation (DT&E). Fairchild-Republic leased back the first YA-10A in 1978, using it to evaluate the night/adverse weather (N/AW) YA-10B concept through the end of 1979. In January 1978 A-10A testing fell under the 6512th TESTS, with the aircraft being marked with its white 'x's on blue stripe fin-flash. In 1983 the tailcode 'ED' was added. On 2 October 1992, the wing was redesignated as the 412th TW, and the squadron the 445 TESTS.

442nd Fighter Wing (AFRes)

Based at Richards-Gebaur AFB, south of Kansas City, MI, the 303rd TFS of the 442nd TFG (AFRes) began conversion from the C-130E to the A-10A on 3 June 1982 with the arrival of its first three of 18 authorised aircraft. The actual conversion of the units from 'Airlift' to 'Fighter' occurred on 1 October 1982, and the 442nd became a Wing on 1 February 1984. Aircraft are marked with a 'KC' tailcode, with black fin-flashes. They gained six OA-10As in mid-1992 to bolster their part of the Air Force commitment to the Army to keep two 'wing equivalents' of A-10s for close air support duties. On 1 February 1992, the 442nd became a Fighter Wing and the 303rd a Fighter Squadron. By mid-1994, as Richards-Gebaur closes, the unit will move to nearby Whiteman AFB, near Knob Noster, MI, with a total of 15 A-10As and nine OA-10As.

Smart 'KC-Hawgs' of the 303rd TFS carry Mavericks and inert AIM-9 Sidewinders for a training mission. Note the 'AFRES' on the engines.

507th Air Control Wing

The 507th ACW, based at Shaw AFB, SC, began transitioning from OV-10As to the OA-10As in 1991. It received its first OA-10As from the inactivating 511th TFS of the 10th TFW at the end of October, with subsequent deliveries in late November and mid-December. These aircraft went to the 21st TASS 'Ravens', which changed its tailcode from 'SR' to 'SF' as it received the new aircraft. The fin-flash was a blue band outlined in white pin stripes with the squadron name in white. On 1 November 1991, the squadron was redesignated as the 21st FS 'Black Panthers', which had previously flown F-4Es as part of the 35th FW at George AFB, CA. With a mix of six OA-10As and 12 A-10As, the squadron sported a fin-flash of black, edged with a white pin stripe, and a red lightning bolt. On 1 April 1992, the 21st FS transferred to the co-located 363rd FW prior to the 507th ACW inactivating on 12 June 1992.

The 507th ACW was a short-lived Warthog operator, being absorbed by the 363rd FW just a few months after transitioning from the OV-10 Bronco.

602nd Air Control Wing

The 602nd Tactical Air Control Wing (TAIRCW), based at Davis-Monthan AFB, AZ, began transitioning from OV-10As to the OA-10As with the activation of the 23rd Tactical Air Support Squadron (TASS) 'Nail FACs' on 1 October 1987. These aircraft were coded 'NF', with dark blue fin-caps marked with three yellow (the squadron's colour) stars. The 23rd TASS was followed by the 22nd TAS Training Squadron (TASTS) on 15 June 1988 (their squadron colour was yellow). The 'Nail FACs', who got their name during the Vietnam War when they flew OV-10As specially modified with the 'Pave Nail' laser designation system, were deployed with the 23rd TFW(P) from 20

Transitioning from the OV-10, the 23rd TASS retained the 'Nail FAC' tailcode when it received OA-10As.

Left: 23rd TASS OA-10s wore a fin-stripe of black with three yellow stars.

November 1990 until March 1991 to participate in Desert Storm. On 1 November 1991, the wing dropped the 'tactical' designation, becoming the 602nd ACW. At the same time the 22nd TASTS was replaced by the 333rd FS 'Lancers' (previously active with the co-located 355th FW), with red as the squadron colour. Also, the 23rd TASS became the 354th FS 'Bulldogs', with blue as the squadron colour. The 333rd FS and 354th FS were absorbed by the co-located 355th Wg on 1 May 1992. The 602nd ACW inactivated on 15 June 1992.

Right: The 22nd TASTS was a training unit.

917th Fighter Wing (AFRes)

Based at Barksdale AFB, Louisiana, the 47th TFS 'Terrible Termites' of the 917th TFG (AFRes) converted from the A-37B to the A-10A on 1 October 1980, becoming the first AFRes 'Warthog' unit. Aircraft were marked with a 'BD' tailcode, with aircraft having green fin-flashes. The group gained formal responsibility for replacement training with the activation of the 46th TFTS on 30 September 1983. On 1 July 1987, the 917th became a TFW in its own right. On 1 February 1992, the units became the 917th FW, the 46th Fighter Training Squadron (FTRS) and the 47th FS. In early 1993, the 47th gained 12 additional aircraft, giving them nine OA-10As and 15 A-10As. The

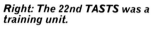

Above: Barksdale A-10s often sport 'Hog's Teeth' markings.

46th FTRS will be replaced by an associate bomber squadron on 1 October 1993, with all A-10 training being consolidated at Davis-Monthan AFB.

Above: The 917th evaluated different colour schemes on two of its A-10s, this being a trial desert scheme. Another scheme involved greys.

As the first Reserve A-10 unit, the 917th was given the type training role, for which the 46th TFTS was established. These aircraft are marked by a blue fin-cap.

The green fin-cap denotes the 47th FS, which is the 917th's operational squadron. This will remain active after all A-10 training has been consolidated at Davis-Monthan.

926th Fighter Group (AFRes)

Based at NAS New Orleans, LA, the 706th TFS 'Cajuns' of the 926th TFG (AFRes) was part of the 434th TFW when it converted from the A-37B to the A-10A between January and June 1982. Aircraft were marked with an 'NO' tailcode, with red fin-flashes. On 1 July 1987, the 926th was transferred to the newly created 917th TFW. Between 31 December 1990 and 18 May 1991, the 'Cajuns' were deployed as part of the 23rd TFW(P) during Desert Storm. On 1 February 1992, the wing, group, and squadron all lost the 'tactical' prefix from their designations. In late 1992, the 706th FS transitioned to the F-16C/D.

Illustrating the 706th TFS's fine showing in Desert Storm, this is the aircraft, piloted by Bob Swain, which shot down a BO 105. The Warthog no longer serves with the 'Cajuns', who now fly the F-16C/D.

930th Operations Group (AFRes)

Based at Grissom AFB, IN, the 45th TFS 'Hoosier Hogs' converted from the A-37B to the A-10A on 1 June 1981, marking its aircraft with an 'IN' tailcode and blue fin-flashes. On 1 July 1987, it transferred from the 434th (which became the 434th Air Refueling Wing) to the newly created 930th TFG (becoming a component of the 442nd TFW of Richards-Gebaur AFB). On 1 February 1992, unit designations changed to the 442nd Fighter Wing, 930th Fighter Group and 45th Fighter Squadron. Then, on 1 August 1992, another reorganisation took place, with the Reserve units at Grissom being restructured under the 434th Wing, with the group becoming the 930th Operations Group (OG). The 45th FS possesses 12 A-10As and six OA-10As.

Flying from Grissom AFB, the 45th FS has been an A-10 squadron since 1981, and has recently added the OA-10A to its regular 'Hogs'. The blue fin-band has remained constant throughout the unit's A-10 history.

3246th Test Wing

Located at Eglin AFB, FL, the 3246th TW was primarily concerned with the testing and evaluation of aircraft ordnance, and operated a variety of front-line USAF types. The fin-band for the unit was white with red diamonds. A-10As were assigned to the wing's 3247th Test Squadron (TESTS). In late 1982, the 'AD' tailcode (for Armament Division) was added, this changing to 'ET' (for Eglin Test) on 30 September 1989. All A-10As had left Eglin by 1992.

The red diamonds on a white band denote the 3246th (now 46th) Test Wing, the USAF's principal ordnance trials unit at Eglin AFB, Florida. This aircraft was the fifth pre-production YA-10A.

Sacramento Air Logistics Center

Based at McClellan AFB, CA, the SM-ALC is the facility responsible for all OA/A-10A maintenance and upgrade work. The Center's Engineering Flight Test (EFT) was the initial operating unit, redesignated the 2874th TESTS on 1 June 1992 and assigned the 'SM' tailcode. On 2 October 1992, it was again renumbered as the 337th TESTS. EFT reports to Air Materiel Command, the modification developer, not Air Combat Command, the user. EFT performs two functions: test fly all aircraft after they have undergone programmed depot maintenance (PDM), and perform qualification testing and evaluation (QT&E) on all new aircraft software and avionics modifications. After determining that modifications (software or hardware) work

as the engineers think they should, the modification is turned over to the user at the USAF WTC at Nellis AFB for OT&E to see if it does what the user wants it to. Only after that testing is the modification released to the operational units.

Proudly wearing the Engineering Flight Test badge, this A-10 was involved in LASTE development work, as evidenced by the night formation lights. The EFT operation is now handled by the 337th TESTS, still based at McClellan AFB.

USAF Tactical Air Warfare Center

Several A-10As were allocated to the USAF's Tactical Air Warfare Center (TAWC) for trials and evaluation purposes. The flying squadron of this unit was the 4485th TESTS, based at Eglin AFB, FL, using a black-and-white check fin-band. All A-10As had left Eglin by 1992.

Another test unit at Eglin is the (previously Tactical) Air Warfare center, which has an 'OT' tailcode for 'Operational Test' and black/white checkerboard fin-stripe. This is one of a small number of A-10s which have been assigned to the Center's flying unit, the 4485th Test Squadron.

Turkish Air Force

In June 1993 it was announced that 50 ex-USAF A-10As would be provided to the Turkish air force. As of this writing, no information as to which aircraft will be transferred was available, but it is rumoured that they will be based at Eskisehir.

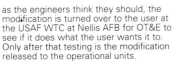

Vietnamese People's Air Force

Photographed by Frank Rozendaal

The Khon Quan Nhan Dan Viet Nam (Vietnamese People's Air Force) has a short but full history. At war almost constantly since its inception, the air arm has amassed considerable combat experience. The air force is now considerably larger than it was at the height of the Vietnam War, and presently fields three front-line divisions, with a total of nine operational fighter and fighter-bomber regiments. These are augmented by two transport and two helicopter regiments, and by a training school with two training regiments. These are based at 13 air bases, and are equipped exclusively with Soviet types, the US-built types inherited from the South Vietnamese having now been grounded through spares shortages, although some remain in storage. Despite the termination of Soviet assistance and a steady decline in serviceability, competitiveness and morale since the days of glory, when Vietnamese pilots notched up an impressive tally of kills against the USAF, the national insignia of a red circle with the Vietnamese Sao Vang (golden star) continues to be carried with pride, and the air arm remains a force to be reckoned with.

Above and right: Massive murals, like this one at the air force headquarters at Bac Mai, recall the heroic days of the Vietnam War when the air force defended the nation against what is still seen as American imperialist aggression. The air force museum in Hanoi provides further memories, including this B-52-killing MiG-21MF.

Above: A MiG-21bis 'Fishbed-N' of the Da Phuc-based 921st 'Sao Do' Fighter Regiment stands alert, armed with R-60 (AA-8 'Aphid') and R-13 (AA-2 'Atoll') IR-homing AAMs.

The Da Phuc flight line displays US-built revetments moved from air bases in the South, and MiG-21s in a mix of colour schemes, including an unusual overall bright blue.

Above: A MiG-21bis of the Kep-based 927th 'Lam Son' Regiment, partners of the 370th Division's 921st Regiment at Da Phuc. MiG-21s also equip the 925th, 929th, 933rd and 935th Regiments, and the 920th, a conversion unit.

Below: Armourers load an Su-22M-3 'Fitter-J' of the 923rd 'Yen The' Fighter Bomber Regiment at Tho Xuan with a Kh-28 (AS-9 'Kyle') anti-radar missile. Other aircraft in the line-up carry recce pods.

Above: Pilots of the 923rd Fighter Bomber Regiment with their Su-22 'Fitters', which include two-seat Su-22UM-3s for training and standardisation. The aircraft are unusual in wearing an overall light-grey colour scheme, rare on this low-level ground attack and recce platform. Another Su-22 unit is the co-located 937th 'Hau Giang' Regiment.

Below: MiG-21 pilots read the army's daily paper as they sit alert at Da Phuc. Their regiment forms one third of the 371st 'Thang Long' Fighter Division, headquartered at the same base. The 370th 'Hai Van' Division is based at Da Nang and the 372nd at Tho Xuan.

Above: The 920th Fighter Training Regiment is based at Phu Cat, and is responsible for MiG-21 conversion training and may also offer lead-in training for the Su-22. The regiment establishment includes a number of single-seat MiG-21bis fighters, allowing the unit to train new pilots in operational tactics and use of the radar, armament and systems of the MiG-21bis.

Below: Workhorse of the 920th Regiment is the MiG-21UM 'Mongol', the two-seat trainer derivative of the 'Fishbed'. MiG-21UMs are also assigned to the front-line MiG-21 regiments, which are the 921st at Da Phuc, the 925th (base unknown), the 927th at Kep, the 929th (base unknown), the 931st at Yen Bai, the 933rd at Phu Cat, and the 935th (base unknown).

Above: *One of 24 L-39 Albatros trainers delivered to the 910th 'Julius Fucik' Training Regiment at Nha Trang; the unit is named after a prominent Czech Marxist.*

Left: *A Vietnamese MiG-21 pilot. The MiG-21s are assigned to three front-line divisions – the 370th (929th and 935th Regiments, plus the Su-22s of the 937th), the 371st (921st, 927th and 931st Regiments) and the 372nd (925th and 933rd Regiments, plus the Su-22s of the 923rd).*

Right: *Wearing a cumbersome Chinese life jacket, a young student pilot removes his helmet after a solo training flight. The ambitious student will be aiming for the multi-role Su-22 force.*

Below: *Vietnam operates the basic unarmed L-39C trainer, 24 of which were delivered during 1980/81. Here one of the Czech trainers is refuelled before a training sortie from its Nha Trang base.*

Above: *The Hoa Lac-based 916th 'Ba Vi' Helicopter Transport Regiment operates the Mi-8 'Hip' and a number of other helicopter types, including Mi-17s, Mi-6s and Mi-24s.*

Right: *Mi-6 'Hook' heavylift helicopters serve with the 916th Helicopter Transport Regiment, and were intensively used during the Vietnamese invasion of Cambodia.*

Above: *Some of the regiment's Mi-8s and Mi-17s wear a pseudo-civilian-type colour scheme and are used for VIP transport duties.*

Below: *916th Helicopter Transport Regiment Mi-8s. The rugged 'Hip' is the workhorse of Vietnam's helicopter transport fleet.*

Above: The Ka-28 'Helix' (seen here) and Ka-25Bsh 'Hormone' are operated from Da Nang and Kien An by the 954th Helicopter Regiment. Massive influxes of Soviet equipment began after the 3 November 1978 Treaty of Friendship, Co-operation and Mutual Assistance signed by the two governments.

Below: Withdrawn UH-1s. After 1975 the air force absorbed many US types. The 935th Fighter Regiment used F-5s, while the 937th was equipped with A-37s, the 917th Regiment used UH-1s, CH-47s, L-19s and U-17s, and the 918th was formed with C-47s, C-119s and C-130s.

Above: C-130s and UH-1s remain in storage at Bien Hoa and Tan Son Nhut. Many were cannibalised for spares over the years, allowing a dwindling number to serve on until very recently. Many US-built types captured by the Vietnamese have been passed to the USSR and its clients for evaluation.

Below: Grounded An-26 'Curls' at Tan Son Nhut. Hang Kong Vietnam originated as the 919th Transport Regiment and was until recently subordinate to VPAF headquarters. An-26s are also operated by the 917th and 918th Transport Regiments at Tan Son Nhut and Gia Lam. With the withdrawal of the C-130 the air force has no heavylift transport assets, and even during the invasion of Cambodia 15 years ago had to borrow Aeroflot An-12s.

Variant Briefing: Part 3

The Operators

Despite its age, the Mirage III and its derivatives remain in widespread service worldwide, in an astonishing number of sub-variants. During the mid-1990s, the aircraft will disappear from the inventories of larger European operators like

Above: The Mirage III continues to enjoy a successful career as a reconnaissance aircraft, despite its relatively short range and its lack of space for onboard sensors. Most Mirage IIIR and 5R operators continue to rely on conventional optical cameras. This is a Swiss Mirage IIIRS.

France and Belgium, but elsewhere Mirages have been upgraded for continued service. Here we present an exhaustive guide detailing all of the squadrons that have operated Dassault's remarkable Delta.

Abu Dhabi

Perhaps influenced by Pakistan, Abu Dhabi placed its first Mirage order in September 1972, calling for 12 Mirage 5AD attack aircraft, two reconnaissance-nosed 5RADs and two 5DAD trainers. A follow-on batch comprised 14 multi-role 5EADs, one 5RAD and a third 5DAD, increasing the purchase to 32 Mirages.

Serial numbers	Type	Quantity
401 to 412	Mirage 5AD	12
201 to 203	Mirage 5DAD	3
501 to 514	Mirage 5EAD	14
601 to 603	Mirage 5RAD	3

The 5ADs were basically 'straight' Mirage 5s, delivered in 1974, but the 5EADs – starting with the first four deliveries on 13 July 1976 – were Mirage IIIEs in all but name, and quite clearly had Cyrano radar and Doppler. Supplies of reconnaissance and trainer variants were completed in July 1976, the last 5EAD arriving in 1977. All had upper surface camouflage of green and sand and most were delivered wearing the Abu Dhabi roundel of red (outer), white and yellow.

In May 1976, the armed forces of Abu Dhabi were joined with those of its smaller

neighbours to form the United Arab Emirates combined military command, embracing Dubai, Sharjah, Ajman, Fujairah, Ras al-Khaimah and Umm al-Qaiwain. Apart from a change of roundel to green, white and black with a red flash at the 12 o'clock position, there was little effect on the Mirage force, which continued to operate from the international airport at Abu Dhabi pending completion of a new military air base at Maqatra/al-Dhafra. Here they formed two units: I Shaheen Squadron, equipped with Mirage 5EADs and 5DADs, and II Shaheen Squadron with Mirage 5ADs and 5RADs.

'Shaheen' is Arabic for 'warrior', but most of the pilots were initially seconded from the Pakistan air force. Under this aid agreement, the PAF could borrow the ADAF/UAEAF Mirages if Pakistan were attacked. Later, when the Mirage force was in need of overhaul, the 26 remaining aircraft were rotated through Pakistan, beginning in 1990, for the PAF workshops at Kamra to overhaul their airframes and engines. Following delivery of Mirage 2000s in 1989, the Mirage 5's role has been less vital, although I Shaheen Squadron is now detached to Sharjah for air defence duties.

Above: Surviving Mirage 5EADs are believed to remain operational with I Shaheen Squadron of the UAE air force at Sharjah. The 5EAD is basically equivalent to the Mirage IIIE with Cyrano radar and Doppler. This aircraft carries underwing fuel tanks inboard, and MATRA R.550s.

Argentina

Against competition from the BAC Lightning and Northrop F-5, the Mirage won an initial order placed on 23 October 1970 for a dozen aircraft, comprising 10 IIIEAs and two IIIDA trainers, to serve with Air Defence Command (Comando Aéreo de Defensa) of the Fuerza Aérea Argentina. Handed over in France from June 1972, they were delivered as air freight inside Argentine air force Lockheed Hercules and did not begin flying until July 1973. A second batch of seven IIIEAs was ordered in 1977 for delivery in 1979, these differing from their predecessors in having the ability to launch MATRA R.530 medium-range AAMs. A further two trainers were supplied in October-November 1982.

There had been a considerable influx of secondhand Mirages resulting from Argentina's belligerent attitude towards its neighbours. In 1978, the prospect of war with Chile over the ownership of islands in the Beagle Channel prompted the purchase from Israel of 24 IAI Dagger As and two Dagger B trainers, which were delivered between 26 November 1978 and 23 December 1980. A further batch of 11 and two was supplied between 29 May 1981 and February 1982. Daggers were armed with Rafael Shafrir IV AAMs as day-fighters, while the Mirage IIIs received MATRA 550 Magic Is in time for the Falklands War of May-June 1982. In contrast to the Mirage IIIs with their I- serial number prefixes, indicating a primary interceptor role, the Daggers were given C- serials, for general-purpose fighter-bomber. They were, however, assigned to Air Defence Command, despite which their main role in the conflict with the UK was attack.

To replace war losses of Mirages, Daggers and other aircraft, Peru supplied 10 Mirage 5Ps on 6 June 1982, these adopting the serial numbers of lost Daggers. A further emergency order to Israel brought 19 war-weary Mirage IIICJs and three IIIBJs, delivered by sea between 18 December 1982 and February 1983, some of them still wearing Arab 'kill' markings from two Middle East wars. During the mid-1980s, the Daggers were progressively modernised by IAI to 'Finger I', 'II' and 'III' standard with a Kfir-type nose with radar ranger and avionics improvements including HUD and INS.

Serial numbers	Type	Quantity
C-720 to C-722	Mirage IIIBJ	3
C-701 to C-719	Mirage IIICJ	19
I-001, 002, 020, 021	Mirage IIIDA	4
I-003 to I-009	Mirage IIIEA	17
C-403, 404, 407, 409, 410, 419, 428, 430, 433, 436	Mirage 5P	10
C-401 to C-424; C-427 to C-437	Dagger A	35
C-425, 426, 439, 439	Dagger B	4

Mirage IIIEA camouflage is brown and two-tone green, this scheme also being applied to the Dagger. Mirage IIICJs and 5Ps are tan and sand. Some Daggers and IIIEAs began changing to overall light blue-grey in the late 1980s.

I Escuadrón de Caza

(Grupo 8 de Caza/VII Brigada Aérea)
Base: Base Aérea Tandil, Buenos Aires
Badge: (VII BA) a Mirage in plan and a map of Argentina

The 1st Fighter Squadron began flying newly delivered Mirage IIIEAs at Base Aérea Militar Dr Mariano Marino, Buenos Aires in July 1973 and had completed conversion of its pilots before the end of the following year. Grupo 8 de Caza formed on 10 December 1975 as parent unit to the squadron, while the arrival of seven more Mirages in 1979 resulted in VII Brigada being formed as the overall controlling unit of 8 Wing and its single squadron. It operated detachments at Comodoro Rivadavia and Rio Gallegos during the Falklands War, losing two aircraft to Sea

Harriers, one of which was finished off by over-enthusiastic army gunners when attempting an emergency landing at Port Stanley, FI. The two trainers delivered in 1982 were added to squadron strength and were soon afterwards augmented by a flight simulator. In December 1987, VII Brigada disbanded, followed by Grupo 8 on 8 February 1988, its aircraft transferring to Grupo 6 at Tandil, where they are currently based alongside Daggers, still in 1 Esc.

Right: I Escuadrón de Caza is a long-term operator of the Mirage IIIEA in the air defence role. This aircraft wears the distinctive badge of V Brigada on the nose, and the VII Brigada badge on the fin.

II & III Escuadrónes de Caza

(Grupo 6 de Caza/VI Brigada Aérea)
Base: Base Aérea Tandil, Buenos Aires
Badge: (Grupo 6) a falcon clutching a bomb; on low-vis aircraft, the head of a falcon in profile

Ex-Israeli Daggers replaced F-86 Sabres in Grupo 6, beginning with first deliveries in November 1978. Two squadrons had formed, although were not fully trained, by the start of the Falklands War. II Escuadrón operated a detachment from San Julian, Santa Cruz during the conflict and III Escuadron did likewise at Rio Grande, Tierra del Fuego. Both units were tasked with attack, although four Daggers were briefly operated from Comodoro Rivadavia as replacements for Mirage IIIEAs late in the

war. Combat losses totalled 11, but the Daggers seriously damaged two British warships. The Dagger upgrade programme 'Finger' began in November 1982. Approximately 20 aircraft remain in service with Air Operations Command (Comando de Operaciones Aéreas) following disbandment of Air Defence Command in February 1988.

Grupo 6 also received the 10 Mirage 5s donated by Peru in June 1982, basing them at Rio Gallegos for at least a year. They were withdrawn for refurbishment and returned to become a component of Grupo 10.

Below: This Grupo 6 Dagger wears a variation of the Grupo badge, using the same colours and elements, but with a stylised G6 replacing the falcon as a centrepiece.

Right: The toned-down version of the Grupo 6 Falcon badge is replacing the ornate shield on the unit's grey-painted Daggers.

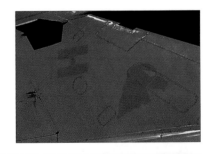

Below: The latest modification to Argentinian Daggers gives them a Kfir-style nose, complete with vortex-generator strakes. The original Grupo 6 badge is worn on the fin. The significance of the M4 code ahead of the roundel is unknown.

Escuadrón 55 'Prudencia y Corajé

(Grupo 4 de Caza/IV Brigada Aérea)
Base: Base Aérea Militar El Plumerillo, Mendoza

Numbered out of sequence, 55 Squadron is named for the 55 Argentine air force personnel killed in the Falklands War. The squadron formed within Grupo 4 early in 1983, flying some of the newly delivered ex-Israeli Mirage IIICJs and replacing Grupo 4's A-4 Skyhawk squadron, simultaneously transferred to Grupo 5. Until June 1986 it was partnered by Argentina's last F-86

Sabre squadron. By mid-1987 it had received the complete force of IIICJs. Escuadrón 55 does not apply the usual prominent serial numbers or badges, but its shoulder patch comprises a yellow map of the Falkland Islands on a blue background, the lower part including a black and white checkerboard.

Elderly ex-Israeli Mirage IIICJs delivered after the Falklands War equip Escuadron 55 of Grupo 4. This is tasked with ground attack duties and forms part of IV Brigada based at El Plumerillo Mendoza. The aircraft seem to have had their Cyrano radar removed.

Dassault Mirage III/5/50 Variants

Escuadrón Cruz y Fiero

(Grupo 10 de Caza/X Brigada Aérea)
Base: Base Aérea Militar Rio Gallegos, Santa Cruz
Badge: a griffon holding a halberd, both before a cross

Gaining its unusual name from an Argentine folk poem, the Cross and Iron Squadron was established at Rio Gallegos when X Brigada was commissioned there on 19 March 1984 to replace the Mirage 5P detachment formerly maintained at the same base by Grupo 6. The squadron was assigned only five Mirage IIICJs until mid-1987, when the aircraft joined 55 Squadron and were replaced by the Mirage 5Ps following their refurbishment to Mara standard. At least two aircraft have been lost in accidents.

Escuadrón Cruz y Fiero forms part of X Brigada's Grupo 10 and is based at Rio Gallegos, where it operates refurbished and modernised Mirage 5Ps from Peru.

Australia

After trials with a Mirage III re-engined with a Rolls-Royce Avon, Australia decided to replace its Commonwealth (North American) CA.27 Sabres with the standard Atar-powered variant and placed an initial order for 30 on 31 March 1961. This quantity was doubled in October 1962 and increased to 100 in May 1963, while 10 two-seat trainers were added in October 1963 and a further six in November 1970. The single-seat contract was split almost evenly between Mirage IIIO(F) interceptors and IIIO(A) attack variants. These were assigned the 'A3' serial range.

Serial numbers	Type	Quantity
A3-1 to A3-25; A3-27 to A3-50	Mirage IIIO(F)	49
A3-26; A3-51 to A3-100	Mirage IIIO(A)	51
A3-101 to A3-116	Mirage IIID	16

Between October 1968 and February 1971, all surviving single-seat aircraft apart from A3-2 were converted to a common standard, the IIIO(F/A).

The first two Mirage IIIOs were built by Dassault, A3-1 making its initial flight on 14 March 1963 before the official hand-over on 9 April. Production of the Mirage at Avalon, Victoria, began with A3-3, first flown there on 16 November 1963. Understandably, the first few aircraft contained some French components to get manufacture under way. The Government Aircraft Factory was the prime contractor, with Commonwealth Aircraft Corporation sub-

contracted to build the wings and fin, for which reason the Mirage was assigned the 'shadow' designation CA.29.

From A3-16, in May 1965, aircraft contained no French-supplied sub-assemblies, apart from 10 mid-production machines which had Dassault-built fuselages to expedite production. A3-100 flew on 4 November 1968. Trainers had French fuselages and local wings apart from the wholly European-built A3-101, which made its first Antipodean flight on 6 October 1966. A3-110 was delivered on October 1967, and the follow-on batch of six was completed between delivery of A3-111 in August 1973 and A3-116's first flight on 18 December the same year. A local modification on some aircraft was a 'wet' wing which gave a further 55 Imp gal (250 litres) of fuel on each side.

Natural metal finish was replaced in service by green and grey upper surfaces with light grey beneath, although the early 1980s saw a change to overall light grey medium-altitude camouflage. Squadrons based at Williamtown constituted No. 81 Wing; those at Butterworth, Malaysia were 78 Wing. The latter had a strength of 42 Mirages, eight of which were detached to Tengah, Singapore. Losses in service totalled 41, including three trainers, before A3-101 of the ARDU made the last official RAAF Mirage flight on 8 February 1989 when it was delivered to Woomera for storage. In 1990, 43 Mirage IIIOs and seven Mirage IIIDs were sold to Pakistan, the type having then been replaced by McDonnell Douglas F/A-18 Hornets.

No. 2 Operational Conversion Unit

Base: Williamtown
Badge: a tiger's head (also a fin stripe of diagonal black and yellow bars)

The first Mirage operator, No. 2 OCU began conversion from Sabres in the second half of 1964, but had to wait two years for its two-seat aircraft. The OCU passed its pilot training role to No. 77 Squadron in January 1985 and converted to Hornets five months later.

Right: No. 2 OCU is now the F/A-18 training unit. This Mirage IIID wears yellow wing bands and fuel tanks for ACM training, in addition to the regular black and yellow tiger stripe fin badge. A practise bomb dispenser is carried under the belly.

No. 3 Squadron

Base: Butterworth, Malaysia
Badge: a phoenix

Sabre-equipped No. 3 Squadron was withdrawn from Butterworth to Williamtown in May 1967 to begin Mirage IIIO(A) conversion and returned to Malaysia in February 1969. It remained there until stood down on 31 March 1986 in preparation for its return to Australia and Hornet conversion.

Right: Relegated to gate guard status, this Mirage IIIO wears the distinctive Phoenix insignia of No. 3 Squadron, which spent most of the Mirage era based in Malaysia at Butterworth.

No. 75 Squadron

Base: Williamtown; Butterworth, Malaysia; Darwin
Badge: a magpie (originally two magpies supporting a badge, surrounded by black and white checks)

The initial operational RAAF Mirage IIIO(F) squadron reformed at Williamtown on 1 August 1965, having discarded its previous Sabres. The unit took the Mirage to Malaysia when it arrived at Butterworth in May 1967 as replacement for No. 76 Squadron's Sabres, but the running-down of the RAAF's presence abroad resulted in its withdrawal to Darwin on 10 August 1983. Responsible for the air defence of the whole of northern

Australia, the squadron built up to 21 IIIOs and four IIIDs by 1987, then started receiving Hornets in May 1988 and flew its last sortie (the RAAF's last operational Mirage mission) on 26 September 1988. It has been at Tindal since 1 October 1988.

Australia's Mirage IIIOs originally wore an overall natural metal colour scheme. No. 75 Squadron's wore an intricate black and white hat-and-checks badge.

Below: The application of camouflage brought a simplified fin badge, with one magpie.

Above: In the final air superiority two-tone grey colour scheme, No. 75 Squadron's tail markings were toned down by substituting light grey for the usual brilliant white.

No. 76 Squadron

Base: Williamtown
Badge: a panther's head

Withdrawn from Malaysia, No. 76 converted from Sabres to Mirage IIIO(F)s in September 1966 and flew in the Williamtown wing until August 1973, when budget cuts and a shortage of aircraft prompted its disbandment.

Right: The short-lived No. 76 Squadron decorated its aircraft with a black and red tail chevron, upon which was painted the unit's panther head insignia. After seven years' service at Williamtown the squadron disbanded in 1973, a move prompted by budget cuts and heavy attrition.

No. 77 Squadron

Base: Williamtown
Badge: an Aboriginal totem representing a ('grumpy') monkey

The second Butterworth Sabre squadron withdrew to Williamtown and began Mirage IIIO(A) conversion in February 1969. Its supplied the 'Deltas' aerobatic team in 1970-71, the 'Miracles' in 1976 and a formation of three in patriotic red, white and blue for the RAAF's diamond jubliee in 1981. These taskings were hardly surprising, as

No. 77 was the sole home-based air defence squadron between 1973 and 1983. It assumed the Mirage conversion role from No. 2 OCU in January 1985, although this lasted only until Course 47 graduated in February 1986. Nevertheless, this and a fleet support duty acquired from the run-down RAN fixed-wing squadrons resulted in No. 77 fielding no fewer than 40 Mirages and 16 Aermacchi M.B.326s in 1985. The unit converted to Hornets from 1 July 1987, but nine Mirages remained in 'B' Flight for fleet support until the end of the year.

Above: No. 77 Squadron's Mirages lined up at Williamtown, showing their Aboriginal 'grumpy' monkey insignia.

Below: This No. 77 Squadron Mirage IIID in overall light grey with toned-down squadron insignia retains high-visibility markings.

Above: As the sole home-based Mirage III squadron at the time, No. 77 provided three red, white and blue aircraft for celebrations in 1981 of the RAAF's diamond jubilee.

Dassault Mirage III/5/50 Variants

No. 79 Squadron

Base: Butterworth, Malaysia
Badge: a winged grenade

Formed on 1 April 1986 from the departing No. 3 Squadron, the RAAF's shortest-lived Mirage unit was assigned an average of only 10 aircraft and eight pilots (plus a DHC-4 Caribou 'hack') to see out the departure of the RAAF from Malaysia. That task was completed when the squadron disbanded in April 1988.

Right: Three Mirage IIIOs of No. 79 Squadron in their final low-visibility air superiority colour scheme. The squadron had a two-year life, covering the Australian withdrawal from Malaysia.

Below: No. 79 Squadron's Mirages inherited the plough rudder marking from the disbanding No. 3 Squadron, which reclaimed them when it transitioned to the F/A-18.

Above: No. 79 Squadron never reached full strength, with an average of only 10 aircraft on strength, plus a de Havilland Canada DHC-4 Caribou hack.

Aircraft Research & Development Unit

Base: Edinburgh
Badge: 'ARDU' logo

Development work, including trials with many types of weapons, occupied the ARDU from the arrival of the first Mirages in Australia until after the last operational squadron disbanded. Three aircraft – A3-2, A3-101 and A3-112 – were maintained in productive service until early 1989.

Right: ARDU operated a large number of Mirages over the years. This one has a test camera in a nose fairing which replaces the usual radome.

During the late 1980s many ARDU aircraft, including some of the Mirage IIIOs, began to adopt a high-visibility Dayglo orange and white colour scheme.

Belgium

Belgium's decision to replace Republic F-84Fs and RF-84Fs by Mirages was announced on 16 February 1968, the initial order being for 54 Mirage 5BAs, 22 5BRs for reconnaissance and 12 5BD trainers. The air force (Force Aérienne Belge/Belgische Luchtmacht) took out options on nine, five and four respectively, and all were eventually exercised. The first of each variant was built by Dassault, but the remainder came from SABCA at Gosselies, with participation by Avions Fairey and other local firms. The full order therefore comprised 106.

Serial numbers	Type	Quantity
BA01 to BA63	Mirage 5BA	63
BD01 to BD16	Mirage 5BD	16
BR01 to BR27	Mirage 5BR	27

Marked MA01, the first Mirage 5BA flew at Bordeaux on 6 March 1970, followed by MD01 (later BD01) on 31 March and BR01 on 16 October 1970. Initial acceptance was of BD01 on 27 April 1970, while the first locally built machines in service were BA02 on 8 August 1970 and BD02 three days later. Application of grey and two-tone green camouflage was by the air force's own maintenance unit, with the result that the pattern differs slightly from aircraft to aircraft. The final delivery was of BA63 on 13 July 1973. Mirage weapons included 2.75-in rockets, Snakeye and BL755 CBUs, napalm and 500-lb, 400-kg and 1,000-lb bombs.

A minimal upgrade was intended to equip the final remaining Mirage squadron for service until 2005. The earmarked 15 BAs and five BDs were altered to five and five respectively (BA04, 11, 46, 60 and 62; BD01, 03, 13, 14 and 15). These began arriving at Coxyde/Koksijde maintenance unit for storage on 18 May 1989, and prototype BA60 first flew in December 1992. The last is due to return from re-work in November 1993, a month before the accelerated disbandment of 42 Squadron. In this Mirage Safety Improvement Programme, SABCA fitted a GEC Marconi HUD, Thomson-CSF TMV 630 laser range-finder and SAGEM nav/attack avionics. Martin-Baker Mk 10 seats had been previously retrofitted under a different contract. By 1993, the Mirage fleet had been reduced by accidents to 35 5BAs, 10 5BDs and 18 5BRs.

Belgium's Mirage era ended in late 1993, with the final disbandment of the remaining unit, No. 42 Escadrille/Smaldeel; this is one of their two-seaters.

The refurbished and fully modernised Mirage 5s are not due to re-enter service after modification, and instead are being stored for later sale. The modification programme was not cancelled, because a heavy cancellation fee would have negated any financial saving. Thus, Belgian front-line pilots will never get their hands on the canard-equipped and comprehensively upgraded and modernised Mirages.

1 Escadrille/Smaldeel

(3 Wing)
Base: Bierset
Badge: a thistle

Delivery of Mirage 5BAs began to 1 Squadron with BA29 in January 1972, making it the second and last unit to receive this variant. The squadron had inherited Belgium's last RF-84Fs when 42 Squadron left Bierset for Florennes in September 1971 and these were operated until the type's final formation flypast on 4 May 1972. Later, two Mirage 5BDs were attached during the 1980s. Late in 1988 the squadron was reduced to a single flight in preparation for F-16s and moved to Florennes in March 1989, its pilots temporarily going to Beauvechain for conversion in July.

The Mirages of No. 1 Escadrille/Smaldeel wore a white thistle fin badge. The squadron converted to the F-16 in 1989.

One Mirage 5BA was decorated in black and gold to celebrate the 70th anniversary of No. 1 Escadrille.

2 Escadrille/Smaldeel

(2 Wing)
Base: Florennes
Badge: a comet

BA03 was received by 2 Squadron on 10 October 1970 as the unit's first single-seat Mirage. Re-equipment was completed with the arrival of BA28 on 27 December 1971, although four trainers were also operated during the 1980s. While Florennes was undergoing refurbishment, the squadron flew from Brustem between February and December 1986. No. 2 stood down on 20 December 1987, with only four Mirages remaining, and passed its last 5BA to 3 Wing in the following April, by which time several F-16s were on strength (the first arriving on 28 January 1988).

Wearing an extra-large white tailcode, this Mirage 5BA was photographed during the 1981 NATO Tactical Air Meet at Florennes. The unit badge was a red comet or shooting star, and was applied to the tailfin in red, outlined thinly in yellow. Mirages gave way to F-16s in 1988.

8 Escadrille/Smaldeel

(2 Wing)
Base: Florennes
Badge: a paper bird on a blue shield

(3 Wing)
Base: Bierset
Badge: a paper bird on a blue shield

The Mirage OCU formed at Florennes on 15 July 1970 with two French-built aircraft and a nucleus of eight pilots fresh from training with ECT 2/2 at Dijon, France. Formally constituted on 1 August, the unit began instructional work on 5 October 1970. On 15 December 1971, by which time it had received 12 BDs and six BAs, it transferred to Bierset. The balance of aircraft allocations was gradually reversed as the conversion burden lessened, so that during the 1980s the squadron comprised 12 BAs and only five trainers (the other two-seaters having been transferred to the squadrons for their own continuation training). Mirage conversion for students coming from flying training was 75 hours.

The nearest approach by Belgian Mirages to combat was on 6 January 1991 when nine 5BAs and one BD of 8 Squadron, plus five of No. 42's 5BRs, were deployed to Erhac, Turkey to boost offensive forces in the event that Iraq attacked Turkey (a NATO member) during the imminent UN operation to liberate Kuwait. They returned home after the Gulf War. No. 8 disbanded on 13 September 1991, but its aircraft and former pilots continued to fly for several months afterwards.

An origami bird on a tilted blue shield marked the Mirage 5BAs of No. 8 Escadrille, which relinquished the type in September 1991.

42 Escadrille/Smaldeel

(2 Wing)
Base: Florennes
Badge: a winged devil holding a telescope

(3 Wing)
Base: Bierset
Badge: a winged devil holding a telescope

All 27 reconnaissance Mirages went to 42 Squadron as RF-84F replacements, beginning with BR01 on 29 July 1971 and ending with BR27 on 19 June 1973. After the arrival of only eight aircraft, the squadron moved from Bierset to Florennes on 15 September 1971. Here it remained, picking up a pair of trainers in the process, although base works resulted in operations transferring to Bierset in February 1986 and Brustem in September, before returning to Florennes in December. The stay was short-lived, for No. 42 moved to Bierset late in November 1988, the final aircraft departing on 25 November. Plans for it to return to Florennes and operate MSIP-modified aircraft were overtaken by budget cuts and, despite a stay of execution from 31 December 1992, the squadron (and the Belgian Mirage) is due to disappear at the end of 1993.

Right: One of the unit's Mirage 5BRs pictured during the 1978 NATO Tactical Air Meet at Wildenrath, with non-standard Roman numeral white fin code and pilot/crew chief names.

No. 42 Escadrille celebrated its 30th anniversary during 1984, decorating one of its Mirage 5BRs with a white tailfin.

This badge was applied to mark the squadron's move from Florennes to Bierset in 1988.

Above: This Mirage 5BR was perhaps the most colourful Mirage ever, with its red and gold leading edges and a massive squadron badge under the belly.

Brazil

The first Mirage order of the Fuerza Aérea Brasiliera was for a dozen IIIEBRs and four IIIDBR trainers placed on 2 May 1970, these gaining the local designations F-103E and F-103D respectively. Hand-over of the first took place in France on 31 May 1972 to begin a programme of training at Dijon, Mont-de-Marsan and Cazaux. Four more single-seat aircraft were ordered in 1978 and delivered the next year, while the loss of three trainers in as many years (1980-82) resulted in the hasty purchase of two ex-French Mirage IIIBEs. Six more ex-French aircraft were ordered to a higher avionics standard, two of them trainers, and handed over from 30 September 1988, their most obvious feature being canards. The cost of these refurbished aircraft was $17,945,865.76 for the batch of four single-seaters and $8,972,932.88 for the two trainers. In December 1989, work began in Brazil to upgrade the remaining 10 EBRs and two DBRs to the same configuration.

Serial numbers	Type	Quantity
4900 to 4903	Mirage IIIDBR	4
4904 to 4905	Mirage IIIDBR	2 (ex-French Mirage IIIBE)
4906 to 4907	Mirage IIIDBR-2	2 (ex-French Mirage IIIBE)
4910 to 4925	Mirage IIIEBR	16
4926 to 4929	Mirage IIIEBR-2	4 (ex-French Mirage IIIE)

Brazil adopted a natty paint scheme of overall light grey with high-vis markings.

1º Grupo de Defesa Aérea

Base: Anpolis
Badge: a Mirage in plan view

1 and 2 Esquadraos are equipped with Mirages, their parent unit being known as 1ª Ala de Defesa Aérea until 11 April 1979. Based at Anpolis, near Brasilia, the wing is the sole flying component of Comando de Defesa Aérea (Air Defence Command).

Right: In service Brazilian Mirage IIIEBRs transitioned from an overall silver scheme to dark grey topsides with light grey undersides. These two aircraft wear the badge of 1 Grupo.

A newly refurbished Mirage IIIDBR-2 seen before delivery to Brazil, and before the application of paint and national markings.

Chile

The territorial dispute which prompted Argentina to buy ex-Israeli Daggers was also the reason why Chile placed an urgent order for Mirages in July 1979. Apart from four South African Air Force Mirage R2Zs, these were the first production aircraft with the 9K50 version of Atar and the first to wear the designation Mirage 50. To meet the needs of the Fuerza Aérea de Chile, Dassault bought back eight low-houred French Mirage 5Fs and modified them to 50FC standard while FAC pilots trained at Dijon and ground crew at Rochefort. The eight were handed over between 26 June and 9 October 1980 and delivered by sea, flying at Antofagasta from August . The balance of the order, being new-build, was longer in arriving. Six radar-equipped Mirage 50Cs were handed over between 27 April 1982 and 6 January 1983, and two Mirage 50DC trainers (reverting to Atar 09C power) on 28 May and 24 November 1982. The second trainer soon crashed, so was replaced with another aircraft wearing the same serial number on 1 June 1987, its appearance suggesting a 9K50 powerplant.

Serial numbers	Type	Quantity
501 to 508	Mirage 50FC	8 ex-French Mirage 5F
509 to 514	Mirage 50C	6
515 and 516	Mirage 50DC	2
516 (No. 2)	Mirage 50DC	1

Chilean camouflage is two-tone blue-grey. The prototype Pantera conversion was 514, which initially flew with the original nose with an added strake before gaining a Kfir-type forward end.

Grupo 4

Base: Santiago/Benitez and Punta Arenas/Ibanez
Badge: (not carried) a bat before a dagger

Re-established on 15 September 1980, Grupo 4 was commissioned at Arturo Moreno Benitez Airport, Santiago on 15 November 1980 as a component of Ala 2 of II Brigada Aérea. In March 1986 it moved base to BA Carlos Ibanez near Punta Arenas, in the far south, there coming under Ala 3 of IV Brigada.

Chilean Mirages wear an exceptionally attractive two-tone blue/grey air superiority colour scheme.

Below: Mirages are operated by Grupo 4, which moved to Carlos Ibanez/Punta Arenas during 1986.

Colombia

An order placed in 1970 secured Mirages as replacements for Canadair-built Sabres in the principal fighter squadron of the Fuerza Aérea Colombiana. Deliveries of 14 Mirage 5COA ground attack aircraft were effected between 21 February 1972 and 17 July 1973, while two Mirage 5COD trainers followed on 13 and 20 March 1972 and two reconnaissance 5CORs on 19 October and 19 November 1973. The first export order for Kfirs was placed by Colombia late in 1981, but both it and a contract to upgrade Mirages to the same standard were cancelled in the following year. Both were reinstated on 6 October 1988 when 13 Kfirs, including one trainer, were ordered, and the single-seaters were rapidly delivered between April and August 1989. They were upgraded from C2 to C7 standard after arrival, but the trainer aircraft was already a TC7 when it was delivered early in 1991.

An ambitious refurbishment programme for the remaining 14 Mirages (to include General Electric F404 engines, as well as new avionics) was reduced in scope and began in 1988 on the two trainers. The work is performed by the FAC's own maintenance unit at Base Arsenal Madrid, Bogota, where the first single-seater, 3026, was converted in 1990. Internal changes have not been announced, but the aircraft may be recognised by their canards (half Kfir size), two extra stores pylons (making nine), nose-mounted ranging radar and inflight-refuelling probes. They are now to Kfir C7 avionics standard, as are the Kfir C2s, upgrading of the latter having begun in 1990.

Serial numbers	Type	Quantity
3021 to 3034	Mirage 5COA	14
3001 and 3002	Mirage 5COD	2
3011 and 3012	Mirage 5COR	2
3041 to 3052	Kfir C2 (later C7)	12
Not known	Kfir TC7	1

All wear grey and green camouflage, with light grey beneath.

Right: A pair of canard-equipped Mirage 5CODs serves with Escuadrón 212 as conversion and continuation trainers. The unit's missile-carrying Eagle badge is visible.

Apart from its lack of a dorsal airscoop, this Mirage 5COA closely resembles an IAI Kfir. Israeli avionics and aerodynamic improvements have been added.

Escuadrón 212

(Grupo 21 of Comando Aéreo de Combate 1)
Base: BAM 5 'German Olano', Palanquero
Badge: a bird in flight

An operator of Mirages since their delivery, 212 Squadron has a current inventory of 11 5COAs, the remaining 5COR and two 5COD trainers, all of which were scheduled to have been upgraded to Kfir C7 avionics standard by 1992. In the past, the unit has provided regular detachments to Barranquila and San Andres.

This crude badge, featuring a fully-upgraded Mirage, is painted on the crewroom wall.

A handful of aircraft wear the Comando Aéreo de Combate 1 badge on their tailfins.

Escuadrón 213

(Grupo 21 of Comando Aéreo de Combate 1)
Base: BAM 5 'German Olano', Palanquero
Badge: (not carried) a dimidiated shield: knight's helmet and lion's face

After basic training of pilots and ground crew in Ecuador on that nation's Kfirs, 213 Squadron received its Kfirs from April 1989 and underwent further instruction in the hands of Israeli personnel. The squadron's aircraft have been raised from C2 to C7 avionics standard.

Right: Colombia's Kfirs serve with the co-located Escuadrón 213. Although prominently marked as Kfir-C2s, the aircraft have been upgraded to a standard approaching that of the Kfir-C7.

The squadron badge of half a knight's helmet and half a lion's face is not carried on any aircraft.

Dassault Mirage III/5/50 Variants

Ecuador

First attempts by the Fuerza Aérea Ecuatoriana to buy Kfirs were thwarted by the US embargo on third party sales of its General Electric J79 engine, so Dassault was contracted in 1977 to supply Mirage F1s. By the time the next batch of combat aircraft was needed the restrictions had been lifted, so 10 Kfir C2s and a pair of TC2s were delivered in 1982, the first batch arriving by sea on 25 March. A third trainer is reported to have been received later.

Serial numbers	Type	Quantity
FAE 901 to FAE 910	Kfir C2	10
FAE 930 and FAE 931	Kfir TC2	2
Not known	Kfir TC2	1

After re-assembly, the first of Ecuador's aircraft made its maiden flight on 19 April 1982. At least four Kfirs have been lost in accidents, including one trainer.

Escuadron 2113 'Leones'

(Grupo 211 of Ala de Combate 21)
Base: Taura

Formerly equipped with BAC Strikemasters, the 'Lions' of 2113 Squadron took a giant leap in capability when they re-equipped with Kfirs in 1982 and were declared operational in 1984. The first loss occurred in 1985 as the result of a birdstrike. From 1985 until the end of the 1980s, the squadron regularly won the annual Copa Taura (Taura Cup) combat competition against entries from the SEPECAT Jaguars and Dassault Mirage F1s forming the remainder of Grupo 211.

Three of Ecuador's Kfir-C2s. Ten single-seaters were delivered in 1982, with three trainers. All wear a badge on the starboard side of the nose and the port side of the fin.

Escuadron 2113 Leones use this triangular Kfir badge as their unit insignia. It is applied to the fin on one side, and the nose on the other.

Egypt

Saudi Arabia paid for Egypt's first batch of Mirages and the aircraft wore RSAF insignia during pilot training in France before delivery. The order of September 1973 covered 32 Mirage 5SDEs and six 5SDD trainers, the first three of each taken from the Armée de l'Air to expedite deliveries. Despite their designation, the single-seat aircraft were to radar-equipped Mirage III standard. Egypt went on to buy 14 5SDEs in December 1975, eight 5SDEs and six 5SDR reconnaissance aircraft in November 1977 and 16 non-radar 5E2s in June 1980, the last of which was delivered in 1984. Although lacking radar, the 5E2s had revised avionics equivalent to the attack-optimised Alpha Jet MS2.

Camouflage is green, sand and chocolate, but some aircraft gained bright orange stripes, with black borders, on the fin and wings for combat conspicuousness.

The Egyptian air force (Al Quwwat Al Jawwiya Al Misriya) formed Mirage regiments at Tanta and Genaclis, the latter housing the recce flight. Tanta had the trainers, providing new pilots with 100-hour conversion courses before their first squadron posting. They then completed 60 hours of qualification flying before being declared operational. Eight Mirages formed a national aerobatic team. Plans to build a local Mirage overhaul facility were abandoned. The Mirage is now used primarily for attack, equipped with Rockeye cluster bombs and defended by a Selenia SL/ALQ-234 jammer.

Serial numbers	Type	Quantity
1001 to 1054	Mirage 5SDE	54 (later 9101-9154)
2001 to 2006	Mirage 5SDD	6 (later reserialled)
3001 to 3006	Mirage 5SDR	6 (later 9021-9026)
9161 to 9176	Mirage 5E2	16

Egypt's Mirage 5SDEs are essentially similar to the Mirage IIIE, with radar and Doppler bulge. This one wears recognition markings on fin, wings and spine.

The Mirage 5E2s operated by Egypt lack search radar and are equivalent to the basic, original Mirage 5 originally designed to meet Israeli requirements.

France

Naturally the largest operator of Mirage III/5s, the Armée de l'Air received 483, including 18 prototypes and development aircraft and 50 Mirage 5Fs which were taken over from an embargoed Israeli order for Mirage 5Js. Eight of the latter were transferred to Chile, resulting in delivery of a similar number of 'pay-backs', the last of which was built in June 1984, over 23 years after the Mirage IIIC's first flight.

Serial numbers	Type	Quantity
201 to 227	Mirage IIIB	27
231 to 235	Mirage IIIB1	5
241 to 250	Mirage IIIB2 (RV)	10
259 to 264, 266 to 276	Mirage IIIBE	17
1 to 95	Mirage IIIC	95
401 to 405, 407, 408, 410, 412, 414, 415, 417 to 419, 421 to 440, 443, 445, 447, 449, 451 to 458, 460 to 463, 466 to 531,	Mirage IIIE	183

533 to 535, 537 to 539, 541, 545 to 556, 560 to 579, 583 to 588, 605 to 625

	Type	Quantity
301 to 350		
351 to 370		
1 to 58		
	Mirage IIIR	50
	Mirage IIIRD	20
	Mirage 5F	58
	Sub-total: 465	
01	Mirage I	1
001	Mirage III	1
01 to 010	Mirage IIIA	10
B01	Mirage IIIB	1
01 to 03	Mirage IIIE	3
01 and 02	Mirage IIIR	2
	Total: 483	

Privately-funded ventures are not included. There have been several conversions to other versions or testbeds and recent sales abroad. Gaps in Mirage IIIE serials are the result of transfers to meet urgent foreign orders.

Military acceptances totalled 464, the number in service reaching its peak in 1974 when, on 31 December, 348 were on charge: 31 Bs, 11 BEs, 55 Cs, 142 Es, 42 Rs, 19 RDs and 48 5Fs. Acceptances of Mirage IIIs up to this time were 400, with a further six following in 1975. The 50 Mirage 5Fs were supplied between 1 October 1971 and 1 April 1974. Numbers delivered and in service at 31 December each year up to 1975 were:

	Delivered	In service
1960	3	2
1961	39	40
1962	98	90
1963	140	127
1964	164	150
1965	220	200
1966	271	245
1967	299	269
1968	329	286
1969	366	305
1970	367	303
1971	381+2 5F	304+2 5F
1972	396+11 5F	313+11 5F
1973	400+42 5F	314+40 5F
1974	400+50 5F	300+48 5F
1975	406+50 5F	294+48 5F

As noted above, the remaining eight aircraft (Mirage 5Fs) were not delivered until 1983-84. Mirage IIIB deliveries began on 27 July 1963, the 10 IIIB-2s following between 27 July 1967 and 17 July 1968, and the IIIBEs between 23 March 1971 and 24 July 1975. The first IIIE was handed over on 27 March 1964 and the first IIIR in March 1963.

Mirage IIIEs and IIIR/RDs were fitted with two standards of radar warning equipment. All IIIRs and early IIIEs (Nos 401 to 459 and 461 to 464, less exports) had only the rear-facing Détecteur Passif Arrière BZ equipment; IIIRDs and later IIIEs (Nos 460 and 466 to 625, plus retrofit to 405) had BZ on the rear of the fin and the Détecteur Passif Avant BU facing forward.

Mirages assigned to interception were under the control of CAFDA (Commandement 'Air' des Forces de Défense Aérienne), and those assigned to tactical strike/attack under FATac (Force Aérienne Tactique). Aircraft of regular fighter squadrons (escadrons) normally wear different badges on the left and right sides of the fin to indicate their two flights (escadrilles), which are usually of World War I vintage. Between two and four squadrons comprise a wing (escadre) at a single air base.

Early aircraft were delivered in natural metal. On 23 August 1968, EC 4 received its first factory-camouflaged IIIE, earlier aircraft having been similarly painted green and grey above with silver below from March 1968. Mirage IIIRs had served in camouflage from the outset (1963), although this was initially compromised by the traditional red/white/blue-striped rudder and yellow outline to the cockades. Even after the last-mentioned was deleted in 1982, France made no attempt to reduce the proportion of white in its national insignia. The IIIB did not go into camouflage until 1980. During the early 1970s at least 13 Mirage IIICs went from natural metal to the blue-grey colours of the Mirage F1 interceptor, although a few of them reverted to old markings by 1977. Those IIICs based in Djibouti from 1978 were camouflaged in 'sand and chestnut'. Inexplicably, Mirage 5Fs entered service in natural metal, the first to receive camouflage (No. 31 '13-SL' at the Clermont-Ferrand depot) returning to its unit on 23 January 1974.

Early in their service lives, Mirage IIIEs received a major overhaul every 500 hours. This was extended to 625 hours in 1982 and 720 hours (or 33 months) in 1990.

2ᵉ Escadre de Chasse

Base: Base Aérienne 102, Dijon/Longvic

The first Mirage III wing converted from Dassault Mystère IVAs and was assigned to FATac for tactical attack and air defence. It was involved in service qualification of the Nord AS20 and AS30 missiles in February 1963 and squadron-level use of the SEPR rocket motor in March 1965. In April 1965, EC 2's Mirages temporarily moved forward to RAF Gütersloh, Germany, armed with AIM-9B Sidewinder and MATRA R.511 missiles, in response to a Soviet blockade of roads to Berlin. Service qualification of the AS11 and AS20 air-to-surface missiles followed in September 1965.

In April 1966, an unannounced intruder in French airspace proved to be a Lockheed U-2 which Commandant Gaudart intercepted at 62,000 ft (19000 m), despite the fact that his SEPR rocket had exploded at 41,000 ft (12500 m). EC 2 converted to Mirage IIIEs in 1967-68 and operated the aircraft until 1 July 1983 when squadrons 1/2 and 3/2 transferred to CAFDA in preparation for receipt of Mirage 2000Cs in a national air defence role. ECT 2/2 similarly switched its allegiance on 1 July 1986.

French Mirages usually have two fin badges, one per side for each of the escadron's subordinate escadrilles. On the starboard side of the fin, this aircraft wears the stork insignia of the 2ᵉ Escadrille, traditionally used by SPA103 – René Fonck's unit.

Escadron de Chasse 1/2 'Cigognes'

1ᵉ Escadrille: SPA3 insignia – *cigogne de Guynemer* (stork badge of air ace Georges Guynemer's squadron), port
2ᵉ Escadrille: SPA103 insignia – *cigogne de Fonck* (stork badge of air ace René Fonck's squadron), starboard
Codes: 2-EA to 2-EZ (radio call FUGEA/FUGEZ)

The famous 'Storks' squadron received its first Mirage IIIC (No. 23 '2-EA') on 10 July 1961 at Mont-de-Marsan and flew the initial three (Nos 24, 25 and 29) to its base at Dijon on 28 July. The first mission was launched on 31 July in the form of a 35-minute sortie by Colonel Simard in No. 25 '2-ED'. The initial loss was of No. 29 (total airframe time 39 hours) on 23 August during a display at Lahr, Germany. The squadron was declared operational on 19 December 1961 with 15 aircraft. Poor serviceability early in 1962 resulted in pilots having to fly Mystère IVAs of EC 3/2 to maintain flying currency, although Mirage IIIBs were used to assist conversion between 1963 and 1966. EC 1/2 passed 10,000 flying hours in September 1964 and 15,000 in January 1966, but began converting to Mirage IIIEs on 24 October 1968 while detached to CEAM at Mont-de-Marsan. The last IIIC was withdrawn on 1 October 1968 and the IIIE ended its service on 23 December 1983 when the squadron stood down to begin Mirage 2000C training.

Below: EC 1/2 wore the stork badge of Guynemer's SPA3 on the port side of the tailfins of their Mirages, but did not initially apply codes.

Unit codes were a contraction of the callsign, with a numerical prefix followed by squadron and individual aircraft letters.

Escadron de Chasse et de Transformation 2/2 'Côte d'Or'

1e Escadrille: SPA65 insignia – *chimère* (dragon)
2e Escadrille: SPA57 insignia – *mouette* (seagull)
3e Escadrille: SPA94 insignia – *Mort qui fauche* (Grim Reaper)
Codes: 2-FA to 2-FZ (radio call FUGFA/ FUGFZ) and 2-ZA to 2-ZZ (radio call FUMZA/ FUMZZ)

The Mirage OCU formed on 1 April 1965 as a regular fighter squadron of IIICs, EC 2/2, had only SPA65, although SPA67 was added in June. On 1 April 1966 it was redesignated CIMIR 2/102 (Centre d'Instruction Mirage) and assigned 12 IIIB trainers previously used by individual squadrons, as well as retaining five IIICs. It became CIMIR 00/329 three months later, then ECT 2/2 on 31 October 1968, gaining IIIBEs from 14 April 1971 onwards, these coded from 2-ZA. As a result of the increase in aircraft strength (15 IIIBEs, 12 IIIBs and five IIICs), SPA94 was added on 6 October 1972 and the distribution of fin badges amended so that each was evenly represented throughout the fleet and might appear on either side. The last Mirage IIIC departed in late October 1975, although four IIIRs were added in May 1983 for regular training (cameras removed), using the 2-ZA code range.

The squadron stood down on 27 June 1986 and passed its aircraft to EC 1/13 on 4 July in order to begin conversion to Mirage 2000Cs. By then, it had flown 103,183 hours in 113,592 sorties in the process of converting 1,311 French and 216 overseas pilots from 16 nationalities. In addition, EC 2/2 had checked out 481 pilots for their combat initiation qualification and 1,089 pilots for night flying, plus renewing the blind flying certificates of 2,712 pilots.

The 1e Escadrille uses the chimera (dragon) of SPA65, as seen on a yellow chevron on the fin of a camouflaged Mirage IIIB.

Because EC 2/2 has three escadrilles, each with a separate fin badge, these are not uniformly worn on one side of the fin or the other; instead, aircraft carry different combinations of insignia. The Mirage IIIB above wears the seagull badge of SPA57, like the Mirage IIIR below. From 1983 ECT 2/2, as the Mirage OCU, operated a quartet of these recce aircraft.

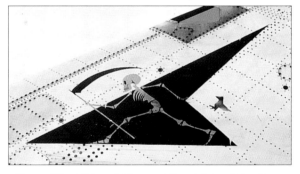

Above: The 3e Escadrille used the sinister Grim Reaper badge of SPA94. Naturally, this was applied on a black chevron.

Left: The three badges of ECT 2/2 could appear to left or right, since each of the unit's aircraft wore two of the three insignia.

Escadron de Chasse 3/2 'Alsace'

1e Escadrille: Strasbourg
2e Escadrille: Mulhouse
Insignia: arms of Alsace (both sides)
Codes: 2-LA to 2-LZ (radio call FUGLA/ FUGLZ)

Training of EC 3/2's pilots and mechanics on the Mirage IIIC began at Mont-de-Marsan on 15 May 1961. Delivery of aircraft started on 4 December 1961, and the first (No. 42 '2-LA') arrived at Dijon on 11 December. A pair of IIIBs was also on charge between 1963 and early 1966. After withdrawing the IIIC on 5 April 1968 when temporarily stood down, the squadron received its first IIIE on 27 September that year and passed its 100,000th Mirage hour in October 1978. It flew the type until withdrawal on 19 July 1985, by which time conversion to Mirage 2000Cs was under way.

A well-worn Mirage IIIE taxis out for a training sortie, laden with massive underwing fuel tanks.

Left: An early Mirage IIIC of EC 3/2 'Alsace', with codes in the original position on the fuselage, and with high-visibility red edges to the intakes.

Right: The familiar arms of Alsace are used as a unit insignia by EC 3/2, on both sides of the fin.

Right: Armée de l'Air Mirage IIIEs were camouflaged in grey and green from 1968, and only the earliest examples were delivered in silver. 'Alsace' flew the Mirage IIIE until conversion to the Mirage 2000 in 1985.

3ᵉ Escadre de Chasse

Base: Base Aérienne 133, Nancy/Ochey

EC 3 was based at BA139 Lahr/Hugsweier, Germany, equipped with North American F-100D Super Sabres carrying US-owned B43 nuclear bombs when it began receiving Mirage IIIEs. On 30 August 1967 it transferred to its present base, where it remained assigned to FATac, although now tasked with defence suppression with the Mirage IVA strategic bomber force (using MATRA AS30 missiles, 250-kg and 400-kg bombs) and interception with AIM-9B Sidewinders. MATRA/HSD AS37 Martel missiles were added in 1970 for anti-radar attacks, these becoming the principal mission after 1975. The third squadron, formed in 1974, is equipped with AS30s.

EC 3 was a Germany-based F-100D wing armed with US nuclear weapons. Mirage IIIEs arrived in 1966, but withdrawal from NATO meant reassignment to the defence suppression role at Nancy.

Escadron de Chasse 1/3 'Navarre'

1ᵉ Escadrille: SPA95 insignia – *oriflamme et martinet* (pennant and martlet), port
2ᵉ Escadrille: SPA75 insignia – *gypaète* (Egyptian falcon), starboard
Codes: 3-IA to 3-IZ (radio call FUGIA/ FUGIZ)

The second of EC 3's original two squadrons to convert, 'Navarre' received its first IIIE (No. 468 '3-IA' from EC 13) on 24 November 1965 but did not fly its last F-100 sortie until the following March. Mirage flying began on 2 May 1965 and continues – having passed 100,000 hours on 23 June 1978 – although re-equipment with Mirage 2000Ns is due in February 1994. The squadron was initially tasked with tactical air defence but changed to attack in 1973.

Silver Mirage IIIEs were never a common sight. This EC 1/3 aircraft carries its fin insignia (SPA95's pennant and martlet to port) on a yellow chevron.

This camouflaged Mirage IIIE displays EC 1/3's 2nd Escadrille badge, the Egyptian falcon insignia of SPA75. Re-equipment with Mirage 2000Ns is due.

Escadron de Chasse 2/3 'Champagne'

1ᵉ Escadrille: SPA67 insignia – *cigogne* (stork), port
2ᵉ Escadrille: SPA75 insignia – *charognard* (vulture), starboard
Codes: 3-JA to 3-JZ (radio call FUGJA/ FUGJZ)

Conversion of EC 2/3 was undertaken at Mont-de-Marsan and Colmar, and it was to the latter that No. 455 of EC 13 was delivered on 29 July 1965 to launch training. The initial delivery of a squadron aircraft (No. 466 '3-JA', the second aircraft with both BU and BZ radar warners) was made on 29 October 1965. Training began on 15 September, although flying with the unit's own aircraft did not begin until 20 December 1965. The first six, plus a IIIB trainer, were ferried to Lahr on 17 January 1966 and the type was operated until the final sortie on 18 December 1990, by which time 90,392 hours had been accumulated. EC 2/3 had a mixed defence and attack role until transferred to attack only in 1979, and now has Mirage 2000Ns.

Above: A well-laden Champagne Mirage IIIE carries a Martel ARM under the centreline, and has external fuel tanks and an ECM pod.

Below: EC 2/3 'Champagne' moved back to Nancy and relinquished its US nuclear weapons when France withdrew from the NATO military structure.

Above: The Mirage IIIEs of EC 2/3 wear the vulture badge of SPA75 to starboard. The squadron was the second of the Lahr-based EC 3 units.

Escadron de Chasse 3/3 'Ardennes'

1ᵉ Escadrille: insignia – *sanglier/barre azur* (wild boar and blue bar), port
2ᵉ Escadrille: insignia – *sanglier/barre gueles* (wild boar and red bar), starboard
Codes: 3-XA to 3-XZ (radio call FUGXA/FUGXZ)

EC 3 received a third squadron on 1 July 1974 when 'Ardennes' was formed to operate the Mirage 5Fs that had begun arriving on 5 June (first was No. 35). They served only until May 1977, accumulating 7,000 hours, before being transferred to EC 13, the Martel missile role passing to EC 2/11's Jaguars. The first replacement Jaguars for EC 3/3 began arriving on 10 March 1977 and the type lasted 10 years until the final six were withdrawn on 29 May 1987. On 1 June 1987 the squadron again equipped with Mirages for conventional attack, on this occasion IIIEs, themselves subsequently made redundant by Mirage 2000C deliveries. 'Ardennes' recommenced operations on 5 August and was up to

EC 3/3 'Ardennes' formed in 1974 with Mirage 5s, but re-equipped with Jaguars between 1977 and 1987, when it received Mirage IIIEs. The same boar's head badge is worn on both sides of the fin.

strength with 15 Mirage IIIEs by October 1987. It is due to be the last Mirage IIIE squadron and will re-equip with Mirage 2000Ds in 1995. On 25 February 1993, No. 539 '3-XO' (finished in Mirage 2000C air

defence camouflage) returned to the squadron after the 897th and last IIIE/IIIBE major overhaul by the technical support groups attached to Dijon, Luxeuil, Colmar and Nancy.

The same boar's head badge is worn against a red band to starboard and blue to port. One aircraft has been operated in Mirage 2000-style camouflage.

4ᵉ Escadre de Chasse

Base: Base Aérienne 116, Luxeuil/St Sauveur

EC 4 was the sole FATac squadron to be assigned to nuclear strike, its previous equipment having been the Republic F-84F Thunderstreak. Declared operational on 18 November 1988 and initially armed with AS30 missiles, among other weapons, for general attack and defensive duties, it received its AN52 nuclear weapons in late 1972. By then, the initial allocation of aircraft had been exchanged for those from No. 519, which were nuclear-capable, and the wing was totally assigned to strike from 1972 onwards. On 28 August 1973, No. 617 made the first live drop of an AN52 at Mururoa Atoll, in the Pacific Ocean.

Right: The Luxeuil-based Escadre de Chasse 4 was the sole nuclear-armed Force Aérienne Tactique Mirage IIIE unit, augmenting the Jaguars of EC 7.

Escadron de Chasse 1/4 'Dauphiné'

1ᵉ Escadrille: SPA37 insignia – *charognard* (vulture), port
2ᵉ Escadrille: SPA92 insignia – *lévrier* (greyhound), starboard
Codes: 4-AA to 4-AZ (radio call FULAA/FULAZ)

The second element of EC 4 to equip, 'Dauphiné' began flying its newly arrived Mirage IIIEs on 1 February 1967 and conducted the final sortie on 28 August 1987 before standing down to receive Mirage 2000Ns.

Left: EC 1/4 flew the Mirage IIIE for 20 years, re-equipping with Mirage 2000s in 1987. The badge of SPA92 was worn.

The SPA37 vulture was carried on the port side of the fins of EC 1/4 Mirage IIIEs. AN52 freefall nuclear bombs were received from 1972.

Escadron de Chasse 2/4 'La Fayette'

1ᵉ Escadrille: SPA124 insignia – *tête de Sioux* (Sioux's head), port
2ᵉ Escadrille: SPA167 insignia – *cigogne* (stork), starboard
Codes: 4-BA to 4-BZ (radio call FULBA/FULBZ)

Crew training began for the Mirage IIIE at Lahr under the guidance of EC 3 on 15 April 1966 and the squadron began operations on 31 October of that year when No. 504 was delivered. The final sortie was flown on 10 November 1988, by which time the squadron had accumulated 130,000 hours on the Mirage IIIE, including a small number on the pair of Mirage IIIBEs it had acquired in 1987. It now flies Mirage 2000Ns.

Above: Escadron de Chasse 2/4 'La Fayette' received its first Mirages in November 1966.

Below: An EC 2/4 Mirage IIIE wearing the famous stork of SPA167 flies in formation with a CIPR 339 Falcon 20SNA. These co-located aircraft were used for providing radar training.

5ᵉ Escadre de Chasse

Base: Base Aérienne 115, Orange/Caritat

Conversion of EC 13 from Mirage IIIC to IIIE freed the latter aircraft to replace EC 5's Dassault Super Mystères in 1966. The wing was the first in CAFDA to receive Mirage IIIs (being declared operational in February 1967) and the second to convert to Mirage F1s after it had flown 58,365 hours on the Mirage IIIC.

Escadron de Chasse 1/5 'Vendée'

1ᵉ Escadrille: SPA26 insignia – *cigogne de Saint Galmier* (stork), starboard
2ᵉ Escadrille: SPA124 insignia – *Jeanne d'Arc* (Joan of Arc), port
Codes: 5-NA to 5-NZ (radio call FUGNA/ FUGNZ)

EC 1/5's pilots began training for the Mirage III at Dijon on 12 April 1966 and flew the first IIIC sortie on 19 July, before returning to Orange with their new aircraft on 31 August. The squadron was officially equipped on 1 September 1966 and remained thus until the first eight Mirage F1Cs arrived at Orange on 21 March 1975.

EC 1/5 applied the stork of SPA26 to port, and Joan of Arc to starboard, both badges on a blue chevron.

Escadron de Chasse 2/5 'Ile de France'

1ᵉ Escadrille: Paris
2ᵉ Escadrille: Versailles
Insignia: a Lorraine Cross and three *fleurs-de-lys* (both sides)
Codes: 5-OA to 5-OZ (radio call FUGOA/ FUGOZ)

Also converted at Dijon in September-November 1966, EC 2/5 took delivery of its first Mirage IIIC on 7 November and returned to Orange on 30 November. Training at home base was completed in February 1967 and the squadron was declared operational a few months later. Mirage F1Cs began arriving in June 1975 and the last Mirage IIIC sortie was flown on 17 November 1975.

Escadre de Chasse 5 became the first CAFDA (air defence command) Mirage III unit, when it re-equipped with surplus Mirage IIICs from EC 13 when that unit re-equipped with multi-role Mirage IIIEs. The wing's second escadron (EC 2/5) 'Ile de France' applied the cross of Lorraine and three fleurs-de-lys on a blue and black shield on each side of the fin, superimposed on a red chevron. EC 2/5 remained with the Mirage IIIC until 1975, when it re-equipped with the Mirage F1, following the lead of EC 1/5 'Vendée'.

10ᵉ Escadre de Chasse

Base: Base Aérienne 110, Creil/Senlis; and BA 188, Djibouti

The fourth and last wing to receive Mirage IIICs, EC 10 was a CAFDA element charged with defence of the Paris region. It later formed a third squadron to operate the aircraft in the French protectorate of Djibouti, East Africa. The unit previously flew Super Mystère B2s but has now disbanded.

This EC 10 aircraft shows obvious signs of having had the colourful fin chevron of its previous operator removed. The small duck insignia of SPA93, which is the adopted insignia of EC 1/10's second escadrille and is worn on the port side of all escadron aircraft, looks almost dowdy.

Escadron de Chasse 1/10 'Valois'

1ᵉ Escadrille: SPA84 insignia – *tête de renard* (fox's mask), starboard
2ᵉ Escadrille: SPA93 insignia – *canard* (duck), port
Codes: 10-SA to 10-SZ (radio call FUISA/ FUISZ)

Pilots of EC 1/10 were detached to Dijon for Mirage conversion by ECT 2/2 in June 1974 and the squadron officially equipped with IIICs on 1 August, having flown its last 'SMB2' sortie on 26 July. The new light blue-grey camouflage for Mirage IIICs was first applied to No. 21 '10-SC' on 27 February 1975 and soon spread to others of the type. Mirage IIICs were operated until May 1981 when 'Valois' began conversion to Mirage F1Cs.

On the port side of their fins the Mirage IIICs of EC 1/10 wear a simple fox head in red. CAFDA squadrons received IIICs when ADTAC units re-equipped with the Mirage IIIE.

Below: During the early 1970s, several Mirage IIICs were repainted in the overall blue grey being applied to the new Mirage F1. One such was this EC 1/10 'Valois' aircraft.

Dassault Mirage III/5/50 Variants

Escadron de Chasse 2/10 'Seine'

Traditions: Cercle de Chasse de Paris (GC III/10-3e)
Badge: a crowing cock (both sides)
Codes: 10-RA to 10-RZ (radio call FUIRA/ FUIRZ)

The second squadron of EC 10 was the first at Creil to receive the Mirage IIIC, its pilots starting conversion at Dijon and Orange in September 1968 just prior to the last 'SMB2' flight on 22 September. Flying with the squadron's own aircraft began on 12 December (Lieutenant Danis in No. 63 '10-RH') and the first aircraft were delivered to Creil from Orange on 24 January 1969, an early highlight being a courtesy visit to Domodedovo, Moscow by six aircraft on 20-26 June 1971. The squadron passed 10,000 flying hours in the second quarter of 1971 and doubled that total in April 1974.

The first use of 500-lb and 1,000-lb bombs was practised at Mont-de-Marsan in April 1973. EC 2/10 became the sole home-based IIIC squadron on 1 June 1981 when EC 1/10 officially became a Mirage F1C unit. Despite what might have been viewed as a disadvantage, it won the Coupe de la Défense Aérienne for 1983 against competition from all CAFDA's Mirage F1C squadrons. EC 2/10 officially disbanded on 1 June 1985 but did not hold its standing-down ceremony until 27 June.

Right: When EC 1/10 converted to the Mirage F1 in 1981, EC 2/10 'Seine' became the only home-based Mirage IIIC squadron. Despite this, the unit won the prestigious air defence trophy in 1983.

Below: From 1973 EC 2/10 began ground attack training using 250- and 500-kg bombs, though it remained an interceptor squadron.

EC 2/10's Mirage IIICs wore the same crowing cockerel insignia on both sides of their tailfins. This was reduced to a minute size on grey-painted aircraft.

Escadron de Chasse 3/10 'Vexin'

1e Escadrille: ERC 3/561 insignia – *mousquetaire gris* (grey musketeer), port
2e Escadrille: ERC 4/561 insignia – *mousquetaire bleu* (blue musketeer), starboard
Codes: 10-LA to 10-LZ (radio call FUILA/ FUILZ)

Formed at Creil on 1 September 1978, 'Vexin' was commissioned at Djibouti on 1 January 1979, replacing the F-100 Super Sabres of EC 4/11 in both defensive and offensive roles. For this, the IIICs were specially modified with provision for MATRA Magic 1 AAMs, plus new radios, air conditioning and re-wiring. Some gained photo-reconnaissance capability through the expedient of fitting cameras in standard drop-tanks. A camouflage scheme of two-tone brown was tried in May 1978 but soon amended to 'sand and chocolate'.

Pilots for 'Vexin' were initially from the Mirage F1 world who had 'down-converted' via IIIRs at Strasbourg and IIICs at Dijon. Delivery flights out to Djibouti began on 21

November 1978, one of the first tasks after becoming operational being Magic firing trials, held during February 1979. EC 10 disbanded on 1 April 1985 and 'Vexin' became an autonomous squadron under direct control of the Air Staff. Accordingly, it changed its aircraft codes to read '3.10-LA' *et seq* and increased in strength from 10 to 11 aircraft.

In 1987, the Djibouti aircraft were fitted with replacement wings which allowed them to use the full flight envelope of -3/+9 *g* and speeds up to Mach 1.7, but retirement was fast approaching. Four aircraft returned to France on 13-14 June 1988 to participate in the annual fighter competition at Cazaux, while Nos 22, 27 and 37 flew the last operational mission in Djibouti on 29 June before 'Vexin' became EC 4/30, equipped with Mirage F1Cs, on 1 July. The last sortie in Africa was flown by four aircraft on 12 August 1988, ending 10 years of operations during which 'Vexin' accumulated 18,000 hours in 24,500 sorties. The highest-houred aircraft was No. 70 '3.10-LF' with 5,200.

EC 10 gained a third escadron in 1978, when EC 3/10 'Vexin' formed at Creil for service in Djibouti. The aircraft were camouflaged in sand and brown, and wore the musketeer insignia of ERC 561.

13e Escadre de Chasse

Base: Base Aérienne 132, Colmar/ Mayenheim

EC 13 was the second Mirage III wing and the first to become operational with IIIEs – being declared as such on 3 January 1966. It has been assigned to the FATac throughout, having been declared operational on 1 September 1962. Mirage IIIEs flew 141,000 hours with the wing until the last was withdrawn in 1992, leaving two squadrons of Mirage 5Fs.

EC 13 replaced its Mirage IIICs with IIIEs in 1965, becoming the first operator of the new variant. This aircraft has its tactical '13-PG' code in the original aft position.

EC 13 at Colmar was France's second Mirage wing, replacing its F-86Ks with Mirage IIICs in 1962. This one wears the swallow badge of SPA100.

Escadron de Chasse 1/13 'Artois'

1e Escadrille: SPA83 insignia – *chimère* (dragon), starboard
2e Escadrille: SPA100 insignia – *hirondelle* (swallow), port
3e Escadrille: SPA155 insignia – *Petit Poucet* (Tom Thumb), starboard
4e Escadrille: SPA160 insignia – *diable rouge* (red devil), port
Codes: 13-QA to 13-QZ (radio call FUHQA/ FUHQZ); 13-FA to 13-FZ (FUGFA/FUGFZ);

EC 1/13 'Artois' retained Mirage IIIEs until it re-equipped with Mirage F1CTs in 1992, becoming the Mirage OCU and gaining Mirage IIIBs and IIIBEs during 1986.

and 13-ZA to 13-ZZ (FUMZA/FUMZZ)

EC 1/13 began Mirage training at Mont-de-Marsan in late November 1961 and took delivery of IIIC No. 56 there on 13 March 1962. This aircraft arrived at Colmar on 3 April, although the official acceptance

ceremony was held on 8 May. Declared operational in February 1963, EC 1/13 did not suffer the wing's first loss until 8 March 1963 when No. 45 '13-QA' crashed. A pair of Mirage IIIBs was temporarily added from July 1963. Conversion to Mirage IIIEs followed between 1 and 30 June 1965. From then on, the squadron was tasked with both attack and air defence. It hosted the 25th anniversary celebrations for the Mirage IIIE on 12 May 1990, the 'VIPs' including Nos 401, 402, 403, 404 and 405, all of which remained in service.

EC 1/13 had assisted EC 2 in training Argentine (1972) and Libyan (1974) pilots but became an OCU itself on 4 July 1986 when it accepted ECT 2/2's fleet of Mirage IIIBs and IIIBEs. These exchanged the '2-' of their tactical codes for '13-' (eg. 13-FA and 13-ZA), although the IIIBs moved into the 13-QA range in 1990. On 29 August 1986 it was officially agreed that EC 1/13 should be increased in size to four *escadrilles* and, accordingly, SPA155 and SPA160 were added, having formerly been the two flights of 'Flandre' squadron. The markings adorned the two-seat Mirages, although SPA160 was disbanded on 1 February 1991 and SPA155 transferred to EC 2/4 on 1 June 1991. The final IIIB sortie – and last in the entire Armée de l'Air – was flown on 15 January 1992, and EC 1/13 passed its IIIBEs to EC 2/13 to continue the small remaining OCU task. Training then began on Mirage F1CTs and the last Mirage IIIE sortie was flown by the squadron on 26 June 1992.

Left: **This Mirage IIIE of EC 1/13 wears a miniscule representation of the dragon badge of SPA83, the escadrille's adopted emblem.**

Above: **One of the former ECT 2/2 Mirage IIIBs. EC 1/13 was increased in size to four escadrilles, the fourth using the badge of SPA160.**

Escadron de Chasse 2/13 'Alpes'

1e Escadrille: insignia – *chevalier/cheval gris* (knight and grey horse), starboard
2e Escadrille: insignia – *chevalier/cheval bai* (knight and bay horse), port
Codes: 13-PA to 13-PZ (radio call FUHPA/FUHPZ)

'Alpes' gained its first IIIC (No. 73 '13-PA') on 29 May 1962, having decamped to Mont-de-Marsan the previous month, and began operations on 1 June. It also operated a pair of IIIBs between June 1964 and 15 June 1966. The squadron began training on Mirage IIIEs in November 1964 at Istres and started flying again in January 1965. It completed training on 26 March and returned to Colmar with 14 aircraft (Nos 417 to 419, 421 to 430 and 432, coded '13-PA' to '-PN') on 1 April, at which time the last IIICs were withdrawn after 5,425 hours in 6,059 sorties. During its time with the Mirage III it was exclusively assigned to air defence. It accepted its third variant in February 1977 when Mirage 5Fs from EC 3/3 arrived as replacements, but for attack roles. Since January 1992, the squadron has been the Mirage III/5 OCU with the AA's remaining Mirage IIIBEs, these changing their 13-Q* codes (when with EC 1/13) to 13-P*. 'Alpes' is expected to disband in 1994 without receiving new equipment

Right: **The size of the escadrille badge was reduced during the late 1980s to reduce its conspicuity. From January 1992 the squadron took over from EC 1/13 as the Mirage III/5 training and conversion unit.**

'Alpes' received Mirage 5Fs made surplus by the Jaguar conversion of EC 3/3. The badge of each escadrille was a knight.

Above: **EC 2/13 operated the Mirage IIIE in the air defence role until 1977, when it re-equipped with Mirage 5s.**

Escadron de Chasse 3/13 'Auvergne'

1e Escadrille: SPA85 insignia – *La Folie* (Joker), port
2e Escadrille: GC II/9-4e insignia – *écu et épée* (sword and shield), starboard
Codes: 13-SA to 13-SZ (radio call FUHSA/FUHSZ)

First of two squadrons to receive Mirage 5Fs, EC 3/13 formed on 1 March 1972, its first aircraft (No. 6 '13-SA') arriving on 5 April. It was not until April 1974 that it was declared operational, but by the end of the year it had built up to 20 aircraft. The squadron temporarily lost three, which were loaned to Zaïre between the autumn of 1975 and 9 April 1976. In its first 20 years of Mirage operations, the squadron flew 72,900 hours. Conversion to Mirage F1CTs was under way in 1993.

Left: **To starboard, the Mirage 5Fs of EC 3/13 'Auvergne' wear the sword and shield insignia of the 2e Escadrille, based on the traditional markings of GC II/9-4. The shield carries a down-turned thumb with the word 'Morietur' above.**

Right: **On the port side of the fin, Mirage 5Fs from 'Auvergne' carry the brightly-coloured, trident-wielding joker insignia of SPA85, adopted emblem of the squadron's first escadrille.**

Left: A Mirage 5F armed with rocket pods underwing, and with an unusual nose marking.

Above: The Mirage 5Fs were originally aircraft built for Israel. Embargoed in 1970, they were held in storage until 1972.

Left: Recalling earlier days, a Mirage 5F was painted silver, with old-style unit markings and fin chevron, to celebrate 20 years of service with EC 3/13.

Below: Although Mirage IIIEs and IIIRs were camouflaged in 1968 the Mirage 5Fs were left in natural metal until 1974.

33e Escadre de Reconnaissance

Base: Base Aérienne 124, Strasbourg/Entzheim

The sole Mirage reconnaissance wing in FATac previously flew Republic RF-84F Thunderflashes and now is equipped with Mirage F1CRs. Squadrons carry the insignia of a single World War I *escadrille* on both sides of the fin. Two flights, simply numbered 1 and 2 Escadrilles, comprise the flying element of each squadron. Until September 1965, squadrons were designated Escadron de Reconnaissance Tactique. The wing had flown 200,000 hours on Mirage IIIs by 1983.

Right: ER 33 gradually replaced its RF-84F Thunderflashes with indigenous Mirage IIIRs during 1963-67. This Mirage IIIR carries the SAL33 axe insignia of ER 1/33.

The insignia of ER 3/33 'Moselle' is a cocotte – a folded paper origami bird. The squadron received its first Mirage IIIR in 1963.

Escadron de Reconnaissance 1/33 'Belfort'

Insignia: SAL33 – *hache* (battle axe)
Codes: 33-CA to 33-CZ (radio call FUICA/FUICZ)

Based at Luxeuil with RF-84Fs, ER 1/33 rejoined the remainder of ER 33 at Strasbourg in January 1967 and immediately began receiving Mirage IIIRs. It received its first Mirage F1CR on 27 November 1975 and completed conversion early in 1986.

Right: Each of ER 33's three squadrons uses a single insignia on the fins of its aircraft, but these insignia have changed in detail over the years. Here ER 1/33's axe is carried on a yellow shield.

Before it converted to the Mirage F1CR in 1985/86, ER 1/33 'Belfort' painted up this Mirage IIIR in overall white with a red cheatline.

Above: When squadron insignia were toned down, ER 1/33's axe lost its outline and was applied simply in red to the fin. Unusually, the squadron codes are carried well back on the fuselage.

Escadron de Reconnaissance 2/33 'Savoie'

Insignia: SAL6 – *mouette du Rhin* (Rhine seagull)
Codes: 33-NA to 33-NZ (radio call FUINA/ FUINZ)

ERT 2/33 received its Mirage IIIRs from January 1964, the first two being Nos 320 and 322, and retired its final RF-84Fs in the following April. Selected to be the first recipient of Mirage F1CRs, it began converting its Mirage IIIR pilots with a ground course at the ETIS F1CR at Reims early in 1983. Training on the squadron's aircraft under EC 24/118 at Mont-de-Marsan followed in April-June 1983, before the first F1CR arrived at Strasbourg on 1 July.

One of ER 2/33's Mirage IIIRDs carries an unusual variation on the usual 'Savoie' insignia of a white Rhine seagull.

Escadron de Reconnaissance 3/33 'Moselle'

Insignia: BR11 – *cocotte* (paper bird)
Codes: 33-TA to 33-TZ (radio call FUITA/ FUITZ)

Pilot training for the Mirage IIIR began in January 1963 at Mont-de-Marsan, where ERT 3/33 received its first aircraft, a Mirage IIIB, on 18 March 1963. It had acquired six ('33-TU' to '-TZ') when the last arrived on 28 May, these two-seaters also being used to assist transformation of the wing's other two squadrons before being transferred in June 1965. Delivery of the Mirage IIIR was begun on 7 June 1963 and flying started on 20 June; four were on charge by 1 July and the squadon was able to return to its home base in September 1963. The first in-service loss of a Mirage IIIR occurred on 25 February 1964 when Lieutenant Roux de Bezieux ejected from No. 305 '33-TA'.

A change-over to the Doppler-equipped IIIRD was initiated with the arrival of the first aircraft on 1 April 1968, working up at Mont-de-Marsan until January 1969. However, the IIIR was used in small numbers to make up strength from 8 November 1978. Re-equipment of ER 33 was completed early in 1988 when 'Moselle' discarded its Mirage IIIRDs in favour of Mirage F1CRs. The final four aircraft in service during 1988 were Nos 356, 358, 360 and 364 ('33-TE', '-TG', '-TI'

Above: To celebrate 90,000 hours on the Mirage IIIR and IIIRD, ER 3/33 'Moselle' painted an aircraft glossy black overall.

Right: This Mirage IIIRD carries a centreline recce pod, and also has rocket pods in the nose of each underwing fuel tank.

and '-TO'), which formed the wholly unofficial squadron ER 4/33 'Beaujolais' at Metz and carried the old GR I/33 badge.

CIFAS 328 'Aquitaine'

Base: Base Aérienne 106, Bordeaux/ Mérignac

Responsible for training strategic force pilots and navigators since 1 May 1964, the Centre d'Instruction des Forces Aériennes Strategique 328 operated Mirage IVAs, Douglas B-26 Invaders, Nord Noratlasses and Lockheed T-33As, later adding Fouga Magisters, Dassault Mystère 20s and D-B/D Alpha Jets. The unit received 10 Mirage IIIB-2s and five IIIBs.

CIFAS 328 was re-organised into three squadrons in 1978, but this made no difference to the unit insignia of a vulture carrying a pair of bombs in its talons. The unit operated a variety of aircraft in its role of training Mirage IV strategic bomber aircrew, including T-33s, Magisters, Mystère 20s, Alpha Jets, Mirage IIIs and, of course, Mirage IVs.

Escadron d'Entrainement 02/328

Insignia: (CIFAS 328) *vautour* (vulture), both sides
Codes: DA to DZ (radio call FUKDA/FUKDZ)

CIFAS was re-organised into three squadrons on 15 July 1978 and its Mirage IIIs assigned to EE 2/328. The squadron also operated Magisters between July 1986 and 31 December 1989. Mirage IIIs assigned to bomber wings for continuation training retained their CIFAS codes, but they were occasionally prefixed by the wing number (91-, 93- or 94-). Reductions in the Mirage IV force resulted in CIFAS disbanding on 1 September 1991. Its remaining equipment of seven IIIB/B-2s, three Mirage IVPs, a Mystère 20 and two loaned Alpha Jets was formed into Escadron de Reconnaissance et d'Instruction 01/328 and made subordinate

to the 91e Escadre de Bombardement. On 30 June 1992, ERI 01/328 also stood down and its Mirage IIIB/B-2s were transferred from Bordeaux to Cazaux.

The 10 Mirage IIIB-2(RV)s of Escadron d'Entrainement 2/328 continued to be used for training Mirage IV pilots in the delicate art of air-to-air refuelling until June 1992, when the unit disbanded. Some aircraft had already been transferred to other units for use as ordinary two-seat trainers, with the gradual rundown of the Mirage IV fleet.

Centre d'Expériences Aériennes Militaires

Base: Base Aérienne 118, Mont-de-Marsan

CEAM is a direct-reporting unit of the air force High Command responsible for trials of equipment. Its components include a fighter trials squadron assigned to long-term development and to the administration of the working-up of the first squadrons to operate a new type or variant of aircraft.

Escadron de Chasse 24/118

Insignia: (CEAM) athlete hurling an arrowhead to the stars, both sides
Codes: 118-AA to 118-AZ (radio call FSDAA/FSDAZ)

Innumerable Mirage IIIs and 5s have passed through Mont-de-Marsan for short-term training and long-term trials. The last aircraft was apparently IIIE No. 495, in use until 1982.

Carrying a Martel test-round under the centreline, this Mirage IIIE wears the 118-series codes allocated to the CEAM at Mont-de-Marsan.

Centre d'Essais en Vol

Insignia: (CEV) the letters 'CEV' in an arrowhead; (EPNER) a paper dart with images of two pilots

CEV is the airborne trials component of the Direction Technique des Constructions Aéronautiques, a military agency responsible for airworthiness testing and certification. Its main base is at Brétigny-sur-Orge, but Dassault fighters are normally evaluated by the unit's two out-stations at Istres (where Dassault's flight test unit is stationed) and Cazaux, for proximity to weapons ranges. Many of the Mirage IIIA development aircraft passed through CEV, including some assigned to its associated test pilots' school at Istres, the Ecole du Personnel Navigant d'Essais et de Réception (EPNER). Mirage IIIB-1s Nos 231-235 were built specifically for CEV trials. Individual aircraft identities, if worn, comprise the last two letters of the aircraft's callsign, in the ranges FZACA/FZAGZ, FZAZA/FZAZZ and FZJOA/FZJOZ. The CEV still flies eight Mirage IIIB/B-1s and five Mirage IIIRs on development work.

Above: This CEV aircraft is actually a Mirage IIIE, though it has been fitted with a Mirage IIIR nose.

Left: A handful of Mirage IIIBs and IIIRs remain on CEV charge, for tests, trials and development work.

Gabon

A former French colony, Gabon ordered three Mirage 5Gs, two reconnaissance 5RGs and two 5DG trainers in mid-1975. The 5RGs were cancelled immediately before delivery (after they had been painted), although the others were delivered to M'vengu in 1978. Two collided in August 1981 and the other three suffered from low serviceability. A further Forces Aériennes Gabonaises order in April 1982 comprised two Mirage 5G-2s, another two 5DG trainers and upgrading of the remaining pair of 5Gs to 5G-2s. Deliveries of the second batch took place on 8 May 1984.

Serial numbers	Type	Quantity
201 to 204	Mirage 5DG	4
401 to 403	Mirage 5G	3
501 to 504*	Mirage 5G-2	2+2
(301 to 302)	Mirage 5RG	0 Cancelled

*Comprising two rebuilds of 5Gs and two from a cancelled Zaïre order (ZAF 411 and 414)

Gabon originally ordered seven Mirages, consisting of three Mirage 5G fighters, two 5DG trainers and two 5RG recce aircraft. The latter were cancelled immediately before delivery. Heavy attrition resulted in the delivery of two 5G2 fighters and two 5DGs, while two surviving 5Gs were upgraded to 5G2 standards.

Israel

The Israeli Defence Force/Air Force (La Tsvah Hagana Le Israel/Heyl Ha'Avir) was an early customer for the Mirage III (in 1960) and first to order Mirage 5s – which were never received. The initial batch comprised 72 Mirage IIICJs supplied between 4 July 1961 and 22 July 1964, lacking provision for the SEPR rocket and with simplified avionics, and five Mirage IIIBJs, delivered 16 February 1966 to 12 January 1968. At least two CJs were converted for reconnaissance with camera noses. The first air combat by a Mirage took place on 20 August 1963 when two aircraft shot down a pair of Syrian MiG-17 'Frescos'. After many more operational missions, the surviving 19 CJs and three BJs were sold to Argentina in 1982.

The IDF/AF system of (deliberately) 'scrambled' serial numbers makes identification of aircraft difficult. The 72 IIICJs had Dassault numbers 101-148, 152, 154-156, 159-160, 162, 165-167, 169-170, 173-174, 176-177, 179-180 and 182-187; five IIIBJs were 236-240. Known Israeli serials are as below, although some aircraft underwent reserialling, often by alteration of the first digit, eg. 758 became 158. For this reason, eight serials are known for the five trainers.

Serial numbers
287, 618, 639, 769, 787, 788, 789 and 98
02, 04, 08, 11, 12, 14, 15, 34, 44, 45, 52, 67, 71, 82, 83, 101, 103, 107, 109, 111, 129, 144, 147, 148, 150, 151, 153, 158, 159, 171, 176 to 178, 180, 259, 287, 296, 406, 409, 458, 459, 507, 522, 524, 534, 620, 649, 684, 703, 712, 719, 720, 725, 729, 730, 732, 733, 741, 743, 745, 748, 749, 753, 755, 756, 758, 764, 768, 771, 775, 776, 778, 779, 780, 785, 833, 915, 941, 942, 948, 951 and 952

Type	Quantity
Mirage IIIBJ	5
Mirage IIICJ	72

A 1966 order for 50 Mirage 5Js and two 5DJs was the subject of a French arms embargo, although the single-seat aircraft were built (completed between 12 September 1967 and 19 June 1969), stored and then delivered to France as Mirage 5Fs. Their replacement was the IAI Nesher, of which 61 were built: 51 single-seat aircraft (IAI numbers S01 to S51) and 10 Nesher T trainers (T01 to T10), the latter reportedly using French-built fuselages. The survivors, when retired in the late 1970s, apparently numbered 37 and four respectively, of which all except 501 (retained for preservation) were sold to Argentina as Daggers.

For the J79-engined Mirage, Israel used codenames Salvo, Barak (Lightning), Ra'am (Thunder) and Radkan (Dancer), but the aircraft became more widely known as the Kfir (Lion Cub). Mirage IIIBJ 988 was used as the J79 testbed, or Technolog, making its first flight on 21 September 1970. It was also used as a test aircraft for canards, with which it flew for the first time on 16 July 1974. Kfir production totalled 212, including 40 to Kfir 1 standard, delivered from 14 April 1975. The canard-equipped C2 was introduced in May 1977 and the C7 in August 1983, prior to closure of the assembly line in 1986. Some Mk 1s gained small canards and became C1s, 25 of them later loaned to the US Navy/USMC. About a dozen of the 212 Kfirs were TC2 or TC7 trainers.

Mirages were delivered in natural metal and later adopted an upper surface disruptive camouflage of sand, brown and green. The latter markings were applied to Neshers and Kfirs, but some Kfir C2s adopted grey overall, first reported in 1977, and this has also been applied to two-seat Kfirs. Mirages, Neshers and early Kfirs were marked on the wings and fin with large triangles of orange with bold black outline.

Delivery of Lockheed F-16 Fighting Falcons resulted in Kfirs being placed in storage and, where possible, sold. By 1987, 45 per cent of the force was in store. Sales and attrition have left the IDF/AF with a little under 150 Kfirs, of which only two squadrons' worth remain operational, these believed to be Nos 121 and 144 at Hatzor.

It is difficult to determine the squadrons which have operated Mirage variants. Those which have been identified tend to be known either by their number or badge, and thus it is possible that some squadrons appear below under both headings.

Serial numbers	Type	Quantity
501, 507,510, 522, 524 to 528, 531, 533, 534, 536 to 539, 541, 541, 543, 549, 562, 563, 565, 566, 569, 572, 574, 582, 586, 598 and 599	Nesher	51
no serials known	Nesher T	10

Serial numbers	Type	Quantity
703, 709, 710, 712, 714, 716, 724 to 728, 731 to 732, 734, 735, 739, 742, 747, 749, 750, 764, 785 to 787, 791 and 794	Kfir 1/C1	40
514, 517, 519, 523, 529, 534, 539, 555, 557, 705 to 708, 711, 718 to 719, 730, 733, 736 to 738, 740, 743, 745, 748, 755, 759, 761, 779, 781, 804, 805, 807, 812 to 814, 821 to 822, 824, 826, 827, 829 to 831, 833, 837, 838, 841, 843, 845, 846, 849, 851 to 855, 857, 858, 860, 862 to 868, 870, 871, 874, 877 to 880, 882 to 885, 887 to 889, 891, 894 to 897, 903, 904, 910, 920, 928, 948, 961, 979 and 987	Kfir C2/C7	160
303, 304, 306, 308 to 310, 611	Kfir TC2/TC7	12

101 Squadron

Badge: a skull; plus blue/white striped rudder (red/white also noted)

101 has been equipped with the Mirage IIICJ, Nesher, Kfir 1 (first operator, April 1975) and Kfir C2 (1977). The unit converted to Lockheed F-16s in 1988, and is based at Hatzor.

111 Squadron

Badge: not known

The unit was equipped with Mirage IIICJs.

113 Squadron

Badge: not known; nose 'sharkmouth'

The unit was equipped with Mirage IIICJ and subsequently converted to Phantoms.

Four Mirage IIICJs of No. 101 Squadron. The unit's distinctive red and white candy striped rudders have not been obliterated by the Israeli censor.

No. 101 Squadron's badge has been taped over on these early canard-less Kfirs, thereby saving the censor some work. Again the candy-striped rudder, first seen on the unit's C-199s, gives the game away.

117 Squadron

Badge: a jet aircraft in plan

The unit was equipped with Mirage IIICJ at Ramat David; its present status is unknown.

Below: The Mirage plan view badge and red fuselage stripe mark this Mirage IIICJ as belonging to No. 117 Squadron.

Above: This camouflaged Mirage IIICJ lacks a fuselage stripe, but has the No. 117 Squadron fin badge.

119 Squadron

Badge: a bat

The unit initially was equipped with the Mirage IIICJ at Eqron, but converted to Phantoms.

121 Squadron

Badge: not known

The unit is a Hatzor-based Kfir operator.

144 Squadron

Badge: not known

The unit is a Hatzor-based Kfir operator.

Right: This two-seat Mirage IIIB wears the red chevron tail marking of No. 119 Squadron.

Below: A rare uncensored photograph of a No. 119 Squadron Mirage IIICJ, with the unit's bat and clouds insignia visible on the fin.

Dassault Mirage III/5/50 Variants

This Mirage IIIC has a rudder chevron which may mark it as an aircraft from No. 190 Squadron.

190 Squadron

Badge: delta-winged aircraft with an eagle's head; blue rudder with white/black/white zig-zag

Previously based at Etam (now in Egypt), the unit is equipped with Mirage IIICJs.

? Squadron

Badge: a wasp

The unit was equipped with Neshers and became the second Kfir 1 operator in 1976. McDonnell Douglas AH-64A Apaches replaced the Kfir 1s in September 1990. (This squadron may be the Nesher unit which had black and yellow checked rudders.)

? Squadron

Badge: not known

This unit was formerly equipped with McDonnell A-4H Skyhawk. It was the third squadron to convert to Kfir 1s, using ex-101 Squadron aircraft, and was declared operational on 28 August 1977.

? Squadron

Badge: black and yellow diamonds on rudder

Equipped with Kfir C1s, this may be the same as the unit immediately above.

? Squadron

Badge: one red and two yellow fin-stripes

The current status of this Kfir C2-equipped unit is unknown.

? Squadron

Badge: bird's head and neck before a setting sun; blue and red fin stripe

The current status of this Kfir C7-equipped unit is unknown.

A line-up of unmarked Kfirs. The black-edged yellow triangles on the fin and outer wings are a recognition aid to prevent confusion with Mirage 5s operated by Arab air arms.

Lebanon

An order for Mirages placed in 1965 concerned 10 IIIELs, two IIIBLs and a supply of R.530 missiles. Following the maiden flight of the first IIIEL on 25 July 1967, the single-seat aircraft were delivered to the air force (Al Quwwat Al Jawwiya Al Lubnaniya) between 11 September 1967 and 11 March 1969, and the trainers on 14 June 1968 and 11 March 1969. Four and one respectively were immediately placed in storage and the others soon followed, apart from L512 which was written off. Attempts to sell the fleet were unsuccessful, although the present condition of the aircraft – if they remain extant after many years of civil war – must now be poor.

Serial numbers	Type	Quantity
L511 to L512	Mirage IIIBL	10
L501 to L510	Mirage IIIEL	2

All were delivered in grey and two-tone green camouflage.

One of 10 Mirage IIIELs delivered to Lebanon, along with two IIIBL two-seaters. Their service life was extremely short, since the entire fleet (apart from a single aircraft written off in an accident) was placed in storage soon after delivery, and the current status of the aircraft is unknown.

Libya

In November 1969, two months after the revolution which brought to power the regime currently led by Colonel Khadaffi, Libya embarked on a major military build-up which included 110 Mirage 5s. Impatient with delivery schedules, the new government arranged for five French Mirage IIIBs of ECT 2/2 at Dijon (Nos 204, 208, 211, 213 and 220) to be painted with Libyan insignia for a flypast over Tripoli to mark the first anniversary of the revolution. The five were thus marked only from 28 August to 4 September 1970 and carried French instructors to monitor the Libyan student pilots nominally in command.

Serial numbers	Type	Quantity
401 to 453	Mirage 5D	53
201 to 215	Mirage 5DD	15
101 to 132	Mirage 5DE	32
301 to 310	Mirage 5DR	10

Training was at Dijon, to where the first 5DD trainer was delivered on 22 December 1970. Initial 5DEs were also delivered to the French base from 3 March 1971, these being equivalents of the IIIE with radar and Doppler. Direct deliveries to Libyan air force (Al Quwwat al Jawwiya al Jamahiriyah al Arabiya al Libyya) of the Mirage 5D attack aircraft started on 5 November 1971, the 5DR reconnaissance machines following from March 1972. All had been received by May 1974, at which time only 24 of the planned 200 local pilots had qualified; there was a similar shortfall in the desired 600 technicians. Many aircraft were refurbished at Dassault's Toulouse plant during the early 1980s, but some were withheld late in 1983 because of Libyan military involvement in Chad. Two of them (and a Mirage F1) were released in 1990 in return for three French hostages held in Lebanon. The aircraft are based at Nasser AB, Tubruq, but few are believed to be serviceable.

Above: Wearing Libya's old national markings, over the original brown, green and dark grey camouflage, this Mirage 5D is equivalent to the basic Mirage 5F/5J attack aircraft, and lacks radar or Doppler.

Right: Wearing the current simple Islamic green roundel and fin flash is a Doppler- and radar-equipped Mirage 5DE. These were delivered from March 1971.

Pakistan

In addition to buying 96 new Mirages in four batches, the Pakistan Fiz'ya acquired 50 secondhand examples from Australia, some of which are being put into service. The first order, in 1967, was for 18 Mirage IIIEP interceptors with MATRA R.530 and Magic AAM armament delivered between 25 October 1967 and 30 April 1969; three IIIRPs between 10 April and 23 June 1969; and three IIIDP trainers, beginning on 30 January 1069. In 1970, the PAF ordered 28 Mirage 5PAs and two more IIIDPs and, in 1975, the reconnaissance element was strengthened with 10 more IIIRPs.

A 1979 contract was for two 5DPA2 trainers delivered from 20 September 1981 and 30 Mirage 5PAs, the last of which arrived on 29 December 1982. Two sub-variants of the latter were received, comprising the 5PA2 with Cyrano IV radar and 5PA3 specially fitted with Agave radar for compatibility with Aérospatiale AM39 Exocet anti-ship missiles. Delivery of the Australian Mirage IIIs, including seven IIID trainers, began by sea in December 1990 for refurbishment and eventual issue to two squadrons. The first conversion was ceremonially rolled out on 30 October 1991.

Serial numbers	Type	Quantity
67.301 to 67.303	Mirage IIIDP	3
70.304 and 70.305	Mirage IIIDP	2
67.101 to 67.118	Mirage IIIEP	18
67.201 to 67.203	Mirage IIIRP	3
75.204 to 75.213	Mirage IIIRP	10
	Mirage III ex-RAAF	up to 43
	Mirage IIID ex-RAAF	up to 7
79.306 and 79.307	Mirage 5DPA2	2
70.401 to 70.428	Mirage 5PA	28
79.429 to 79.446	Mirage 5PA2	28
79.447 to 79.458	Mirage 5PA3	12

Pakistan's fleet of newly-built Mirages, like this Mirage 5PA3, is being augmented by an influx of ex-RAAF aircraft which are being overhauled at Kamra before entering Pakistani service.

PAF upper surface camouflage is green and mid-grey. Overhaul of the ex-RAAF aircraft is undertaken at the PAF's own Mirage rebuild factory at Kamra, from where the first French-built aircraft and engine were returned to service in February 1981. It is probable that some of the ex-RAAF aircraft will be broken down for spares.

Mirage IIIEPs participated in the short 1971 war between India and Pakistan, opening the score with a BAC Canberra on 4 December. In all, 10 claims were made: five HS Hunters, two Su-7 'Fitters', the Canberra and two aircraft on the ground. IAF claims of six Mirages were dented by a PAF post-war parade of all 23 in service at the time the conflict began.

No. 5 Squadron

(No. 34 Wing)
Base: Sargodha and Rafiqui
Badge: a falcon clutching a Sidewinder

Re-equipped from F-86F Sabres at Sargodha in late 1967, No. 5 was the first PAF Mirage squadron and flies IIIEPs and IIIDPs. It transferred to Rafiqui after the Sargodha wing converted to F-16 Fighting Falcons in 1984-85, operating in the all-weather interception role. No. 5 gathered the IIIRP reconnaissance fleet after re-equipment of Nos 18 and 20 Squadrons, and therefore currently operates all Mirage III variants.

This No. 5 Squadron Mirage IIIRP is fitted with new RWR equipment above the windscreen arch (forward hemisphere) and spine (rear hemisphere).

No. 5 Squadron also operates Pakistan's surviving Mirage IIIEPs, two of which are seen here. These can use the MATRA R530 and R550 Magic AAMs, as well as Sidewinders of various sub-types.

No. 8 Squadron

(No. 32 Wing)
Base: Masroor
Badge: a sword and shield

De-activated as a Martin B-57 unit in 1970, No. 8 reformed at Masroor in May 1982 to receive Mirage 5PA3s for anti-shipping operations, and later added half of No. 33 Squadron's complement of 5PA2s.

No. 8 Squadron is tasked primarily with anti-shipping duties, and operates the Exocet-compatible, Agave-radar-equipped 5PA3.

The Mirage 5PA2 is externally identical to the PA3, though it has a Cyrano IVM radar, as fitted to later Mirage F1 variants. It serves with Nos 8 and 22 Sqns.

No. 9 Squadron

(No. 34 Wing)
Base: Rafiqui

(No. 32 Wing)
Base: Masroor

Disbanded as an F-104A Starfighter unit at Sargodha, No. 9 reformed at Rafiqui in January 1973 to operate Mirage 5PAs. It became part of No. 34 Wing when this formed at Rafiqui in June 1976, and was additionally issued with IIIDPs and 5DPs to become the Mirage OCU on 15 June 1977. On 31 August 1981 it moved to Masroor where it stood down for F-16 conversion on 23 March 1984, passing its aircraft to No. 22 OCU.

Right: This Mirage 5DPA2 is typical of the two-seaters used by No. 9 Squadron before the aircraft passed to No. 22 OCU.

Below: The Mirage 5PA is a true Mirage 5, an optimised attack aircraft lacking radar and Doppler.

No. 18 Squadron

(No. 34 Wing)
Base: Rafiqui
Badge: an eagle's head

Disbanded as an F-86 Sabre squadron in September 1980, No. 18 reformed in October 1981 with Mirage 5s and six IIIRPs from No. 20 Squadron. It converted to Chengdu F-7P Skybolts in 1988 and passed its IIIRPs to No. 5 Squadron.

No. 18 Squadron operated Mirages between 1981 and 1988, when it passed most of its aircraft to No. 5 Squadron. The unit formed with a mix of Mirage 5s and IIIRPs.

No. 20 Squadron

(No. 34 Wing)
Base: Rafiqui
Badge: a spread eagle

A former Lockheed RT-33A unit disbanded in June 1972, No. 20 was reformed in June 1977 to fly the Mirage IIIRP and 5PA. Six of the reconnaissance aircraft went to No. 18 Squadron in October 1981. On 7 May 1986 No. 20 converted to Shenyang F-6s (later Chengdu F-7s) and transferred its former equipment to No. 5 Squadron.

No. 22 OCU

(No. 34 Wing)
Base: Rafiqui
Badge: a Mirage in plan

A new squadron, No. 22 formed on 22 June 1984 to fly Mirage 5s and currently has a mixed fleet of 5PAs, 5PA2s and 5DPs.

Right: A line-up of No. 22 OCU Mirages. Nearest the camera is a Mirage 5PA2. The squadron badge is a Mirage in plan view.

Above: A Mirage 5DP of No. 22 OCU, which serves as Pakistan's Mirage conversion and standardisation unit.

No. 33 Squadron

(No. 34 Wing)
Base: Rafiqui
Badge: none known

Formed as the initial operator of Mirage 5PA2s in 1981, No. 33 was a short-lived squadron which divided its equipment between No. 8 Squadron and No. 22 OCU.

Below: A Mirage 5PA2 of the type operated by No. 33 Squadron. This sub-variant was fitted with a Cyrano IVM radar as used by the Mirage F1. This had air-to-air, air-to-ground, sea-search, mapping, terrain avoidance and other modes, but was not compatible with the AM39 Exocet missile.

Combat Commanders School

(No. 38 Wing)
Base: Sargodha
Badge: letters 'CCS' within a circle; later, a sword before a radiant sun

Formed on 7 June 1976 for advanced training, the CCS operates a squadron each

of Mirage 5PAs and Shenyang F-6s, named the 'Skybolts' and the 'Dashings' respectively. The aircraft provide four/five-month combat commanders courses, three-month weapons courses, and four/five-week fighter integration courses.

Below: The basic Pakistani Mirage 5PA is a simple, non-radar, Mirage 5 fighter-bomber.

Peru

Mirage deliveries to the Fuerza Aérea Peruana began on 7 May 1968, the first two contracts covering 14 Mirage 5Ps delivered by 21 December 1969 and two 5DP trainers supplied on 30 September and 17 October 1968. In total, 40 aircraft were eventually received from no less than 10 individual contracts (codenamed Martello 1-10), several of which covered only one or two attrition replacements (usually with duplicated serial numbers).

Serial numbers	Type	Quantity	
182 to 191	Mirage 5P	10	Martello 1
192 to 195	Mirage 5P	4	Martello 2
101 to 107	Mirage 5P	7	Martello 4
188	Mirage 5P	1	Martello 5
108 to 114	Mirage 5P3	7	Martello 6
193	Mirage 5P3	1	Martello 7
184	Mirage 5P3	1	Martello 8
191	Mirage 5P3	1	Martello 9
190 and 194	Mirage 5P4	2	Martello 10
196 and 197	Mirage 5DP	2	Martello 1
197	Mirage 5DP	1	Martello 3
198	Mirage 5DP	1	Martello 4
199	Mirage 5DP3	1	Martello 6
198	Mirage 5DP3	1	Martello 10

On 6 June 1982, 10 Mirage 5Ps were loaned to Argentina as emergency aid for the Falklands War, but did not enter service before hostilites ended a week later. They were later purchased and currently serve the FAA. Remaining aircraft were upgraded under a March 1982 contract to 5P4 and 5DP4 standard with a fixed refuelling probe, new RWR, HF radio and laser range-finder. The 5P4 is reported to be fitted with Agave radar and carry AM39 Exocet anti-ship missiles, but none has been seen in radar configuration.

Above: Peruvian Mirage 5Ps were delivered in standard Armée de l'Air style grey and green camouflage. National insignia originally included a massive red/white/red fin stripe, later replaced by a smaller fin flash.

Escuadrón de Caza 611

(Grupo Aéreo 6)
Base: Chiclayo (BA Capitan José Abelardo Quinones Gonzales)

611 Squadron is currently the sole component of 6 Wing, but when initially delivered the Mirage 5 was operated by 12 and 14 Squadrons of the same wing. There are, at most, 15 single-seat aircraft and three trainers remaining in Peruvian service.

Peruvian Mirage 5Ps later adopted a sand and stone camouflage, as seen here. Ten aircraft were loaned and then sold to Argentina.

Saudi Arabia

In the wake of the Arab-Israeli war of 1973, Saudi Arabia paid for a batch of 38 Mirages for Egypt to replace Soviet-built types lost during the war. Public opinion and Israeli sensibilities made it desirable to conceal the true recipient, so the aircraft were given SD (Saudi) designations and were painted in Saudi markings (with roundels and fin flags, but without the distinctive Arabic Royal Saudi air force logos) for delivery and pilot training at Dijon. The batch consisted of 32 Mirage 5SDEs and six two-seat Mirage 5SDD trainers, the single-seaters being virtually identical to the Mirage IIIE operated by the Armée de l'Air. Saudi Arabia's tenuous Mirage connection ended with the delivery of the aircraft, directly to Egypt, from October 1974.

Three Mirages wearing Saudi Arabia's distinctive green and white markings. These are actually Egyptian aircraft, seen prior to delivery, as described above.

South Africa

After evaluation of the Mirage III at Marignane in May 1961, the South African air force (Suid-Afrikaanse Lugmag) placed an initial order in April 1962 and eventually received 58 new-built aircraft. These were 16 IIICZ interceptors received between 18 December 1962 and 9 March 1964; three IIIBZ trainers (14 December 1982 to 9 December 1964); four reconnaissance IIIRZs (24 November 1966 to 22 February 1967); 17 multi-role IIIEZs (2 February 1965 to 15 March 1972); three IIIDZ trainers (4 July to 18 September 1969); 11 IIID2Z trainers; and four IIIR2Zs. The four R2Zs were the first production Mirages with the 09K-50 version of Atar. Further aircraft appear to have been acquired recently from an undisclosed source, as evidenced by serials up to 866, noted in 1992. (SAAF aircraft converted to Cheetah retain their original serial numbers.)

Serial numbers	Type	Quantity
816 to 818	Mirage IIIBZ	3
800 to 815	Mirage IIICZ	16
839 to 841	Mirage IIIDZ	3
843 to 853	Mirage IIID2Z	11 to Cheetah D
819 to 834 and 842	Mirage IIIEZ	17 to Cheetah E
835 to 838	Mirage IIIRZ	4
854 to 857	Mirage IIIR2Z	4
? to 861	Cheetah D	4? (858 to 861?)
862 to ?	Cheetah E	5? (to at least 866)

Remaining Mirage IIIBZs and IIICZs were withdrawn in October 1990, only two having been lost in service. One IIIRZ has been placed in a museum.

Mirage IIICZs and EZs arrived in natural metal finish and did not adopt the olive drab and deep buff upper surface camouflage, with light grey beneath, until 1971 (following some experiments with different schemes). The IIIRZ was delivered in NATO green and grey and served until 1976 before going into SAAF colours. Cheetahs receive an overall light grey camouflage during conversion.

The 'Flying Cheetahs' of No. 2 Sqn put up a this formation. Most original Mirages have been converted to Cheetah standards or retired.

No. 2 Squadron

Base: Waterkloof and Hoedspruit
Badge: a winged cheetah

Delivery of Mirage IIICZs began (as airfreight) to No. 2 Squadron at Waterkloof in April 1963, replacing the Canadair-built Sabre 6s previously in service. Strength was augmented by IIIEZs between July 1965 and August 1966, when they passed to No. 3 Squadron. A tactical reconnaissance element was incorporated in No. 2 Squadron on the arrival of Mirage IIIRZs in November 1966, the R2Z variant joining in 1974. The squadron moved to Hoedspruit in 1975 where it remains in the reconnaissance role.

Above: No. 2 Squadron finally re-equipped with the Cheetah when it took over the aircraft of No. 89 CFS.

Below: This gaudy Mirage IIICZ was specially painted for the celebration of 25 years of Mirage operations by the 'Flying Cheetahs'.

Above: When first delivered, No. 2 Squadron's Mirages were in highly-polished natural metal finish, with red fins and fuselage stripes.

Below: Mirage IIICZs were toned down until little more than the squadron badge remained.

Dassault Mirage III/5/50 Variants

No. 3 Squadron

Base: Waterkloof
Badge: a hornet

Although reformed in August 1966 when it absorbed No. 2 Squadron's Mirage IIIEZs, No. 3 remained subordinate to its companion at Waterkloof until declared autonomous in February 1975. On 4 April the same year it received its first Mirage F1 and passed its fleet of IIIEZs, IIIDZs and IIID2Zs to No. 85 AFS.

The Mirage IIIEZ served with No. 3 Squadron until replaced by the Mirage F1 in 1975, when the survivors were passed to No. 85 ACS.

No. 5 Squadron

Base: Louis Trichardt Air Base
Badge: a pegasus

Converted to Impala IIs in 1981, the Citizen Force (ie, reservist) No. 5 Squadron moved to the newly completed Louis Trichardt AB on 1 January 1988 and re-equipped with Cheetah EZs, being declared operational in the following April.

Right: No. 3 Squadron's IIIEZs later went through a conversion programme to emerge as Cheetah EZs. As such they equipped No. 5 Squadron.

No. 5 Squadron's Cheetahs wore a toned-down Pegasus badge on their fins, but are now believed to have been passed to No. 2 Squadron.

No. 85 Air Combat School

Base: Pietersburg
Badge: a diving sea bird

Formed on 1 August 1972 from the un-numbered Advanced Flying School at Pietersburg, No. 85 AFS initially operated de Havilland Vampires but was entirely equipped with Mirage IIIDZs and Atlas Impala Is a year later. Re-equipment of No. 3 Squadron resulted in the addition of Mirage IIIEZs in 1975, together with newly delivered (1974) IIID2Zs. A Sabre Mk 6 flight was operated by the AFS between 1976 and April 1980, while Impala IIs were received later, the unit then being renamed No. 85 Air Combat School. No. 85 ACS transferred its single-seat Mirages to No. 5 Squadron in January 1988.

Above: The diving bird insignia of No. 85 ACS, which took over No. 3 Squadron's aircraft during 1975, initially augmenting them with vintage F-86 Sabres.

Right: One of No. 85 ACS's Mirage IIID2Zs lands.

No. 89 Combat Flying School

Base: Pietersburg
Badge: a lion rampant

Formed on 1 July 1986, No. 89 CFS received two-seat Cheetah Ds as they emerged from conversion, but is due to be combined with No. 5 Squadron at Louis Trichardt in the near future, when Pietersburg AB is closed.

Left: No. 89 CFS decorated its Cheetah Ds with a rampant lion badge, seen here in colourful form.

Above: The rampant lion insignia is seen in toned-down form on the fins of two Cheetah Ds.

Spain

Having evaluated a Mirage IIIC in April 1962, Spain's air force (Ejercito del Aire Español) waited until 1968 to order 24 Mirage IIIEE interceptors and six IIIDE trainers, to which it assigned the local designations C.11 and CE.11 respectively. Hand-overs of single-seat aircraft began on 9 April 1970, and after training at Dijon the first six aircraft were delivered to Manises on 13 June 1970. The first IIIDE was delivered on 15 July 1970.

Serial numbers	Type	Quantity
CE.11-25 to CE.11-30	Mirage IIIDE	6
C.11-1 to C.11-24	Mirage IIIEE	24

In 1978, Mirages were equipped with a Thomson-CSF BF radar warning receiver on the fin leading edge. Plans for a comprehensive Mirage mid-life update were abandoned in July 1991 and the aircraft withdrawn from service in 1992.

Right: One of the 24 Mirage IIIEEs delivered to Spain during 1970. Spain abandoned plans for an ambitious Mirage III upgrade in 1991, and instead opted to retire the aircraft in 1992.

Ala de Caza 11

Base: Manises/Valencia
Badge: three birds (bustard, hawk and blackbird) diving

When delivered to Ala 11, early Mirages were assigned to component Escuadrón 101, although Esc 103 was soon formed to accept the second half of the order. In May 1971 the squadrons were renumbered 111 and 112. Code numbers on the aircraft noses were changed as a consequence and amended again in 1987 when only the wing number (11-) was applied as a prefix, instead of either 111- or 112-. Aircraft wore NATO grey and green camouflage throughout their service, the only other change of marking being a drastic reduction in size of the St Andrew's cross on the rudder during the mid-1980s.

Replacing F-86 Sabres, Mirages armed with MATRA R.530FEs and AIM-9B (later 9J) Sidewinders became the first of a new generation of interceptor in Mando de Combate (Air Combat Command), but were later augmented by McDonnell Douglas F-4C Phantoms and Mirage F1s. In later years, their lack of electronic warfare equipment resulted in the change to a 75 per cent assignment to air-to-surface missions. Escuadrón 112 disbanded on 31 December 1989 to release aircraft for the planned upgrade, and Esc 111 returned its final C.11s on 1 October 1992 when they were replaced by Mirage F1CEs and EEs.

Equipped with 10 C.11s and four CE.11s, Esc 111 flew its final operational warfare missions on 30 September 1992 and a ceremonial seven-ship formation on the following day, rounding off 75,000 sorties and 80,500 flying hours by the 'Plancheta' (Flat Iron) in Spanish service. On 23 October 1992 the last ferry flight completed assembly of the 22 surviving Mirages at CASA's Getafe plant from where they have been offered for sale, perhaps to Argentina.

Below: Wearing small rudder markings, this is one of Ala 11's last Mirage IIIEEs.

Below: A 'Winder-armed IIIDE. They initially had a larger St Andrew's cross.

Above: Until 1987 codes were prefixed 111- or 112- to show the user squadron.

Above: The Patrol Azur insignia dates from the Civil War.

Switzerland

An order for 100 licence-produced Mirage IIIs was placed in June 1961 after the Swiss air force and anti-aircraft command (Kommando Der Fleiger- Und Fliegerabwehrtruppen) had evaluated a Mirage IIIA and a IIIC in January of the previous year. Local manufacture and the costs associated with incorporating the Hughes TARAN avionics system as a replacement for Cyrano and other French equipment caused a price crisis and reduction of the contract to 57, although four more trainers were added later. A single Mirage IIICS was obtained for trials and delivered in December 1962.

The Dassault-built prototype IIIS flew on 13 December 1963, and it and the second aircraft were delivered on 28 February and 1 June 1964. A further 34 came from the FFA factory between 27 October 1965 and 7 February 1969. A French-built prototype IIIRS reconnaissance aircraft flew on 5 November 1964 and was delivered on 27 July 1967. FFA manufacture accounted for 17 more between 28 March 1968 and 12 June 1969. A pair of IIIBS trainers arrived from France, the first of which flew on 21 October 1963 and was delivered on 30 November that year. Two IIIBSs followed in 1970-72, the second of which was assembled locally, and Dassault delivered two IIIDS variants on 27 January and 3 February 1983.

Serial numbers	Type	Quantity
U2001 to U2004	Mirage IIIBS	4
J2201	Mirage IIICS	1
J2011 and J2012	Mirage IIIDS	2
R2101 to R2118	Mirage IIIRS	18
J2301 to J2336	Mirage IIIS	36

The IIIS is a multi-role aircraft able to launch Hughes HM 55 Falcon AAMs and Aérospatiale AS30 ASMs, the current air defence armament now being the AIM-9P Sidewinder. All the IIIRSs remain in service, as do 30 IIISs, both types having been modernised in the ISMA programme (Improved Swiss Mirage Aircraft) with canards, a Martin-Baker Mk 10 zero-zero ejection seat, braking parachute, increased stores pylon capacities (including Israeli 160-Imp gal/727-litre drop-tanks), ECM/ESM/IRCM equipment and (for the IIIRS) infra-red reconnaissance pods.

Interceptor Mirages were delivered in natural metal and the reconnaissance aircraft in upper surface green and grey. Following upgrading in the late 1980s, an overall two-tone light grey has been adopted, this having first been seen on the two IIIDSs when they were delivered.

Above: One of Switzerland's Mirage IIIRS reconnaissance aircraft banks away from the camera ship, showing off the layout of the camera nose and the bulged nosewheel door.

Left: Switzerland's Mirage IIIS interceptors were based on the airframe of the IIIE. They were delivered in natural metal.

Above: The TARAN 18 radar necessitates a pattern of holes on the starboard side of Swiss Mirage IIISs.

Dassault Mirage III/5/50 Variants

Fliegerstaffel 3

Base: Groupement Aérodrome 4, Sion
Badge: a bulldog's head

On 1 January 1992, 3 Squadron was disbanded as a militia Hunter unit at Ambri and its 'number plate' transferred to the Mirage IIIRS detachment permanently based at Payerne.

Fliegerstaffel 4

Base: Groupement Aérodrome 1, Payerne
Badge: a witch over a four-leaved clover

Previously a Hunter squadron of the Militia at Raron, 4 Squadron disbanded on 1 January 1992 and was immediately reborn at Payerne to fly the four Mirage IIIRSs previously operating as an undesignated detachment of 10 Squadron.

Below: A No. 10 Staffel Mirage IIIRS, wearing the unit insignia on its tailfin. Reconnaissance aircraft are going through what amounts to the same FFA upgrade programme as the Swiss fighters and trainers, with new RWRs and fixed canard foreplanes. Vortex generators are not fitted to the pitot on the IIIRS, unlike the upgraded IIIS airframes.

Fliegerstaffel 10

Base: Flugplatz Abteilung 10, Buochs (Stans)
Badge: a stylised eagle's head

All reconnaissance Mirages were issued to 10 Squadron, which has its peacetime HQ at Dubendorf. On 1 January 1992 the detachments of four aircraft each at Sion and Payerne were given squadron numbers 3 and 4.

Above: Fliegerstaffel 10, once the sole IIIRS operator, has always had detachments at Sion and Payerne, but these have now been given their own squadron identities.

Fliegerstaffel 16

Base: Flugplatz Abteilung 10, Buochs (Stans)
Badge: a dragon over the number 16

One of two squadrons operating the Mirage IIIS, Fliegerstaffel 16 has its peacetime HQ at Payerne and a war base at Buochs. Its primary role is attack.

Right: The IIIS fleet has always been pooled between Fliegerstaffeln 16 and 17, and the aircraft therefore wore each unit badge, on opposite sides of the fin.

Below: Fliegerstaffel 16's dragon badge is clearly visible here, on the fin of an AIM-9P-wielding Mirage IIIS. Squadron badges were dropped when camouflage was introduced during the late 1980s.

Left: Switzerland's two Mirage IIIDS trainers were delivered in grey camouflage, and was the first aircraft in this scheme.

A fully modernised Mirage IIIS, with modifications including new RWR and canards, and improved gun blast deflectors.

Fliegerstaffel 17

Base: Groupement Aérodrome 1, Payerne
Badge: an eagle

The second Mirage IIIS squadron is based at Payerne, which is also its war station, in the air defence role.

Right: An AIM-9P Sidewinder-armed Mirage IIIS wearing Fliegerstaffel 17's diving eagle fin badge. Switzerland's Mirage IIIS interceptors were delivered with provision for radar-guided AIM-26B Falcon AAMs, and used AIM-9Bs to augment these. They now tend to rely on late-model AIM-9s, since the AIM-26 is to all intents and purposes obsolete. They could also operate in the ground attack role, the Nord AS30 ASM being one of the weapons of choice, but now being replaced by the AGM-65.

Below: This Mirage IIIS carries an ACMI pod under the port wing, to allow it to use an instrumented air combat manoeuvring range – in this case the BAe-operated range over the North Sea, where the Swiss are regular customers.

Right: An unmodernised Mirage IIIS taxis with RATOG bottles fitted below the rear fuselage.

United States

The DoD designation F-21A was issued to cover Kfir C1s obtained under short-term lease to the Navy and Marine Corps for use as aggressor aircraft. Pending delivery of its Lockheed F-16N Fighting Falcons, the USN arranged for 12 Kfirs to be delivered in 1985, while 13 more were ordered by the USMC in 1986. All had been in storage at Hatzor. The first batch was assigned the serials 163298 to 163309, but all aircraft wore their IDF/AF serial prefixed by 999 to make a six-digit number which would conform to computerised spares requisitioning procedures.

Serial numbers	Quantity
999703, 999709, 999710, 999726, 999728, 999732, 999735, 999739, 999742, 999747, 999786 and 999791	12 (USN)
999708, 999716, 999724, 999725, 999727, 999731, 999734, 999749, 999750, 999764, 999785, 999787 and 999794	13 (USMC)

USN aircraft were delivered in light blue and two-tone grey upper surface camouflage, those of the USMC having three colour schemes. All have now returned to Israel.

The US Navy and US Marine Corps both operated leased IAI Kfirs as adversary aircraft, replacing them with F-16Ns and F-5Es respectively.

VF-43 'Challengers'

Base: NAS Oceana, Virginia
Badge: a mailed fist crushing a MiG

Pilots of VF-43 converted to Kfirs with the IDF/AF before their first three aircraft arrived by sea in April 1985. They displaced Northrop F-5Es, although the squadron retained its McDonnell Douglas A-4E/F and TA-4J Skyhawks. All were in service by the following June, maintained under contract by IAS, a US subsidiary of IAI. America paid only for the maintenance, the lease of the aircraft being without charge. After returning creditable 90 per cent serviceability in spite of being flown 300 hours per year, they were withdrawn from service in March 1988, having been replaced by F-16Ns. VF-43's F-21s flew 9,700 hours in 9,800 sorties.

Above: IAI Kfir-C1s were withdrawn from storage and refurbished before being leased to the US Navy as F-21As. The US Navy's VF-43 operated 12.

Right: US Navy Kfirs wore a three-tone blue-grey camouflage scheme, with toned-down national markings and the VF-43 insignia on the fin.

VMFT-401 'Snipers'

Base: MCAS Yuma, Arizona
Badge: none

The first eight of 13 Kfirs for the USMC's adversary training squadron were shipped from Israel in July 1987, allowing VMFT-401 to be commissioned with its new equipment on 13 August 1987. Later availability of ex-USAF Northrop F-5E/Fs obviated the requirement for a foreign aircraft and the Kfir was withdrawn on 28 September 1989.

Below: Some of the US Marine Corps' Kfirs wore the same grey colour scheme as the US Navy aircraft.

Above: Another scheme worn by USMC F-21As was a dark brown, dark green and sand camouflage.

Below: Some VMFT-401 aircraft were painted in one of the standard Israeli camouflage schemes.

Venezuela

The first Venezuelan air force (Fuerzas Aéreas Venezolanas) order for Mirages was a mixed batch of six 5Vs delivered from November 1972, six IIIEV interceptors from May 1973 and three IIIDV trainers from February 1973. An attrition-replacement IIIEV was added in 1977, but continued losses reduced the fleet to six single-seat and two trainer aircraft by 1989, when a contract was placed with Dassault for upgrading to Mirage 50EV/DV standard. At the same time, Venezuela ordered more aircraft in the form of six new 50EVs, three 5Ms from an undelivered Zaïre contract converted to 50EVs, and one new 50DV. The first refurbished FAV aircraft was redelivered on 22 October 1990 and the new-built trainer in March 1991. The Mirage 50EV has canards, Cyrano IVM3 radar, SHERLOC RWR, AN/ALE-40 chaff/flare dispensers, a Thomson VE-110C HUD, ULISS 81 INS and the ability to carry Magic 2 AAMs and Exocet anti-ship missiles. FAV serial numbers are wildly scrambled, as is apparent below.

Serial numbers	Type	Quantity
5471, 7381 and 7512	Mirage IIIDV	3
0624, 2843, 3039, 4058, 6732, 8940 and 9325	Mirage IIIEV	7
1297, 1506, 2473, 5706, 7162 and 9510	Mirage 5V	6
not known	Mirage 50DV	1
0160, 5504 and others	Mirage 50EV	9

Upper surface camouflage is two-tone green, plus brown.

Right: The original Mirage 5V was a non-radar-equipped fighter-bomber, similar to the Mirage 5F. The survivors are being upgraded to modernised Mirage 50EV configuration.

Grupo Aéreo de Caza 11

Base: Base Aérea El Libertador, Palo Negro

Initial Mirage deliveries were made to 12 Wing at Barquisimeto, where Escuadrón 34 equipped with Mirage 5s. On 26 July 1973, 11 Wing formed at Palo Negro with 34 Squadron as its first unit, soon adding Escuadrón 33, equipped with the Mirage IIIs. By 1990, No. 34 had temporarily lost all its Mirages to the upgrade programme in France and No. 33 was down to three aircraft. Both were scheduled to be fully operational with Mirage 50s by 1993.

Right: The Mirage IIIEV is essentially similar to the Armée de l'Air Mirage IIIE, though it does not have an undernose Doppler bulge. The Mirage IIIEV served with Escuadrón 33, while the Mirage 5s served with co-located Escuadrón 34. After the Venezuelan aircraft have been modernised, all will be to a common configuration, with refuelling probes, canards and long noses, and with the same weapons and avionics systems.

Above: A Mirage IIIEV taxis out from the squadrons HAS complex at El Libertador.

Below: Their recent upgrade has revitalised Venezuela's Mirages, adding to their capability.

Above: One of Venezuela's Mirage IIIDVs upgraded to full 50DV standard, including refuelling probe and canard foreplanes. The vortex generators on the nose are particularly noteworthy.

Zaïre

Grandiose plans for three squadrons of Mirages had been reduced to one by the time Zaïre's air force (Force Aérienne Zaïroise) ordered 14 Mirage 5Ms and three 5DM trainers, but even six of the former fell victim to financial problems in between being built and the time of their intended delivery. Just 11 aircraft were delivered in 1975, of which at least five (including two trainers) have been lost in accidents.

Serial numbers	Type	Quantity
M401 to M408	Mirage 5M	8
M201 to M203	Mirage 5DM	3

Of the undelivered aircraft, M411 and M414 went to Gabon, M413 to Egypt (9161), and M409, M410 and M412 to Venezuela. Green and sand upper surface camouflage was applied to FAZ Mirages.

211ᵉ Escadrille

Base: Kamina

Re-equipment of 21ᵉ Escadre de Chasse et d'Assaut with Mirages progressed only as far as its first squadron, which is partnered by 212 Squadron, still flying Aermacchi M.B.326s. Serviceability of the few remaining Mirages is believed to be poor.

Below: The Mirage 5 proved too sophisticated for Zaïre, and serviceability was poor. Three of the 11 aircraft delivered were two-seat Mirage 5DMs, but two of these (and three single-seaters) have been written off.

Left: Zaïrean Mirage 5s were deployed to Chad in that nation's struggles with Libya. This aircraft was written off during operations in Chad, the victim of a landing accident. The unusual two-tone green camouflage colour scheme worn by the aircraft is noteworthy, as is the toned-down national insignia. The Mirages were delivered to 211ᵉ Escadrille of 21ᵉ Escadre de Chasse et d'Assaut at Kamina. One of the squadron's two-seaters reportedly wore a large French roundel and EC 3/3 insignia in Chad.

Mountain Home Super Wing

Photographed by Randy Jolly and Jim Benson

An air force within an air force, the 366th Wing is the first of the so-called 'Super Wings'. Wielding enormous firepower in the form of fighters, bombers and tankers, the 'Gunfighters' are ready to move out at a moment's notice to fight in any part of the globe.

Left: Among the mixed bag of types operated by the 366th Wing is the Lockheed F-16C/D. These provide a multi-role attack/air defence function.

Above: Having its own dedicated tankers allows the wing to deploy rapidly, while the F-15E (right) provides the interdiction muscle for strike operations.

Left and below left: F-15Es of the 391st Fighter Squadron during a tanking session on their way to a bombing exercise. The F-15E is a highly versatile warplane, able to carry large and varied loads into well-defended airspace. This aircraft is armed with free-fall bombs, in this instance inert 2,000-lb-class Mk 84s. They are fitted with the standard low-drag general-purpose fins, indicating a medium-level drop where the aircraft does not have to avoid fragmentation damage. The 391st FS is known as the 'Bold Tigers', and carry an orange/black tiger stripe on the fin-tip.

Above: An F-15E crew prepare for a mission. The twin LANTIRN pods that hang down from the intakes provide the 'Mud Hen' with full night/adverse weather capability, incorporating attack and navigation FLIR, terrain-following radar and laser designation.

Right: The E's crew concentrate on refuelling. Their mount is widely regarded as the world's most capable multi-role warplane.

Below: Even with a full bombload, the F-15E is fast and agile at low level. This allows it to penetrate hostile air space at low level, using TFR commands and FLIR imagery.

Left: View from the back seat as an F-16D takes on fuel at 22,000 ft from one of the wing's **KC-135R** tankers. The cockpit has two **MFD**s (multi-function displays) for showing navigation, systems and weapons data. The dial on the left is the radar warning display, showing information of hostile emitters.

Above: The F-16 is a true multi-role warplane, and can easily switch from air-to-air to air-to-ground missions. This aircraft is configured for a medium-level bomb attack, carrying triplets of Mk 82 500-lb-class **LDGP**s on the wing pylons. The centre pylon has the **AN/ALQ-131 ECM** pod.

Left: *The 'Vipers' of the 366th Wing are F-16C/D Block 25s, fitted with the Pratt & Whitney F100-PW-200 engine. Consequently they are fitted with the small inlet, and are not provided with LANTIRN compatibility.*

Above: *In the 366th Wing organisation, the F-16 is primarily used as an attack platform, as the dedicated air defence mission is assigned to the F-15C. The F-16 squadron is the 389th FS 'Thunderbolts'.*

Below: *Two 'boss-birds' together. The front aircraft carries markings for the 366th Wing, and the word 'Gunfighters' in the fin-stripe. The rear aircraft is marked for the 389th FS commander, and has the unit's yellow lightning bolt fin-marks.*

Mountain Home Super Wing

Above: With the customary 'Eagle Driver' patch on his shoulder, this F-15 pilot 's task is to defend the strike aircraft of the 366th Wing. The F-15C squadron is the 390th FS 'Wild Boars' which, like the 389th and 391st, used to fly F-111s from Mountain Home.

Below: F-15s and F-16s face each other between sorties. The exercises of the 'Gunfighters' regularly involve all of the wing's aircraft types to maximise co-ordination between the disparate forces under the commander's control.

Above: 'Wild Boars' of the 390th FS on patrol. The squadron's air defence tasking is fully integrated with the overall wing mission, the Eagles being used primarily in a sweep and fighter escort role.

Left: The 390th FS 'boss-bird' takes on fuel from a Mountain Home KC-135R. It is wearing the new standard 'Mod Eagle' grey scheme, and has the unit's 'Wild Boars' legend superimposed on the blue fin-band. The legend itself is written in white on a black bar which leads into a boar's head.

Right: An F-15E crew return from their mission past a line of 390th FS F-15Cs. In addition to its own assets, the 366th Wing can quickly call on other USAF units to support a rapid deployment. Most likely are the defence suppression outfits – EF-111A Ravens from Cannon AFB and F-4Gs from Nellis AFB. Further support could come rapidly from reconnaissance and AWACS units.

Above: The 'Gunfighters' 'big stick' is the B-52G, seen here carrying AGM-142s. Although assigned to the 366th Wing, these are not based at Mountain Home, flying instead from Castle AFB, California, with the 34th Bomb Squadron.

Left: Configured for conventional bombing, this Mountain Home 'white-tail' lugs a heavy load of free-fall bombs from the runway. The use of the heavy stores adaptor beam on the wing pylons allows the carriage of 45 bombs.

Right: The 366th's heavies in action – a conventional bomb-armed B-52G edges up to a KC-135R. It is rumoured that the 34th BS aircraft will be the last B-52Gs in active service, and that they will be replaced by Rockwell B-1Bs.

Above: The tankers assigned to the 366th Wing are from the 22nd Air Refueling Squadron, based at Castle AFB alongside the B-52s. These will move to Mountain Home eventually to consolidate all the wing's assets at one base. The tankers are painted with a green fin-band, although the central aircraft here is marked for the 22nd ARS commander, and sports the wing's 'Gunfighters' name and dropped-shadow tailcode.

Below: Emphasising the 366th Wing's conventional warfare role, the B-52s have been issued with the AGM-142 Have Nap stand-off precision attack weapon. Developed by Rafael of Israel as the Popeye, this missile has a 50-mile range and uses inertial guidance for most of its flight. As it approaches the target, the nose-mounted EO/IR seeker allows an airborne operator to control it to a precise aim-point. A 1,955-lb (887-kg) warhead is fitted.

Australasia

Long traditions, a proud history which includes service alongside the mother country in both World Wars, and common origins as Empire-era off-shoots of the British Royal Air Force have given the RAAF and RNZAF a common organisational and rank structure, and similar uniforms and insignia. This continues despite the air forces' present statuses as fully independent organisations with a determinedly Pacific/Far Eastern orientation.

Despite New Zealand's expulsion from the ANZUS defence agreement, it continues to have close links with Australia, exemplified by the presence of A-4Ks at RAN Nowra.

In spite of growing republican sentiments which may soon result in the RAAF becoming the AAF, the Royal Air Forces of Australia (RAAF) and New Zealand (RNZAF) have many common bonds which will outlast the office of Governor General of Australia. In close proximity – at least in relation to the vast geographical area of South East Asia – and sharing a common outlook and language, these two countries possess air arms cast in the image of the RAF. Political and cultural ties with the UK may have been diluted in recent years, yet both the RAAF and RNZAF maintain traditions inherited from their progenitor and remember with pride their predecessors who fought with the RAF in Europe before Pearl Harbor brought World War II closer to home.

Korea, the Malaysian confrontation and Vietnam saw RAAF and RNZAF aircraft again in combat, but for the past two decades the Antipodean air forces have been facing a seemingly insoluble problem which has only recently begun to tax the West's forward planners: lack of a potential enemy. Recent dissolution of the USSR – so unsettling to Western military forces – has had little effect in Australasia, where defensive posture was never dictated by the presence of the Soviet navy. More important will be the forthcoming contraction of the US presence and influence in the South Pacific and South East Asia.

As the origin of current front-line aircraft makes apparent, the USA has replaced Great Britain as the 'natural' source for combat equipment in the RAAF, RNZAF and Royal Australian Navy (RAN). The ANZUS (Australia, New Zealand and US) defence agreement was the vehicle for close collaboration between these three English-speaking nations until New Zealand's expul-

sion in August 1986. Precipitated by anti-nuclear policies of the Wellington government, which resulted in supposedly allied USN ships being refused entry to New Zealand's ports, this exclusion caused noticeable damage to Australasian defence. New Zealand lost its status as an ally of the US, resulting in it being denied access to intelligence and restricted in the acquisition of advanced technology. A new government, elected late in 1990, tacitly dropped the most restrictive anti-nuclear rules but has been unable to capitalise on better relations because of cuts in funding available for new equipment. More harmonious relations between Australia and the US allow for the latter to have receiving and control stations for intelligence-gathering satellites at Pine Gap near Alice Springs and Nurrungar in the Woomera area. A US naval communications centre at Northwest Cape, Western Australia, has recently passed into national hands.

As the USA is to the UK, so is Australia to New Zealand. The larger, more prosperous and more ethnically mixed Australia is a land of great diversity and the logical leader of the partnership. New Zealand, though boasting geographical features including glaciers, fjords and active volcanoes, is more the 'little England' of less harsh climate, constrained by its smaller armed forces to play a subordinate role. That said, its responsibilities are far from insignificant, for its territory includes islands up to 500 miles (805 km) from the main pair and a separate group 2,000 miles (3200 km) distant, plus a self-governing dependency (the Cook Islands). The latter doubles the sea area over which New Zealand has sovereignty. A major air force would have difficulty in policing such a vast area; for the RNZAF, contemplation of such an operation would be an excursion into fantasy.

The Office of Australia's Chief of the Air Staff is allocated this superbly decorated Pilatus PC-9. The PC-9 has now replaced the Aermacchi M.B.326 for basic pilot training.

Even the national aerobatic team, the RAAF's 'Roulettes', have lost their 'Macchis', a withdrawal that was expedited after the discovery of structural problems.

As part of a major reorganisation during recent years, the RAAF has lost all of its helicopters to the army, including Ecureuils used for training and SAR.

Australia

Spanning 2,500 miles (4025 km) from east to west, Australia has a population approaching 16 million – equivalent to half a square kilometre of land for every man, woman and child. Being close to the equator, the northern areas were less popular with European settlers, resulting in a legacy of uneven occupation which favours the south-eastern

region. RAAF bases tend to reflect this pattern in defiance of the self-evident truth that any threat to Australian sovereignty will most likely come - as did the Japanese in 1942 - from the north. Then, the defence strategy for invasion was to fall back to positions in the south, poisoning water supplies in the process. That is not an option today for two

The RAAF retired its Chinooks in June 1989 as an economy measure. All 11 survivors are now scheduled to be upgraded to CH-47D standard for service with the army.

The Hawker Siddeley 748s of No. 32 Squadron, RAAF, are used by the School of Air Navigation at East Sale for training student navigators and AEOs for Australia and New Zealand.

Reflecting the close co-operation between the RAAF and RNZAF, an Australian F/A-18 Hornet buddy refuels from a New Zealand Skyhawk. Co-operation between the two nations was hampered by New Zealand's expulsion from ANZUS, especially where the USA was involved.

Having lost its last A-4 Skyhawks in 1984, the Royal Australian Navy has become an all-rotary-wing air arm, at least in so far as the front line is concerned.

In a misguided attempt to save money, Australia has passed over the initial pilot training and screening role to private contractors, and has lost the Airtrainer-equipped No. 1 FTS.

Australia's S-70B-6 Black Hawks were originally delivered to the RAAF, but were officially absorbed by the army in February 1989, following a 1986 government directive.

Above: The F/A-18 Hornet forms the backbone of Australia's air defence, and also serves in the strike fighter role.

Below: The 'Roulettes' aerobatic team re-equipped with the Pilatus PC-9 in 1988, initially flying as a pair, then as a six-ship.

Privatisation and contractorisation has come to Australia in many forms. Civilian firms are now responsible for fleet requirements and providing target facilities for the Navy.

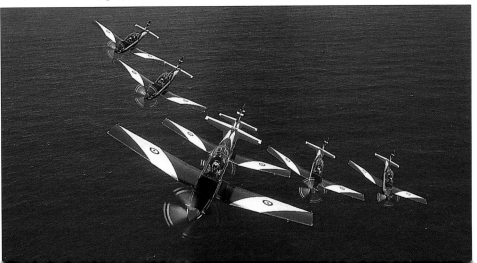

reasons: air and sea resupply would allow a beach-head to be expanded rapidly and, in any event, it is likely that an attacker would not wish to conquer all of Australia, settling instead for political concessions in respect of land occupied.

The three armed services are now concentrating more of their efforts in the 'Top End' of Australia. Infrastructure and population do not permit a full-blown realignment of military bases, but experience is being accumulated in operating regular detachments in the area and the means are being assembled to get there in a hurry, if need be. This requires regular combined forces exercises and even, in the case of the army, changing olive-green camouflage dating from the Vietnam era to a mottled pattern of tan, green and black which more accurately represents the northern scrub land. Patrol of northern waters has the dual purpose of dissuading illegal activities, the thousands of miles of deserted coastline being a gift to smugglers.

Until April 1988, forward-basing policy involved the RAAF supplying a permanent squadron (previously two) of Dassault Mirage IIIs at Butterworth, Malaysia. The replacement McDonnell Douglas Hornets now make only two deployments per year to the same base to keep crews familiar with operating in the area. Australia is a key element, with the UK and New Zealand, in the Five-Power Defence Agreement of 1971, which provides the means by which Malaysia and Singapore can receive military assistance in the event of being attacked. Regular exercises are held to test the readiness of the associated Integrated Air Defence System, the RAF periodically detaching combat aircraft from the UK to participate.

Nearer to home, military assistance is provided to the former possession of Papua New Guinea, which gained independence from Australia in September 1975. Finance and training is given to the PNG Defence Force and, although there is no formal defence treaty, an understanding between the two governments would most likely result in Australian armed forces being used to defend Papua if it were to be threatened. Indonesia, once viewed as the pro-Moscow threat, has more cordial relations with Australia which extend to occasional joint convoy protection exercises. Plans are for these to be augmented by Indonesian participation in air defence exercises over northern Australia.

Coincident with the withdrawal of the

RAAF to Australian territory, a programme was launched to provide a chain of 'bare bases' along the northern coastline and raise the former bare base at Tindal to fully operational status. The last-mentioned received its initial resident unit when the Hornets of No. 75 Squadron moved in on 1 October 1988, although the official opening did not take place until 31 March 1989. Tindal, located in the north-central region, is the first RAAF base to have dispersals and protected aircraft pens along lines long common is Europe. RAAF Curtin, in the north-west, was opened in June 1988 as the vanguard of the new emergency bases and the first major military airfield built since the end of World War II.

In December 1992, a go-ahead was given for construction by 1999 of RAAFB Frederick Sherger, near Weipa on the north-eastern peninsula of Cape York. Like Curtin, it will have an underground operations room and dispersed facilities, but nothing stronger than a wall-less maintenance 'hangar' to protect its aircraft. Except for times of air defence exercises, bare bases are manned by a skeleton staff, although Curtin is used as a transit base for Lockheed Orion maritime patrollers. Even so, its temporary use by No. 75 Squadron's Hornets in Exercise Western Reward required 65 truckloads of supplies to be brought from throughout Australia. Existing airfields at Darwin, Learmonth and Townsville complete the coverage of the northern coastline.

Learmonth, another pre-existing bare base, was also activated for a fortnight in October 1992 for Exercise Western Reward. This was the first product of closer defence links being forged between Australia and Singapore outside the Five-Power Agreement and involved eight Northrop F-5Es, four Lockheed F-16A Fighting Falcons and a Lockheed KC-130B tanker of the RSAF operating with RAAF Hornets, General Dynamics F-111Cs and Boeing 707 tankers. Bilateral defence exercises are expected to become increasingly common in the region, as evidenced by the 1992 agreement under which Singapore is allowed to base fighter aircraft in Australia for 10 months of each year. Australasian democracies are reluctant to enter into additional treaties of a formal nature, but are keen to develop defence liaison through other routes. In this way, Australia could further strengthen its position as a 'first among equals' in Australasian defence.

No. 1 Squadron's F-111s wear a variety of tail flashes, the newest with the unit's crest.

This stylised '1' and Kookaburra is worn by No. 1's display mount.

No. 1 Squadron's F-111s commonly wear a simple yellow flash, with no superimposed insignia. The yellow patch on the nose is a waterproof cover for the avionics bay.

A No. 6 Squadron RF-111C lands. No. 6 Squadron's F-111s wear a blue fin flash, usually with the unit's boomerang insignia in a central white disc.

No. 6 Squadron painted one aircraft in special markings to celebrate 20 years of F-111 operations. No. 6 operates four RF-111Cs, four F-111A(C)s and four standard F-111Cs.

Royal Australian Air Force

Autonomous since 1921, the RAAF has recently completed a re-equipment programme for its front-line fighter force and organised units for rapid redeployment to northern bases in addition to the longer-standing commitment to forward defence in Malaysia and Singapore. Central to this new strategy has been the formation, in July 1988, of the tri-service Northern Command, which combines RAAF, army and navy units in Northern Territory and the Kimberley area of Western Australia (WA). Omitted from

the balanced force needed to defend the 'Top End' of the country from attack is a squadron of at least three airborne early warning aircraft which has long been sought by the RAAF.

Instead, following trials with a prototype Jindalee over-the-horizon radar (OTHR) at Alice Springs, two stations were authorised in 1991 at Laverton, WA, and Longreach, Queensland (Qld), the co-ordination centre for their data being at Edinburgh. Due for completion by 1997, these are far from a per-

The sensor pack contains a Honeywell AN/AAD-5 IRLS, two TV cameras, low-altitude KA-56E (two) and high-altitude KA-93 panoramic cameras, and a pair of KS-87C oblique cameras.

Australia's original batch of 24 F-111Cs has been augmented by four ex-USAF F-111As delivered in 1982 and modified to a similar standard, these offsetting the operational losses up to that time. One more has been lost since, along with one of the four aircraft converted to RF-111 standards.

No. 6 Squadron's traditional crest incorporates a boomerang and the appropriate motto 'Nous Reviendrons'.

Instead of the ornate full crest, the blue fin-flash of No. 6 Squadron's F-111s sometimes bears a simple boomerang in a plain white disc.

A recce F-111 was planned from the start and a single RF-111A was flown with Westinghouse AN/APD-8 SLARs, IRLS and KA-55/KA-56 cameras. The production RF-111D was cancelled and it was not until 1979 that the first of four F-111Cs was converted to RF-111C configuration.

fect solution to the problem of locating a hostile force, in view of the comparative newness of OTHR. Reported to be capable of picking up an air or sea contact at ranges up to 1,000 nm (1,150 miles; 1850 km), Jindalee officially replaces plans for a large AEW aircraft such as the Boeing E-3 Sentry. Although a short-range airborne warning aircraft is still seen as necessary to complement Jindalee, its procurement seems unlikely and the RAAF will have to make do with more air-transportable (Hercules) tactical radars for control of Hornet interceptions. Also in 1988, Australia initiated a programme to develop a National Air Defence and Airspace Control System and re-organised its 'sharp end' – Operational Command – for increased responsiveness to the new defence strategy.

Aircraft of all three armed services are serialled in a recently unified system which has some aspects of a local type designation. A type number is assigned to aircraft on entry into service – some of the early digits now having been used three times. Letter prefixes are 'A' to indicate the RAAF/army and 'N' for the navy; for example, A21 – F/A-18 Hornet RAAF; N22 – Eurocopter Squirrel RAN; A23 – Pilatus PC-9/A RAAF; N24 – Sikorsky S-70B RAN; A25 – Sikorsky S-70A AAAC. Any aircraft exchanged between forces will modify their prefixes, such as AAAC Bell JetRanger A17-005 which became RAN N17-005, or RAN Aermacchi M.B.326 N14-087 to RAAF A7-087, an allocation dating from the days of separate A and N numbering series. The final three digits may begin at 001 or be based on the aircraft constructor's number or previous serial. National markings featuring a red kangaroo were introduced gradually during the mid-1950s to replace the cockade inherited from the United Kingdom.

Operational Command

Subordinate to the RAAF HQ at Canberra, Operational Command is located at Glenbrook, near Sydney, New South Wales (NSW), with responsibility for combat aircraft, air transport and operational training. Its 1988 reorganisation created five component groups, each equipped to perform a specific function: Strike-Reconnaissance, Tactical Fighter, Maritime Patrol, Air Lift and Tactical Transport Groups. Most of these groups contain a single wing, the maintenance element of which is a squadron numbered 400 or above, e.g., No. 482 Squadron of No. 82 Wing.

Strike/Reconnaissance Group (No. 82 Wing)

Ordered in 1963 for 1968 delivery at a cost for 24 aircraft of $A112 million, the General Dynamics F-111C eventually arrived in RAAF service during 1973, priced at $A324 million. In spite of this less than propitious start to its career, the F-111 has become a valued element of the RAAF and a potent weapon for both reconnaissance and strike (or 'attack', if 'strike' is restricted to its NATO context of nuclear delivery). Exclusive to Australia – indeed, the RAAF is the only foreign 'Aardvark' user – the F-111C is a hybrid of F-111A and FB-111A, including the latter's increased wing span, strengthened undercarriage and higher operating weight, but retaining lower-powered Pratt & Whitney TF30-P-3 turbofans and early-style air intakes.

To make good attrition, four ex-USAF F-111As were bought in 1982 and delivered from May. They were modified at Amberley by No. 3 Aircraft Depot, the F-111 major overhaul centre, where wings and undercarriage were brought to F-111C standard although the original wing carry-through box was retained. More recently, in October 1992, it was announced that Australia was to buy 15 surplus F-111Gs from the USAF, together with 12 spare engines. By mid-1993, four of the F-111Gs had been transferred to McClellan AFB, California, in preparation for ferrying to Australia in September, the others due before the end of the year after service at Cannon AFB, New Mexico. F-111Gs will be stored as a long-term source of spare parts and only a few will enter service in future years to replace any of the existing force lost in accidents. It is now envisaged that the F-111 fleet's life will be extended 10 years to a new retirement date of 2020.

Survivors of the original 24 aircraft have been subjected to several modification programmes, beginning in May 1979 with the first flight at GD's Fort Worth plant of a prototype RF-111C conversion. Three more followed from the RAAF's No. 3 Aircraft Depot by 1981, all having a sensor pack in the weapons bay comprising two TV cameras, an IR linescan, two low-altitude panoramic cameras, one high-altitude panoramic and a split pair of vertical cameras. The remaining 16 F-111Cs were modified with the ability to carry Ford Aerospace AN/AVQ-26 Pave Tack target tracking and designation systems, as fitted to USAF F-111Fs, although only 10 of the underfuselage pods were purchased, to be moved between aircraft. All four F-111A(C)s were similarly upgraded. Once again, all but the first modification were performed by No. 3 AD, from where redeliveries began in September 1985.

Pave Tack gives precision delivery capability with the 500-lb Mk 82 and 2,000-lb Mk 84 bombs in their laser-guided form as GBU-12 and GBU-10. The RAAF has also obtained the winged CBU-15 version of Mk 84 but can use it only within visual range, as the datalink pods necessary for long-distance TV guidance have not been funded. In anti-shipping roles, the F-111C/A(C) may carry up to four McDonnell Douglas AGM-84 Harpoon sea-skimming missiles, trials of which began at NAS China Lake, California, in July 1982, on an F-111C of the RAAF's Aircraft Research & Development Unit. For close air support – a hazardous duty for such a high-value asset – the F-111 can be armed

with the locally-designed Karinga cluster bomb. AIM-9L Sidewinder AAMs provide self-defence and the Texas Instruments AGM-88A HARM is being incorporated to add offensive or defensive anti-radar capability.

One problem hindering integration of new weapons in the 'Pig' (as its crews affectionately call the F-111) has been the dated analog avionics. Following the scrapping of a 1986 plan to replace F-111s in the late 1990s by a follow-on batch of 25 Hornets, an Avionics Upgrade Programme (AUP) to include conversion of 70 per cent of systems to digital operation via a MIL STD 1553B digital databus was launched in 1988. Rockwell was awarded the contract in August 1990 and is also upgrading the AN/APG-110 terrain-following and AN/APQ-113 attack radars and flight control system, as well as fitting a new navigation and communications suite, including a dual Honeywell H-423 ring-laser gyro INS. The programme involves all 22 aircraft, including the RF-111Cs, the first (A8-132) having been delivered to Rockwell at Palmdale, California, in May 1991 - incidentally, wearing a new overall-grey colour scheme being considered as a replacement for the current green and brown. Ground testing was due to begin in mid-1993, leading to a first flight in February 1994 and a year of performance testing beginning in the third quarter of the year. The remaining 21 will be modified at Amberley by Hawker-de Havilland, the first roll-out also due in July 1995. The total cost of upgrading the fleet, buying surplus F-111Gs and investing in related test equipment is estimated to be $A700 million, compared with the $A7,000 million which would have been needed to fund new aircraft as replacements. Amberley, near Brisbane, Qld, has been the home of RAAF bombers since the days of the Avro Lincoln and currently hosts Nos 1 and 6 Squadrons sharing the F-111 fleet. No. 1 is a pure F-111C operator, with 10 aircraft, while No. 6 has the non-standard RF-111Cs and F-111A(C)s as well as four F-111Cs, including one detached to the ARDU for trials. The latter unit is also responsible for crew training. No. 1 Squadron identifies its aircraft with a yellow lightning flash and a kookaburra badge, while No. 6 employs a boomerang marking and blue flash.

Strike/Reconnaissance Group (No. 82 Wing)

UNIT	EQUIPMENT	BASE
No. 1 Squadron	F-111C	Amberley
No. 6 Squadron	F-111A(C), RF-111C, F-111C	Amberley

Tactical Fighter Group (No. 81 Wing)

For many years, budgetary constraints have obliged the RAAF to operate a single type of aircraft for both interceptor and fighter-bomber duties. Dassault's Mirage III served

well in these roles until a protracted evaluation of potential replacements eventually resulted in the McDonnell Douglas Hornet becoming the current defender of Australian

Above: The winged grenade badge of No. 3 Squadron, as worn on the unit's F/A-18s.

No. 3 Squadron's Hornets wear a representation of the Southern Cross on their fins.

Above: A No. 3 Squadron F/A-18 armed with a practice bomb dispenser/rocket launcher. The Hornet fulfils tactical fighter and air defence roles in Australian service.

Above: No. 2 OCU Hornets wear a tiger's head and black/yellow chevron.

The fin of No. 77 Squadron's 75th anniversary aircraft, with the unit's Fleur-de-Lys.

Above: No. 77 Squadron's markings are a simple black chevron on the fin, and a stripe along the spine bisected by the unit's 'grumpy monkey' badge.

Above: One No. 77 Squadron Hornet wears an experimental overall dark grey colour scheme. Squadron markings are thinly outlined in white.

Above: A No. 2 OCU Hornet pulls hard, its LERXes generating the powerful vortices which give the F/A-18 its magnificent high-Alpha capability. The unit has a mix of single- and two-seat F/A-18s and provides Hornet conversion and advanced fighter combat instructor training.

This Avon-engined Commonwealth Sabre is operated in No. 75 Squadron colours, and is the last airworthy example of the variant.

Above: No. 75 Squadron's current mount, the F/A-18, is less gaudily decorated, with a diamond pattern on the fin-tip and a magpie on the spine.

Above: No. 77 Squadron celebrated its 75th anniversary during 1991, and painted up the boss's F/A-18 in this subdued but attractive colour scheme. Four RAAF Hornet units form No.81 Wing (the Tactical Fighter Group) at RAAF Williamtown, with only No. 75 Squadron elsewhere, at Tindal.

skies. The Air Staff Requirement for a Mirage successor was issued in December 1971 under the initials TFF - Tactical Fighter Force – but changes of government and re-ordering of priorities, combined with assessments of numerous candidates, considerably extended the selection process. At length, on 20 October 1981, the Hornet was pronounced the winner and recipient of an order for 75 aircraft, including 18 two-seat operational trainers.

A requirement for significant local participation in the programme was met by final assembly in Australia of all except the first two aircraft. The US-built machines were the initial pair of trainers, handed over in America on 29 October 1984 following the maiden flight on 13 August. After crew training with the US Navy at NAS Lemoore, California, the two arrived in Australia on 7 May 1985 to join the first aircraft from the assembly line at Avalon, Victoria (Vic). This was the third trainer, rolled out on 16 November 1984 and flown on 26 February 1985. Prime contractor was the Government Aircraft Factory (which became Aerospace Technologies of Australia in 1987), while Commonwealth Aircraft Corporation (Hawker de Havilland Victoria from 1986) handled assembly and testing of General Electric F404 turbofans required for the project: 158, plus 17 assembled from modules and seven built in the USA. The last of the F/A-18B trainers was received in December 1988 and the final F/A-18A on 16 May 1990.

The Hornet had been chosen for its twin-engined safety factor, scope for further upgrading and ability to carry a wide range of ordnance, including radar-guided AAMs for all-weather interception. Changes to the American specification include addition of HF radio, ILS/VOR (replacing the carrier landing system), provision for a reconnaissance pack, landing light, Martin-Baker seat harnesses, improved video/voice recorder and fatigue data recorder, and the deletion of the catapult attachment points on the nosewheel leg. Standard armament includes the AIM-7 Sparrow and AIM-9L Sidewinder AAMs, AGM-88 HARM anti-radiation missile, AGM-84 Harpoon for anti-shipping missions, 2,000-lb laser-guided bombs, free-fall/retarded bombs and practice weapons. A few have a reconnaissance pallet in place of the internal 20-mm M61 cannon.

No. 2 OCU became the initial Hornet operator in 1985, starting its first conversion course in August with three students, all four of the aircraft then delivered to the RAAF and the six instructors trained by VFA-125 at Lemoore. The first of two Sperry Corporation simulators was delivered to Williamtown in June 1985, while less sophisticated training aids – such as one to familiarise pilots with HOTAS controls – have also been installed. In addition to pilot conversion, the OCU runs 18-week Advanced Fighter Combat Instructor courses once every two years, the graduates receiving postings either to the three Hornet operating squadrons or the OCU staff.

Likewise, at Williamtown, No. 3 Squadron took delivery of its first pair of Hornets on 29 August 1986, a former existence as a Mirage unit having ended in Malaysia on the previous

31 March. No. 77 Squadron at Williamtown was issued with Hornets from 29 June 1987, No. 75 – the third and final ex-Mirage unit – following from May 1988. The last-mentioned re-equipped at Darwin prior to its transfer to the Northern Territory (NT) base of Tindal in October 1988, its remote location qualifying it for the services of a pair of ASTA Nomad light transports assigned to the base for liaison and transport of urgent spares and supplies. Having made goodwill visits to Malaysia and Singapore in 1986, Hornets went overseas on business in March-April 1987 when six of No. 3 Squadron and three of No. 77 took part in Exercise Willoh 87 in New Zealand. Regular Asian deployments began in September 1988, with the intention of having Hornets deployed in either Singapore or Malaysia for a total of 16 weeks per year.

Exercise Pitch Black, a little later in 1987, was a more elaborate test of Australian air defences, involving USAF B-52s and F-4s as well as Australian F-111s and other aircraft types all enlisted on the 'enemy' side. As the only Hornet squadron then equipped, No. 3 was assisted by Mirages of Nos 75 and 77, making their last appearance in a major exercise. Also in 1987, Hornets of No. 3 Squadron operated from Clark AFB, Philippines, during Exercise Cope Thunder. Deployments of Hornets to Asia have been expedited by the availability of Boeing 707 tankers, the first such non-stop flight being made by six aircraft of No. 3 Squadron which undertook the 4,350-mile (7000-km) flight to Butterworth on 18 September 1990. Closer to home, the improved northern defences were tested in October-November 1992 by Exercise Aces North, in which Tindal's No. 75 Squadron was heavily involved in repulsing attacks from USAF and USMC aircraft.

The remarkably low number of just four Hornets had been lost during the first eight years of service. Survivors are expected to remain in use until at least 2010, assuming the aircraft reach their full fatigue life of 6,000 hours. In 1992, Canada and Australia began a joint programme of fatigue testing in view of the fact that their more severe usage of the aircraft (in comparison with the US Navy) was expected to curtail operational life. By timely modification, it is hoped to restore - and possibly exceed - the 6,000-hour limit. Ensuring that there are sufficient pilots to fly the Hornet has been another unforeseen problem. Many were tempted to civilian operators during the 1980s and, after the situation stabilised in 1991, there was an unsatisfactory one-to-one ratio. The target is two pilots per Hornet, to be achieved over an unspecified period.

No sooner had the last Hornet rolled from the Avalon assembly line than ASTA began an upgrade programme for the fleet, bringing the RAAF aircraft up to the operational equivalent of the F/A-18C and D. The first modified Hornet was completed in September 1990 and most have now followed it into the factory for a rebuild that takes approximately 10 weeks. Aircraft capabilities currently exceed RAAF resources in some areas

– for example, a newly-gained provision for carrying the AIM-120 AMRAAM has yet to be utilised. New mission computers, armament control processor, stick-top, data storage set, data transfer equipment, revised flight management system, improved ECM and the addition of target designation capability have all been incorporated. In terms of 'add-ons', however, the RAAF has only made use of the ability to integrate a Northrop AN/ALQ-162 radar jammer and add the Texas Instruments AN/AAS-38 FLIR/designator pod. In the longer term, it is planned to upgrade the Hughes AN/APG-65 radar to AN/APG-73 standard and convert the 16,000-lb st (71.1-kN) F404-400 reheated turbofans to -402s of 17,600 lb st (78.3 kN).

Tactical Fighter Group, commanded by the OC RAAFB Williamtown, includes all four Hornet operators, as well as two training squadrons (discussed below) with Aermacchi M.B.326s. The four Williamtown squadrons form No. 81 Wing, the ground element of which includes No. 481 Squadron, responsible for Hornet maintenance and the training of technical personnel. The OCU has 14 aircraft in approximately equal measures of both versions; the other three squadrons use 16, of which one is an F/A-18B. A tiger's face upon a black and yellow flash is applied to the fins of OCU Hornets, the other three squadrons having both a fin marking and an element of their badge applied to the spine, flanked by a black arrow. No. 3 Squadron has its official fleur-de-lys and a Southern Cross tail decoration; No. 75, an Australian Magpie and black/white fin-top diamonds; and No. 77 an oriental lion (colloquially known as a 'grumpy monkey'), complemented by a black 'speedbird' on the fin. In 1992, No. 77 was experimenting with at least one Hornet in an overall dark grey camouflage.

In combination, the Hornets, Jindalee radars and reconstructed northern airfields form the basis of the National Air Defence and Airspace Control System. NADACS also includes three control and reporting units, each equipped with a Westinghouse AN/TPS-43 radar. No. 2 CRU is at Darwin and No. 3 CRU at Williamtown, while No. 114 CRU is a mobile unit normally at Amberley. Formerly comprising No. 41 Wing, the three have been attached to No. 81 Wing since 1990.

Providing training and support, Nos 25 and 76 Squadrons are now the sole users of the Aermacchi M.B.326H following the type's replacement by Pilatus PC-9s within Training Command. Co-production by Commonwealth Aircraft Corporation in 1967-72 gave the RAAF 87 'Macchis', to which eight survivors of 10 naval examples were added in mid-1983. Of these, 82 had completed a life-extension programme by 1985, measures including new components for wings, fuselage and fin, as well as cockpit and avionics improvements. No. 25 Squadron (which has the badge of a black swan swimming) at Pearce is assigned to post-graduate tactical and combat training as well as provision of RAN fleet requirements off the West Coast. At Williamtown, in the east, No. 76 Squadron formed on 1 January 1989 with 16

Above: No. 75 Squadron, based at far-flung Tindal, operates a pair of GAF Nomads for liaison and light transport duties. These wear No. 75 Squadron markings on the fin.

Above: A toned-down M.B.326H of No. 25 Squadron. Based at Pearce, it is used as a holding unit for pilots from the PC-9, providing a short fast-jet tour before type conversion.

Above: The formation of No. 25 Squadron was made possible by the re-equipment of No. 2 FTS with the PC-9. Some aircraft initially wore the orange and white training colours.

Above: No. 76 Squadron operates four Commonwealth CA-25 Winjeels in the forward air controller training role, with another FAC-converted airframe in storage.

Above: The grey/green NATO-style camouflage with light grey undersides (as worn by this Macchi) has largely given way to an overall dark grey.

Above and right: No. 76's M.B.326s wear overall grey, with red/black fin stripes.

Left: The black swan badge of No. 25 Squadron, as applied to an orange/white 'Fanta can Macchi'.

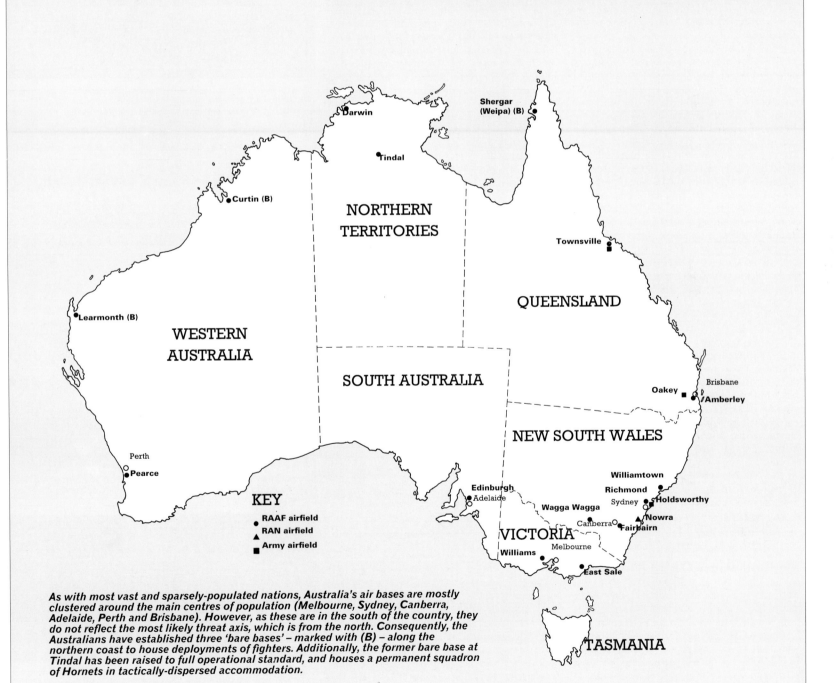

Shergar (Weipa) (B)

Darwin

Tindal

Curtin (B)

NORTHERN TERRITORIES

Townsville

QUEENSLAND

Learmonth (B)

WESTERN AUSTRALIA

SOUTH AUSTRALIA

Oakey — Brisbane

Amberley

NEW SOUTH WALES

Perth
Pearce

Williamtown
Richmond
Sydney — Holdsworthy

Edinburgh
Adelaide

Wagga Wagga

KEY

● RAAF airfield
▲ RAN airfield
■ Army airfield

Canberra
Fairbairn
Nowra

VICTORIA

Williams

Melbourne

East Sale

TASMANIA

As with most vast and sparsely-populated nations, Australia's air bases are mostly clustered around the main centres of population (Melbourne, Sydney, Canberra, Adelaide, Perth and Brisbane). However, as these are in the south of the country, they do not reflect the most likely threat axis, which is from the north. Consequently, the Australians have established three 'bare bases' – marked with **(B)** – along the northern coast to house deployments of fighters. Additionally, the former bare base at Tindal has been raised to full operational standard, and houses a permanent squadron of Hornets in tactically-dispersed accommodation.

'Macchis' for lead-in ground attack training for the Hornet and F-111 forces, as well as army and navy support and provision of dissimilar air combat targets for Hornets.

No. 25 ('City of Perth') Squadron is unusual in that it was raised to 'regular' status on 1 December 1989, having been a unit of the RAAF Emergency Reserve. Its companions are No. 21 ('City of Melbourne') at Laverton, No. 22 ('City of Sydney') at Richmond, No. 23 ('City of Brisbane') at Amberley and No. 24 ('City of Adelaide') at Edinburgh, each staffed by Reservists who serve between 32 and 100 days per year to support the aircraft stationed at their base. Initially, No. 25 continued to rely heavily on Reservist support as it built up towards a planned strength of 20 aircraft - most of them camouflaged - made surplus by the re-equipment of co-located No. 2 FTS. Newly graduated pilots fly between one and two years on the M.B.326 before posting to the Hornet OCU.

Despite the comparatively recent upgrade, M.B.326s have suffered serious structural problems which have left the RAAF and the other armed forces short of comparatively inexpensive air support. When examination of an aircraft which crashed in November 1990 revealed the probability of wing failure, the fleet of 69 was grounded for examination. By the end of 1992, two badly affected 'Macchis' had been repaired for trials with beefed-up wings, but this potential solution proved unsatisfactory. Instead, it was decided early in 1993 to buy 19 sets of new wings from Aermacchi and to rotate low-houred machines through squadron usage to achieve a pool of 29-30 aircraft in use at any one time. Even the rewinged aircraft are expected to be subject to operating restrictions, prompting plans (abandoned in June 1993 before implementation) for the RAAF to buy flying time on New Zealand's M.B.339CBs.

A long-standing RAAF requirement (AFST 5045) for an M.B.326 replacement began to make progress in mid-1993 when the Chief of Staff toured Europe to fly in the BAe Hawk 100, Aermacchi M.B.339C, CASA C.101DD Aviojet and Dassault Alpha Jet NG. The McDonnell Douglas T-45 Goshawk has also been assessed. Requirements are for up to 35 lead-in trainers for the Hornet to enter service in 2000. Additionally, there is a move to acquire a 'day fighter' to be based on the chosen trainer, but that will depend upon the finance available. A licence-production agreement of March 1991 between British Aerospace and ASTA for the BAe Hawk 100/200 clearly indicates one likely dual-role contender for the order.

TFG's equipment is completed by the Commonwealth CA-25 Winjeel, a radial-engined trainer sometimes confused (at least by those old enough to remember that aircraft) with the Percival Provost. An indigenous design (the Aboriginal name, one of which is assigned to all local aviation products, means 'Young Eagle') dating from 1949, the Winjeel is used for training forward air controllers. Having entered the role for no better reason than that there was a surplus of these machines in the pilot training fleet at the same time that Australian involvement in the Vietnam War was increasing the demand for FACs, it has proved to be a rugged and dependable platform from which to learn the controller's task.

Of 14 Winjeels converted for FAC with additional radio equipment and a centreline rack for 12 Mk 18 smoke grenades, four have been lost. At any time four of the survivors are in service and the remainder are stored at Dubbo, NSW, along with four unconverted trainers. Operational aircraft have been attached to No. 2 OCU (from 1968), then No. 4 FAC Flight (from 1 April 1970), but now form 'C' Flight of No. 76 Squadron. Transferred to the last-mentioned on its formation on the first day of 1989, Winjeels wear grey and green camouflage and the squadron's fin badge of a panther's head. Supplementary duties include aerial reconnaissance, range safety patrols and training for army Air Contact Officers who normally organise air attacks from the ground. Recently fitted with ADF, DME and a transponder, the aircraft are expected to remain in use for several more years.

Tactical Fighter Group

UNIT	EQUIPMENT	BASE
Direct Reporting		
No. 25 Sqn	M.B.326H	Pearce
No. 81 Wing		
No .3 Sqn	F/A-18A	Williamtown
No. 75 Sqn	F/A-18A	Tindal
No. 76 Sqn	M.B.326H Winjeel	Williamtown
No. 77 Sqn	F/A-18A	Williamtown
No. 2 OCU	F/A-18A/B	Williamtown
Base Flight	Nomad	Tindal

Maritime Patrol Group (No. 92 Wing)

Adopting UK practice, Australia assigns its maritime patrol force to the air arm, rather than naval aviation. Since retirement of Lockheed P-2 Neptunes from No. 10 Squadron at Townsville, Qld, in December 1977, MPG has been equipped entirely with Lockheed P-3 Orions and based wholly at Edinburgh, South Australia (SA). Its two operational squadrons, Nos 10 and 11, are backed by No. 292 Squadron (part of Training Command) as the OCU (borrowing aircraft as required) and No. 492 Squadron with 650 technicians for the maintenance task, the whole comprising No. 92 Wing. There is a continuous presence of two Orions at Butterworth, Malaysia, maintained by the squadrons on four-month rotations.

Australia's first Orions were P-3Bs deliv-

Above: A No. 12 Squadron P-3C Update II Orion lands at Butterworth, Malaya, where Australia maintains a permanent two-aircraft Orion detachment.

Above: Even before the toning down of the RAAF Orion fleet, No. 10 Squadron's markings were not very colourful, consisting of a harpooned shark on a white band.

Above: Australia's Orions were toned-down during the late 1980s and early 1980s, losing their colourful squadron and national insignia. This aircraft belongs to No. 11 Squadron.

Above: The Falcon 900s of No. 34 Squadron at Fairbairn have replaced a collection of HS.748s, Falcon 20s and BAC One Elevens.

Above: The port Flight Refuelling Mk. 32B HDU (hose drum unit) of a No. 33 Squadron Boeing 707-338C. All four -338Cs have been converted as tankers.

No. 11 Squadron re-equipped with P-3C Update II.5s between 1984 and 1986. These aircraft are locally known as P-3Ws, and have Elta ESM equipment in place of the AN/ALQ-78.

All Australian Orions have British Marconi AQS-901 sonobuoy processing equipment, and use Australian Barra buoys. This aircraft wears No. 11 Squadron markings.

Above: A P-3W, (better known as a P-3C Update II.5) of No. 11 Squadron drops a Barra Sonobuoy. The Aussie Orions have British GEC-Marconi AQS-901 sonobuoy processing equipment. Weapons options include the AGM-84 Harpoon ASM and Mk. 46 torpedos.

Many Australian Orions wear the badge of No. 492 Squadron, a non-flying unit which maintains the aircraft.

Above: Australia replaced its ageing P-3Bs with P-3C Update IIs (No. 10 Squadron) and Update II.5s (No. 11 Squadron). No. 11's badge is a gull.

ered to No. 11 Squadron in 1968. The P-3C Update II was ordered in May 1975, 10 aircraft going to No. 10 Squadron between May 1978 and January 1979 following the first hand-over (in the USA for training with VP-31 at Moffett Field) the previous February. Their arrival coincided with the introduction of a 200-nm (230-mile/370-km) exclusive economic zone around Australia's 12,000-mile (19310-km) coastline, but reductions from 1,200 to 700 hours per year in individual Orion flying hours introduced in 1987/88 have resulted in inshore patrols being taken over by civilian Rockwell Shrike Commanders, IAI Seascans and GAF Nomads. Three radar-equipped Nomads and 12 'visual' Commanders fly 7,450 hours per year on inshore tasks over northern waters, augmented by the 4,600 hours contributed by three more elaborately-equipped Seascans penetrating up to 600 nm (690 miles/1110 km). To this, the RAAF adds just 250 Orion hours, including nocturnal operations from Darwin and Townsville using night-vision goggles or flares to investigate suspect vessels.

The first P-3Cs to be exported, No. 10's machines differed from their USN counterparts in having British GEC-Marconi AQS-901 sonics processing equipment and the Australian Defence Department Barra sonobuoy in place of American equivalents. The decision to install the Barra system (which is also in RAF Nimrod MR.Mk 2s) was not taken until after the first batch of Orions was ordered, although it was retrofitted shortly after the P-3C-IIs were delivered. McDonnell Douglas AGM-84 Harpoon anti-ship missiles were added to the armoury of Mk 46 torpedoes and Mk 82 500-lb (226-kg) mines in 1981 and first test-fired in April of the following year.

Differences between the digital P-3C and analog P-3B were such that plans to upgrade No. 11 Squadron's aircraft with AQS-901/Barra were shelved and an order placed in June 1982 for 10 P-3C Update II.5s, which

'City of Sydney' is one of two Boeing 707-338Cs acquired in 1983 to augment the first pair of ex-Qantas aircraft. All four were converted to two-point 'probe-and-drogue' tanker configuration, the first being redelivered in April 1991. Two 707-368C aircraft acquired in 1988 were to have been converted to flying boom tankers for the F-111 fleet.

were supplied between November 1984 and May 1986. Fitted with AQS-901 (in Australia) from the outset, they received the local designation P-3W to differentiate them from earlier aircraft. These same Orions had their AN/ALQ-78 ESM equipment replaced by new kit from Elta of Israel in 1991, installation being by AWA Defence Industries. The remaining nine Update II aircraft are understood to be scheduled for ESM upgrading in 1993/94. Under normal circumstances, Orions could also be differentiated by their squadron insignia on the fin: a speared Northern Chimaera (fish) for No. 10 and seagull for No. 11, although the aircraft are actually operated in a pool and drawn by units as needed. Furthermore, from 1990, some began appearing in overall light grey toned-down markings, devoid of badges and serial numbers.

A comprehensive upgrade package has recently been compiled for the 19 surviving Orions following budget authorisation in August 1992. This will include new MAD, acoustic processor and flight instruments, corrosion treatment, new radar (replacing AN/APS-115), a nav/comms upgrade (satcom, GPS and other features) and 3,528 lb (1600 kg) of weight-saving modifications. Work is due to begin in December 1996 and be completed by August 2001, implying that the Orion is scheduled for service until at least 2010. Also announced in 1992 was the

intended purchase of three ex-USN P-3Bs for 'circuit-bashing' and similar non-operational tasks - a sensible step which only highlights the ill-advised move of trading in all the RAAF's P-3Bs to help in financing the second P-3C order.

Orions hone their crews' skills in the annual Fincastle Trophy competition against their counterparts in Canada, New Zealand and the UK, and participate in the biennial Rimpac series of international maritime exercises off Hawaii. They also practice target location for the F-111 force, passing co-ordinates via a secure radio link so that the 'Pigs' can make their attack with precision. Rescue operations are regularly mounted for civilian ships in difficulties, while the residual fisheries protection task typically involves a six-hour transit of the 'Top End' between Townsville and Darwin, surveying 180,000 sq miles (150500 km²) of sea by radar en route.

Maritime Patrol Group (No. 92 Wing)

UNIT	EQUIPMENT	BASE
No. 10 Squadron	P-3C Orion	Edinburgh
No. 11 Squadron	P-3C Orion	Edinburgh

Air Lift Group

With the exception of the DHC-4 Caribous assigned to tactical operations, all RAAF transports and tankers are operated by ALG from its bases at Amberley, Fairbairn and Richmond. Stage lengths which for most air forces would be regarded as international are mere local hops in a country the size of Australia. The most regular out-of-country flights are those to support the Australian detachment in Malaysia, for which reason the RAAF invested in its first pair of ex-Qantas Boeing 707s in April 1979. In June 1983, another pair arrived on newly formed No. 33 Squadron at Richmond from the same source, while two more bought second-hand from Saudi Arabia via Boeing were delivered in March 1988. Though often considered as VIP aircraft, the Boeings fly only 15 per cent of their time in this role. Round-the-world flights every flew months collect and deliver spare parts from suppliers in the USA and Europe and move personnel to new postings, the usual aircraft fit for such missions being 60-80 passengers and six-eight freight pallets.

Also in 1988, Hawker de Havilland Victoria was awarded a contract to convert the first four 707s to tankers using kits supplied by Israel Aircraft Industries and a pair of Mk 32B underwing hose pods from Flight Refuelling Ltd in the UK. The first conversion was due for redelivery in April 1990, but it was delayed a year to 11 April 1991 because of compatibility problems. The primary role for these four tankers is refuelling the Hornet force, although the additional capability has not lessened the ability of the aircraft to perform their passenger and freight carrying

roles, as no extra tanks are fitted. Following an accident, only one of the third pair of 707s remains for regular transport duties. These had been provisionally earmarked for 'flying boom' tanker conversion in the mid-1990s to back up the F-111 arm of the RAAF. No. 33 undertakes its own training, its aids including a simulator bought from Qantas with the first two 707s. It has recently transferred from Richmond to Amberley due to congestion at the former, joint-user airport.

Having been the second after the USAF to order Lockheed Hercules, Australia operates two squadrons of C-130s at Richmond, its original A models having long ago retired. A dozen C-130Es supplied to No. 37 Squadron in 1966-67 operate principally in the strategic role, undertaking long-range transport flights within Australia and to more distant destinations, generating some 9,500 hours per year. This is based on a daily on-line total of seven aircraft, including one assigned to crew training. No. 36 Squadron's aircraft are 12 newer C-130H versions, supplied between July and October 1978 and dedicated to tactical missions. Again, the unit aims to have seven serviceable at all times, of which one is for pilot training and another for tactical training. Shorter flights result in annual generation of about 8,500 flying hours. No. 486 Squadron provides maintenance and operates the Hercules simulator.

No. 36's aircraft carry the fin badge of a rampant horse and No. 37's are marked with a winged globe, yet the easiest method of distinguishing a C-130E from a C-130H is

Above: A20-261 is the survivor of a pair of ex-Saudia Boeing 707-368Cs acquired in 1988 and at one time slated for conversion to boom-equipped tankers.

Above: The C-130Hs of No. 36 Squadron wear an unusual three-tone camouflage, being dedicated to tactical missions. A toned-down squadron badge is worn on the fin.

DHC-4 Caribou fly mainly with Nos 35 and 38 Squadrons at Townsville and Amberley. A handful serve with other units.

One of Amberley-based No. 38 Squadron's DHC-4 Caribou shows to advantage the tan, green and black camouflage scheme selected for the aircraft during the late 1980s.

Above: This de Havilland Canada DHC-4 Caribou wears an experimental three-tone green and black camouflage which was evaluated against the brown scheme above.

No. 36 Squadron's Lockheed C-130H Hercules taxi out for a mass mission. Although primarily a tactical squadron, No. 36 does occasionally use its aircraft in support of No. 37 Squadron's regular missions, flying between Australia's far-flung air force bases.

The squadron crest of No. 36 Squadron has a prancing horse as its centrepiece.

Above: A heavily graffitied C-130H of No. 36 Squadron after winning the USAF's 1989 Airlift Rodeo competition, at which USAF and other free-world tactical transport units demonstrated their prowess.

Above and below: The No. 37 Squadron crest as worn on the unit's C-130Es.

Above and below: No. 37 Squadron's C-130Es wear a smart grey and white colour scheme, with a blue cheat line and Royal Australian Air Force titles in red. One has received a special anniversary scheme.

by the latter's tactical camouflage. The No. 36 Squadron 'H's are regularly operated at low level during cargo-dropping operations in support of the army, such missions requiring a high standard of flying from the aircraft's captain. Newly-posted pilots must spend some 18 months as second-in-command before being allowed to begin tactical conversion, during which they will be trained to fly down to 250 ft (76 m) at speeds between 200 and 260 kt (229 and 298 mph; 369 and 480 km/h), using the terrain to mask their approach to the drop zone. Some C-130H missions are flown to assist No. 37 Squadron in its regular weekly or twice-weekly flights between air bases.

The route-flying squadron is not entirely without more interesting missions, and frequently makes aeromedical evacuations throughout Australia and as far afield as Papua New Guinea, Fiji, Noumea, Cocos Islands and Norfolk Island. Each medevac mission carries a medical team which is sometimes required to undertake surgery on patients during the return sortie. To assist the longer-range flights, retrofit of No. 37's aircraft was authorised in 1989 with Litton LTN 92 ring-laser gyro inertial and GPS navigation systems. RAAF Hercules have flown in support of many UN operations, as well as responding to natural disasters such as the devastation of Darwin by a cyclone on Christmas Day 1974. When civilian pilots went on strike between August and December 1989, the RAAF replacement service (Operation Immune) flew 6,524 hours and carried 172,287 passengers – the Hercules force being responsible for the greatest proportion of sorties, having contributed five aircraft to fly alongside three BAe 748s (one RAN) and two Boeing 707s.

Formerly equipped with a variety of BAe 748s, BAC One-Elevens and Dassault Falcon 20s, No. 34 Squadron standardised on the Dassault Falcon 900 in 1989, taking delivery of five between September and November that year. The RAAF's VIP squadron is based at Fairbairn, ACT, joint-user airport for the Australian capital, Canberra. Leased for 10 years, with on option on a further five, the Falcon 900s, with their 3,000-nm (3,450-mile/5552-km) range, are well suited for trans-Australia flights .

Air Lift Group (No. 86 Wing)

UNIT	EQUIPMENT	BASE
No. 33 Squadron	Boeing 707	Amberley
No. 34 Squadron	Falcon 900	Fairbairn
No. 36 Squadron	C-130H Hercules	Richmond
No. 37 Squadron	C-130E Hercules	Richmond

Tactical Transport Group

Having been required, by government order, to transfer its helicopters to Army Aviation, the RAAF's tactical air transport component now consists only of veteran DHC-4 Caribous. Plans to replace these machines during the early 1980s with a joint-venture STOL transport to be designed with Canada (the DHP-72) were defeated by development costs estimated for the new design. Similarly, a proposal to buy two more squadrons of Hercules fell victim to defence economies imposed in 1987. Acquisition of a Caribou follow-on is now planned for the late 1990s, current studies favouring a mixture of Boeing CH-47 Chinooks and four Hercules. The latter would probably emerge as 'C-130J' Hercules IIs to be bought at the same time as up to a dozen more for replacement of the C-130E fleet. A project office was established late in 1992 to study the C-130E replacement question. A mid-1993 contract with Boeing for 11 CH-47Ds (see Army Aviation) indicates this option to be the most likely.

Retirement of seven Caribous – one-third of the force – was announced late in 1992, at which time No. 38 Squadron moved from Richmond to Amberley to become a non-operational training squadron with just four aircraft. The remainder continue to serve in No. 35 Squadron at Townsville and its SAR and liaison detachments of one aircraft each at Pearce and Darwin. In all, Australia received 29 Caribous, all but four of which formed the main delivery between March 1964 and August 1965. Of these, 12 saw service with the RAAF in Vietnam. Until recently, squadron strengths had been reversed, with No. 38 as the major unit with 13 aircraft and No. 35 being half-equipped with Bell UH-1 helicopters. Townsville (No.

35 Squadron) is conveniently close to Laverack Barracks, home of the army's Operational Deployment Force.

Able to deliver 30 fully-equipped troops to a 750-ft (228-m) airstrip, the Caribou can operate closer to the front line than the C-130H; albeit with a smaller load. Unlike their Hercules-operating counterparts, Caribou aircrew are equipped to sleep under canvas close to their aircraft while ground staff maintain the engines and airframe in the open. Pilots were are also trained in night operations from airstrips, using aids no more sophisticated than a handful of lights to mark the runway, but now have the advantage of night-vision goggles. Navigation at a tactical operating height of 150 ft (46 m) has been simplified by retrofitting GNS 500 navigation equipment. Caribou colours began changing in 1987 from olive drab to a disruptive camouflage of black, green and tan, while retaining the squadron badges of a wallaby (No. 35) or a lion, passant (No. 38).

Tactical Transport Group

UNIT	EQUIPMENT	BASE
No. 35 Squadron	Caribou	Townsville
No. 38 Squadron	Caribou	Amberley

Training Command

Formed in February 1989, Training Command is the instructional element of the old Support Command. Remaining ground-based functions were simultaneously transferred to Logistics Command, notably Nos 2 and 3 Aircraft Depots at Richmond and Amberley respectively for storage and repair of aircraft, and No. 1 AD at Laverton, responsible for other equipment. No. 7 Stores Depot at Toowoomba closes in February 1994. Technical instruction establishments of Training Command include the School of Technical Training with its fleet of grounded airframes at Wagga Wagga.

Pilot training in the RAAF has undergone profound changes since No. 126 Course at No. 1 FTS graduated on 11 June 1992 and its base at historic RAAFB Point Cook prepared for closure as an airfield after 78 years and the passing out of over 7,000 pilots. In fact, Point Cook had ceased to exist officially in 1989 when it and nearby Laverton were merged as RAAFB Williams in preparation for the arrival of Air Force HQ from Canberra. Point Cook also holds the RAAF Museum. Laverton airfield closed at the end of 1992, becoming an unlicensed strip used by PC-9s visiting Hawker-DH for overhaul. The 'Fanta can'-coloured 'Plastic Parrots' (orange and white NZAI CT-4A Airtrainers) that provided 52 hours of primary instruction at Point Cook have been sold.

Now, the RAAF grades its young hopefuls at a civilian school before they begin flying recently built Pilatus PC-9/A Turbo Trainers with No. 2 FTS at Pearce, on the west coast. Previous residents of Pearce were Aermacchi M.B.326s, withdrawn when No. 155 Course ended in July 1990. However, Singapore has

made a 25-year agreement to base 29 SIAI-Marchetti S.211 jet trainers at Pearce from September 1993 to alleviate pressure on its crowded airspace. Up to 50 Singaporean students per year pass through the RAAF base for a 120-hour/40-week course, using some facilities specially built and paid for by the RSAF.

Under an agreement signed on 6 March 1992, BAe-Ansett's flying school at Tamworth, NSW, has been responsible since February 1993 for the first 15 hours of screening for future pilots of the RAAF and RAN, using Mudry CAP 10Bs and ex-RAAF Airtrainers. (It also provides instruction up to 'wings' standard for Australian Army and Papua New Guinea Defence Force students, beginning January 1993 and September 1992 respectively.) After their course at Tamworth, RAAF candidates progress to No. 2 FTS for 158 hours on PC-9/As in nine months, the fighter pilots then receiving 75 hours of weapons and air combat lead-in training with No. 76 Squadron's M.B.326Hs, as described under Tactical Fighter Group.

The PC-9 purchase stemmed from an unhappy decision of December 1985 to terminate development of the Hawker-DH A.10 Wamira turboprop trainer because of delays and cost escalation in preparing a prototype to meet the AFTS 5044 requirement. Gaining its 'A' suffix though fitment of PC-7-type low-pressure tyres for grass airfield operation (it was originally destined for Point Cook) and a Bendix EFIS (Electronic Flight Information System, or 'glass cockpit'), the PC-9 entered service when the first Swiss-built pair was handed over in October 1987, three months late due to electrical problems

Although No. 1 FTS and its Airtrainers (seen above) have gone, the aircraft is still used for screening potential RAAF pilots by the BAe/Ansett flying school.

No. 2 FTS at Pearce operates the PC-9 in the pilot training role. It was selected in favour of the indigenous Wamira. This aircraft has an instrument training hood erected.

The Pilatus PC-9 offers jet-like handling and performance, and has a cockpit designed to simulate a jet fighter, while using a fraction of the fuel of a jet-powered trainer.

The Chief of the Air Staff's unique blue PC-9 is based at Fairbairn. The aircraft is used for liaison flying and to keep desk-bound officers in current flying practice.

No. 6 Squadron provides an F-111 for use by ARDU. This aircraft was used for compatibility trials of the AGM-84 Harpoon anti-ship missile.

The CFS 'Roulettes' formation display team operates PC-9s in a smart and highly conspicuous red and white colour scheme, as befits Australia's national aerobatic team.

Above: The Central Flying School at East Sale uses the PC-9 for instructor training and standardisation.

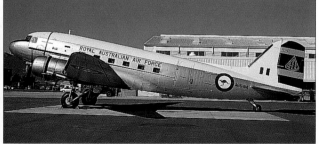

A 'Macchi' tail decorated with a non-standard version of the No. 2 FTS badge.

The PC-9s of No. 2 Flying Training School do not usually wear unit markings, unlike the 'Macchis' they replaced. This aircraft, however, has a small crest on the nose and a large badge on the rudder.

Above: The Aermacchi M.B.326Hs of No. 2 FTS gave way to the PC-9 from May 1989, although many of the aircraft were passed straight over to the co-located No. 25 Squadron, which functions as a holding unit for pilots emerging for No. 2 FTS. Some of these pilots then go to No. 76 Squadron for fighter lead-in training.

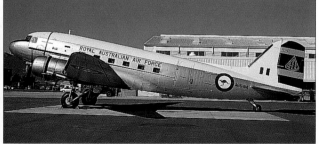

Above: The immortal Douglas C-47 Dakota continues to serve with the RAAF, a number of these aircraft serving with ARDU for trials and transport duties.

Above: This grey C-47 was used to test a camouflage scheme intended for the P-3 fleet.

with Australia's first EFIS-equipped military aircraft. Hawker-DH at Bankstown assembled a further 17 from kits – the first three delivered on 19 December 1987 – and built another 48 locally for an RAAF total of 67, the last in May 1992. One early aircraft was assigned to the Chief of Air Staff at Fairbairn.

Responsible for training flying instructors, the Central Flying School (CFS) at East Sale, Vic, received the two Swiss-built PC-9/As on 24 November 1987. This unit has also now given up its M.B.326s and CT-4As and is equipped only with the PC-9/A. Aermacchi phase-out began on 25 August 1990 when the first aircraft (A7-029, with 6,100 hours 'on the clock') was flown to Wagga Wagga for use as an instructional airframe. In addition to its routine task, the CFS provides the 'Roulettes' aerobatic team of six aircraft. The team made a gradual conversion from M.B.326s, starting with a pair early in 1988-89 season and only accepting its six dedicated aircraft during 1990.

No. 2 FTS, meanwhile, received a first batch of five PC-9/As on 16 May 1989. These were used to train an experimental group of eight students as part of Course 151 (158 hours in nine months) beginning on 9 August as a prelude to full-scale instruction starting in August 1990. The school had built up to a fleet of 37 by the end of 1991, these wearing the No. 2 FTS badge of a black swan in flight before a torch of learning. Similarity to co-located No. 25 Squadron's marking (see Tactical Fighter Group) is no accident, for a black swan is the emblem of Western Australia. Since Course 155, training at the FTS has been entirely on the PC-9/A, initially with the undesirably high allocation of three students per instructor as a consequence of earlier high RAAF pilot losses to the civilian sector. The preferred ratio is two-to-one.

Completing the overhaul of air training, the School of Air Navigation (SAN) expanded its operations in June 1993 with the admission of students from the RNZAF following the latter's retirement of its Fokker F27s on cost grounds. An agreement of 22 October 1992 provides for joint training on the BAe 748s of No. 32 Squadron at co-located East Sale of navigators and air electronics officers from both air forces. The SAN's eight 748-228s were reassigned to No. 32 Squadron when it formed on 1 July 1989, a further addition being two transport-configured 748-229s transferred from No. 34 Squadron in November 1989 and February 1990. Two attempts – in 1984 and 1989 – to take over the navy's pair of 748s have been unsuccessful and these aircraft remain firmly in RAN hands.

One further flying unit concentrates on R & D, rather than training. The Aircraft Research and Development Unit at Edinburgh comprises the R & D Squadron, Flight Test Squadron and Maintenance Squadron with modern equipment such as the Hornet and PC-9/A, as well as three veteran Douglas C-47s. Plans to retire four of the latter in 1982 (for use as targets for trials of the indigenous Karinga cluster bomb) caused such an outcry that the RAAF withdrew the grounding order. C-47s are assigned to general support, a more unusual trial undertaken by one (sold in 1989) being the modelling of the overall grey colour scheme later adopted by some Orions. ARDU has an ASTA N.24 Nomad similar to the two N.22s assigned to No. 75 Squadron for general support. Other duties of ARDU include dropping/launch clearance for new combinations of aircraft and weapon, plus support of the RAAF Institute of Aviation Medicine. The unit's badge consists simply of 'ARDU' within a triangle.

Having lost its helicopters to the Army, the RAAF uses a civilian contractor to provide SAR cover once the responsibility of Eurocopter (Aérospatiale) Squirrel flights of No. 5 Squadron at Darwin, Pearce and Williamtown. In 1987, however, the Williamtown flight was reassigned to a civil Bell 205A, while this and other stations were converted to Bell 212/412s soon afterwards.

Early in 1993, Lloyd Helicopter Group was contracted to provide a Sikorsky S-76A+ at five main bases. The helicopters, including four bought from the Royal Jordanian air force and upgraded, were due to be in position before August of the same year, equipped for crews wearing night-vision goggles.

Above: Civilian-registered aircraft like this Shrike Commander operate in the coastal patrol role, conducting fishery protection, drug interdiction and other duties.

Training Command

UNIT	EQUIPMENT	BASE
CFS	PC-9/A	East Sale
No. 2 FTS	PC-9/A	Pearce
No. 32 Squadron/SAN	BAe 748	East Sale
No. 292 Squadron	P-3C Orion	Edinburgh
ARDU	various	Edinburgh

Above: Shrike Commanders are augmented by IAI Seascans (Westwinds) and by radar-equipped Nomads, which are known as Searchmasters in customs service.

Royal Australian Navy

Two front-line helicopter squadrons and one general support unit are all that has survived from a drastic pruning of RAN aviation resources a decade ago. With the morale-sapping cuts now in the past, the navy can look forward to a modest expansion of its helicopter force as new platform-equipped frigates are delivered, but it will never regain the days of splendour personified by the late, lamented 15,170-ton aircraft-carrier HMAS *Melbourne*. When the UK withdrew its bargain offer of 'Harrier-carrier' HMS *Illustrious* after the 1982 Falklands War, Australia was forced to consider a newly-built vessel of the same class to follow on from the ageing *Melbourne*. The additional cost, allied to the fact that BAe Sea Harriers would have to be bought because existing McDonnell Douglas A-4G Skyhawks could not operate from a deck lacking catapults and arrester wires, resulted in a newly elected government abandoning the entire carrier concept in March 1983.

Melbourne, meanwhile, had paid off on 30 June 1982 and its Skyhawk (805) and Grumman S-2G Tracker (816) squadrons disbanded on 2 July. Trackers continued with land-based patrols of the 200-nm (230-mile/370-km) limit until replaced by civilian Rockwell Shrike Commanders in December 1983. They were then offered for civilian disposal, while the Skyhawks (10, including two TA-4G tandem-seat trainers) were sold to New Zealand. One of the support squadrons (724) disbanded in August 1984, its target facilities work being reassigned to the civilian contractor, Hawker Pacific, which operated two Learjets. Lloyd Aviation took over the task in 1986.

The RAN follows Royal Navy practice in having operational squadrons numbered in the 800s and support units in the 700 series, but bowed to US convention in 1969 by adopting role prefixes: HS-816 and HS-817 are the current anti-submarine helicopter

squadrons, and HC-723 flies everything else, including the only two fixed-wing aircraft on RAN charge. In a further connection with the UK, aircraft carry three-digit 'side numbers' in addition to their serials, these mostly in the 800-899 range. Accompanying 'deck letters' were abandoned following the demise of HMAS *Melbourne* ('M'), as the sole land base is now HMAS *Albatross* (formerly 'NW') at Nowra, NSW.

The mainstay of naval aviation is the Sikorsky S-70B-2 Seahawk, a helicopter which, though versatile, is far from a complete replacement for carrierborne attack aircraft. Current strategy calls for the RAAF to provide air cover for the fleet, thereby limiting it to wartime operations within range of shore bases. However, 'fleet' is a potentially misleading term, as warships would often have to operate autonomously in view of their small numbers in relation to the vastness of Australian waters. Seahawks are intended to fly in support of their parenting frigates, searching for submarines and surface vessels as well as providing mid-course guidance for McDonnell Douglas RGM-84 Harpoon anti-ship missiles, eight launchers for which are on each of the six new RAN frigates.

Because of a mismatch of time scales, the RAN's 3,962-ton, US-built FFG-7 frigates began arriving long before their helicopters. HMAS *Adelaide* (the name ship, pennant number 01) was commissioned on 15 November 1980, followed by Canberra (02/March 1981), Sydney (03/January 1983) and Darwin (04/July 1984). Local shipyards built two more: *Melbourne* (05, commissioned February 1992) and *Newcastle* (06/November 1993). *Adelaide* was transferred to west Australia in 1992 and joined by Sydney in the following year, the remainder operating from the east coast. NSR 16/74, the accompanying helicopter requirement, was finalised in October 1984 when Sikorsky was awarded a contract for eight Seahawks, having beaten

Above: For the Gulf War, three RAN Aérospatiale AS 555 Squirrel (Ecureuil) helicopters were painted dark grey, armed, and deployed on Darwin, Adelaide and Success.

Above: Six Squirrels were delivered for service with HC-723 from May 1984. These have not been navalised, but do feature a lightweight Doppler navigation system.

Above: HC-723's Squirrels are augmented by Bell 206 JetRangers. This one carries a winch for SAR duties. Both types were delivered in a smart blue and white colour

Above: The Coastwatch titles worn over a standard civil paint job, as seen on the Shrike Commander pictured to the left, have been superseded by a red/white customs colour scheme.

Above: This Squirrel is painted in the tactical light grey colour scheme, but retains high-visibility national markings and titles.

Above: This S-70B-2, photographed on the deck of an RAN frigate after its return from the Gulf War, carries an unidentified store on its port stub pylon. The aircraft deployed to the Gulf were the first two Sikorsky-built S-70B-2s. Inset: the badge worn by the aircraft in the main picture.

Above: Nose art on one of the three Squirrels deployed to the Gulf.

Above: 7.62-mm machine guns on the Gulf AS555s led to the 'Battle Budgies' tag.

Above: The final Ecureuil deployed to the Gulf was nicknamed 'Stealth One', and received this bizarre nose art.

competition from the Aérospatiale AS 332F Super Puma and SA 365N Dauphin, plus Westland's Lynx Series 3. A further eight were ordered in May 1986.

The RAN Seahawks are unusual in two respects, both of which were responsible for delays in their service entry. A requirement for maximum price offsets resulted in plans for all except the first pair to be assembled in Australia, but although Hawker-DH began work on its first (the RAN's third) helicopter on 22 January 1988, shortage of skilled personnel threatened unacceptably late delivery. Accordingly, the six airframes constituting the remainder of the first batch were returned to, or retained in, the USA for completion by Sikorsky, which delivered the first to Nowra on 3 February 1989, 'only' four months late. ASTA assembled the second batch of Seahawks, of which the last was delivered on 11 September 1991.

Second and most significant of the customisation measures for Australia is the modified avionics suite. The S-70B-2 RAWS (Role Adaptable Weapon System) version of Seahawk has Thorn-EMI SuperSearcher radar in place of Texas Instruments AN/APS-124, plus Collins advanced integrated avionics, including cockpit control and displays, navigation receivers and communications transceivers, a tactical data system and target hand-off link. The initial two US-built helicopters – the first flying at West Palm Beach on 4 December 1987 – were assigned to avionics proving, assisted by the third when integration problems became apparent. Difficulties continued after the helicopter entered service, but now appear to have been fully overcome.

Hand-over of the first Seahawk in the USA eventually took place a year late on 12 September 1989, and was followed by delivery to Nowra on 4 October. After a further 12 months, the Seahawk Introduction and Transi-

Above: This HC-723's (Helicopter Transport Squadron 723) JetRanger wears navy titles and deck numbers over its army camouflage. The legend on the nose, above the '891' modex, reads 'Battle Budgie'. Navy JetRangers are used primarily for training.

tion Unit was eventually formed to begin working up the operational squadron, accordingly becoming HS-816 on 1 June 1991. Even then, it was 23 July 1992 before 816 Squadron was commissioned, the first ship's flight having formed the previous September. However, that is not to say that the RAN's Seahawks had never previously been to sea, for *Darwin* and *Adelaide* took one each to the Arabian Gulf for Desert Shield/Desert Storm, embarking them on 14 August 1990. Hot weather performance of the RAN S-70s is assisted by uprated (9 per cent) GE T700-401C 1,900-shp (1417-kW) turboshaft engines in all except the first pair which, nevertheless, have provision for later upgrading from straight -401s.

Effort expended on getting the RAN Seahawk right has been justified by the high degree of autonomy which individual flights of HS-816 have gained. Carrying 32 A-size sonobuoys (half of them in ready-to-launch racks) as well as homing torpedoes, radar and MAD, the helicopter can search for surface or sub-surface contacts and launch its own attack under the guidance of the on-board tactical co-ordinator and the sensor operator. More complex than either the SH-60B or SH-60F flown by the US Navy, the S-70B-2 has cockpit lighting compatible with night-vision goggles and is expected to adopt further upgrades, such as FLIR, as they become available.

The belated decision on a helicopter type for the six frigates meant that the first three ships had to be expensively modified after delivery, as the FFG-7 class was designed to accommodate a six-ton Kaman SH-2 Seasprite. Taking a year for each, this involved rebuilding the stern to lengthen the heli-deck by 8 ft (2.4 m) and installing the RAST recovery gear. *Sydney* was completed in February 1989, *Adelaide* in November 1989 and *Canberra* in December 1991, and all can now take the 10-ton Seahawk, two of which can be hangared as a wartime complement, compared with one as the usual issue. Rough weather operations are assisted by the RAST or 'beartrap' system, which winches down the helicopter and grips it securely to rails while it is winched into the hangar. Up to 10 more Seahawks may be ordered for the equipment of eight 3,600-ton 'Anzac'-class frigates to be delivered between October 1995 and 2004: HMAS *Anzac*, *Arrernte*, *Warumungu*, *Stuart*, *Parramatta*, *Ballarat*, *Toowoomba* and *Perth*, pennant numbers 150-157 respectively. They have space for only one helicopter.

Competing aircraft for the 'Anzac' contract are the Bell 412 and Eurocopter AS 555. The single-engined version of the latter is a familiar sight in RAN markings. In order to build up helicopter operating experience aboard frigates between the first FFG-7 delivery and the availability of Seahawks, six AS 350B Squirrels (Ecureuils) were delivered to HC-723 from 14 May 1984, additionally joining the survey vessel HMAS *Moresby* in 1987. Installation of a lightweight Doppler navigation system was about the only concession to naval operations enjoyed by the Squirrels, their landing skids and lack of corrosion-proofing being distinct disadvantages afloat. The absence of a second engine might legitimately be included as a distinctively un-naval feature in view of the usual safety margins for over-water operation. Fortunately, none was lost and the only structural problems reported concerned minor airframe cracking from being secured to the deck in high seas.

Squirrels had their unexpected moment of glory when *Darwin*, *Adelaide* and support vessel HMAS *Success* each took one to the Gulf in 1990-91, complementing Seahawks aboard the two first-mentioned. For this, the helicopters were painted grey over their peacetime blue and white colour scheme. Unofficially dubbed 'Battle Budgies', they were fitted with a 7.62-mm pintle-mounted machine-gun in the cabin doorway.

Relegated to utility tasks following commissioning of the Seahawk force, Westland Sea Kings of HS-816 arrived in Australia during 1975 and initially flew from the carrier *Melbourne*. The 10 Mk 50s were augmented in 1983 by two Mk 50As, but trials aboard FFG-7 frigates reached the not-unexpected conclusion that they were too big to fly from the decks of these vessels. Using Plessey Type 195 dipping sonar and Mk 44/46 homing torpedoes, Sea Kings spent the 1980s providing anti-submarine coverage out to 100 nm (115 miles/185 km) from the Australian coast. This at an end, the remaining seven (including both Mk 50As) have had more time to concentrate on their many other tasks, such as fleet replenishment and utility transport, military and civilian SAR, and support for the Australian Special Air Service. In this third category, it is believed that the Sea King's radar gives it an advantage over army helicopters for covert insertion of forces at night. Coincident with withdrawal of the last of an earlier generation of Westland Wessex in 1990, Sea Kings were given composites main rotor blades to extend their operational lives.

The last four Bell UH-1C Iroquois were also retired in 1990, but HC-723 operates the 206B-1 Kiowa from the same manufacturer. Two remain from four supplied from the army in 1974, their seagoing exploits concerning the support vessels HMAS *Stalwart*, *Tobruk* and *Success*, from which Sea Kings may also be operated. HC 723's Electronic Warfare flight has two BAe 748s that were originally delivered in June 1973 as navigation trainers. In 1977, Sanders Associates received a contract to convert one with electronic jamming equipment and chaff dispensers, a proliferation of ventral aerials and radomes being an easy identification feature. Crewed by seven, including three systems staff, the aircraft provides surface radar and communications operators of all three armed services with experience of various forms of electronic distraction. The pair has been on charge to 723 Squadron since VC-851 disbanded on 31 August 1984, the unmodified aircraft (which has the ability to carry the jamming kit) acting as a general-purpose transport.

Other fleet support work is being undertaken from 1 March 1991 by six New Zealand A-4K/TA-4K Skyhawks which

Above: Probably the most colourful Australian Sea King ever was this aircraft, smartly decorated to celebrate the anniversary of Australian naval aviation.

Above: The standard Australian Sea King scheme consists of white topsides and light grey fuselage. Delivery of the S-70B-2 has allowed Sea Kings to switch to the utility role.

Above: The Sea Kings of HS-817 have started to receive a more tactical overall grey colour scheme, although national markings, navy titles and codes have not been toned down.

Above: After their withdrawal from anti-submarine duties with HS-817, the Wessexes of HC-723 were employed in the utility role until replaced by Sea Kings in 1990.

Above: 1990 saw the retirement of the navy's last Bell UH-1Cs. Four of these served with HC-723, and they gave way to Sea Kings supplanted in the ASW role by S-70B-2s.

Above: An S-70B-2 of HS-816 shows off its SAR capability, a vital secondary role for this versatile machine. For SAR duties the aircraft is fitted with an external rescue winch.

Above: A non-running torpedo mounted on the port pylon of an S-70B-2. Australia has a need for 10 more ship-board ASW helicopters for service on the new 'Anzac'-class frigates.

Above: Banking away from the camera ship, an S-70B-2 shows off its underside. The distinctive shape of the radome for the MEL Super Searcher radar is clearly apparent.

Above: Until 1991 HC-723's HS.748s wore a blue and white colour scheme. The primary EW aircraft was then painted light grey, unlike the second, which serves as a transport.

Above: This Learjet 35A belongs to Fleet Support Pty which provides fleet target facilities. The company replaced Lloyd on this contract, which had taken over from Hawker Pacific.

Above: This formidable array of sonobuoys can be carried by the Sikorsky S-70B-2.

Above: One HS.748, N15-710, was converted by Sanders Associates as an EW trainer in 1977, and has been progressively modified and upgraded ever since.

Above: The insignia of HC-723's EW flight, worn on the unit's two Hawker Siddeley 748s.

were deployed with six pilots and 47 ground crew to Nowra from No. 2 Squadron at Ohakea to provide target and air combat facilities under a five-year agreement. The aircraft, which took up station on 26 February, complementing the civilian Learjets, are no strangers to Nowra, as some are the very same Skyhawks which the RAN sold to the RNZAF a few years earlier. Other targets in naval use are the GAF Jindivik drones stationed at Jervis Bay. First flown in August 1952, the Jindivik remained in production (apart from a short interruption) to meet Australian, UK and other orders until 1993. Non-flying aircraft will be found at HMAS Narimba, Schofields, Sydney.

Above: Projections below the forward fuselage of N15-710 include a ram air turbine and antennas. Previously used as a navigation trainer, the aircraft is now used for EW training.

Above: The ventral antennas, radomes and chaff/flare dispensers fitted below the rear fuselage of HC-723's Elint HS.748.

Naval Aviation

UNIT	EQUIPMENT	BASE
HC-723	Squirrel, Kiowa, BAe 748	Nowra
HS-816	Seahawk	Nowra
HS-817	Sea King Mk 50/50A	Nowra

Air Power Analysis

Australian Army Aviation Corps

The AAAC entered the 1990s as a considerably expanded force with both new equipment and squadrons freshly transferred from the RAAF. This move to increase army mobility and place the improved capability under closer control of the ground forces has been advantageous to the latter, although the mothballing of the RAAF's Chinook medium-lift fleet has left the soldiers with a significant gap in their air support. That shortcoming is, after some procrastination, being addressed, the intention being to equip the army properly for operations in the empty 'Top End' of Australia as a parallel to the RAAF's Bare Base and Jindalee OTH radar programmes. A major step, literally in this direction, will be the transfer of one aviation squadron to Darwin in 1995.

A comparatively new force, AAAC was constituted on 1 July 1968 from observation units administered until a few years before by the RAAF. Moving in 1973 to its present HQ at Oakey, near Brisbane, Qld, it officially received the RAAF's Bell UH-1H Iroquois and Sikorsky S-70 Black Hawks on 15 February 1989, although the transfer was phased over several years following the government directive of November 1986. Duties of the AAAC include light transport (fixed- and rotary-wing), air observation, liaison and communications, casualty evacuation and photography. Significantly absent is attack capability in the form practised by the AH-1 Cobra or even an unarmoured helicopter carrying anti-tank missiles. Australia evaluated the Agusta A 129 Mangusta, Eurocopter AS 565M Panther, MBB BK-117A-3 and Sikorsky S-76 with the intention of taking delivery of an initial batch of 34 to 40 in 1992, but no order has yet materialised.

As Army Aviation Centre, Oakey is home of one of the two aviation regiments as well as the School of Army Aviation, a base squadron and 5 Base Workshop Battalion. The base squadron supplies air traffic control, fire service, accommodation and all other support facilities, while 5 BWB is a component of the 1st Electrical and Mechanical Engineers Group and responsible for repair and modification of the army's aviation-related material. Additional duties are the maintenance of the school's aircraft and trade training of aircraft engineers. Two of the AAAC's six operational squadrons are based at Oakey, the others being distributed to three other bases. Of these, two are virtually twins: Townsville/Garbutt Qld, and Townsville/Laverack Barracks, both of these covering north-east Australia. Finally, one squadron is based at Holsworthy Barracks, Sydney, NSW. As a consequence of the vast area of Australia without an army aviation presence, it is not unusual for detachments as small as one helicopter to be dispatched great distances for several weeks or months, their progress supported by civilian airstrips and fuel stores at remote police stations.

The longest-established helicopter equipment is the Bell 206B-1 JetRanger, which rejoices in the official name of Kalkadoon but is universally known as the 'Sky Scooter'.

The first 12 arrived from US production in 1971 and a further 44 were assembled by Commonwealth Aircraft Corp., including those loaned to the RAN (two of which are still maintained by 5 Workshops). No. 161 (Reconnaissance) Squadron at Holsworthy, No. 162 (R) Squadron at Laverack Barracks and No. 171 (Operational Support) Squadron at Oakey are the components of 1 Aviation Regiment (Reconnaissance), each of which is issued with nine Bell 206s. Despite their named roles, squadrons all undertake battlefield surveillance, casualty evacuation and SAR support for the civilian authorities, Oakey's unit having the additional role of liaison for HQ 1 Division, the controlling authority for both the AAAC regiments. No. 162 is a rapid-reaction squadron attached to the Army's 3rd Brigade and accordingly keeps as much of its support equipment as possible in air-transportable containers ready for immediate despatch.

Although not to OH-58 Kiowa standard, the JetRangers are optimised both for military missions and operations in Australia, with uprated (400 shp/298 kW) engines and an extra hour's fuel for the latter. A secure speech system and a distinctive HF whip aerial protruding from the rear of the cabin are complemented by large doors to permit loading of up to two stretchers and the provision for optional rescue hoist, cargo hook and floats. For safer tactical flying, cable-cutters were fitted in 1987. JetRanger crews now have the advantage of night-vision goggles and some helicopters have gained GEC-Marconi FLIR 2000 in recent years. Performance with the optional Minigun armament is less than sprightly in the Australian summer heat.

Rationalisation of the fixed-wing fleet during 1992 resulted in withdrawal and sale of the AAAC's Pilatus PC-6B1/H2 Turbo-Porters, of which 13 remained out of 19 delivered from 1968. Replacement has been by a follow-on purchase of ASTA (GAF) Nomad turboprop twins. The first batch of 11 N22B Nomad Missionmasters was received between 1975 and 1977 and augmented in 1982 by a further pair. In 1987, when civilian sales had slumped, the Australian government bought the last 11 aircraft from storage, allocating five N22Cs and four long-fuselage N24s to the AAAC and the balance to the RAAF. The former were delivered in 1991-92 to supplant Turbo-Porters at Oakey with No. 173 (General Support) Squadron and the School of Army Aviation.

Partnering No. 173's Nomads in 5 Aviation Regiment (Air Mobility) and also forming an element of the School at Oakey, the S-70A-9 Black Hawks of 'A' and 'B' Squadrons at Townsville/Garbutt have boosted AAAC efficiency since their introduction in the late 1980s. It was the RAAF which placed the initial order for 14 of these utility helicopters in 1986, all bar the first of them assembled by Hawker-DH. A follow-on contract of May 1987 added 25 more, for a total of 39, the last of which was handed over on 1 February 1991. No. 9 (RAAF)

Above: The Australian Army Aviation Corps was founded in 1968, but until 1989 operated only a handful of Bell 206B-1 JetRangers in the observation role.

Above: Virtually all Army Aviation Corps aircraft and helicopters now wear the same brown, green and black camouflage as this JetRanger.

Above: The long nose instrumentation boom on this S-70A-9 identifies it as an aircraft on loan to ARDU. The S-70A-9 is broadly equivalent to the US Army's UH-60A.

Above: The Army Aviation Corps gained Bell UH-1Hs when it took over the RAAF's helicopter fleet. This aircraft is fitted with an external rescue hoist, and a stretcher litter.

Above: Included among the helicopters taken over from the RAAF were the Squirrels of No. 5 Squadron, which are now operated by the ADF helicopter school at Fairbairn.

Squadron began equipping at Amberley in February 1988, passing its Bell UH-1B Iroquois to Nos 5 and 35 Squadrons. On 15 February 1989, No. 9 moved to Townsville/Garbutt and became 'A' Squadron, while the Iroquois Flight of No. 35 (the other half of which still exists at Townsville with Caribous) was incorporated as 'B' Squadron the following July. The authorised strength of the two squadrons is 33 Black Hawks plus six of the eight UH-1H Iroquois converted to 'Bushranger' gunships. Eight Black Hawks participated in their first major exercise, Kangaroo 89, between July and September 1989 and five were taken to Papua New Guinea the following year for overseas training.

The Iroquois remain from total deliveries of 24 UH-1Bs, two UH-1Ds, 29 new UH-1Hs and some 25 more of the last variant from US Army stocks. In the share-out of RAAF helicopter assets, the 29 surviving UH-1Hs were disposed of as six to reconnaissance duties, eight as gunships, 11 for training and four transferred to the Papua New Guinea Defence Force. The Training Flight of No. 5 Squadron became the Australian Defence Forces Helicopter School (ADFHS) at RAAFB Fairbairn on 1 January 1990 and its 18 Eurocopter (Aérospatiale) AS 350U Squirrels (Ecureuils) began adopting 'ARMY' titles to reflect the fact that the unit is under the administrative control of Training Command, as is the School of Army Aviation. ADFHS, which decorates its Squirrels with the badge of a black hawk, is due to transfer to Oakey in 1994-95.

A further change in instructional procedures has followed the retirement of RAAF Airtrainers and the re-allocation of AAAC basic training to the BAe-Ansett Flying College at Tamworth, NSW. Beginning in January 1993, prospective pilots now attend one of the two 21-week/60-hour courses which pass through Tamworth each year, graduating with their 'wings' before reporting to Oakey for further training. Here, they are converted to the JetRanger (eight on strength), perhaps returning at a later stage for upgrading to Iroquois (five), Black Hawk (six) or Nomad (five). The school also administers conversion to night-vision goggles, involving 15 hours of flight in two weeks, while observation pilots are assigned 26 rounds of 105-mm artillery on which to practise reporting the fall of shot. The school's rotary-wing instructors are trained by the US Army at Fort Rucker or the RAF's CFS detachment at Shawbury, their fixed-wing equivalents passing through the RAAF's CFS. Also trained at the Aviation School are observers and loadmasters for the UH-1 and S-70.

The Black Hawk force is able to airlift a complete 150-man company, plus most of its equipment, to northern Australia in a single wave. However, even with this greatly improved carrying power, shortcomings were noted at the heavier end of the airlift spectrum during the Kangaroo 89 exercise – the largest tri-service operation for 40 years – which closely followed the retirement of the RAAF's Boeing CH-47C Chinooks on 30 June 1989. Costing 3.5 times more than a Black Hawk per hour of flight, the 11 remaining Chinooks of Amberley's No. 12 (RAAF) Squadron were

Above: Australia's Sikorsky S-70A-9 Black Hawks were delivered to the RAAF, serving with No.9 Squadron before transferring to A Squadron of the Army's 5th Aviation Regiment on 15 February 1990. The last aircraft of the order were delivered directly to B Squadron instead of the RAAF's No.35 Squadron.

Above: Australia's S-70A-9s are based at Townsville in mixed squadrons which also include UH-1Hs converted to 'Bushranger' gunship configuration.

Above: Pylons can be used for the carriage of long range fuel tanks. 39 S-70A-9s were procured, in batches of 14 and 25.

Above: When the UH-1H is used in the gunship role, small deflector plates are installed in the leading edge of each door.

Above: Eight of the RAAF's 29 surviving UH-1Hs went to the Army as gunships, six for recce, and eleven for training. Four were given to New Guinea.

Above: The Army's PC-6 Turbo Porters have now been replaced by the indigenous ASTA Nomad. This one wears an unusual overall white scheme.

Above: The Army Nomads mostly wear a similar tactical camouflage to that applied to RAAF Caribous and to the now retired PC-6s.

doomed to premature disposal by a combination of funding shortages and poor serviceability. The fact that they could undertake tasks for which the Black Hawk was not designed failed to feature in the calculations. Positioning of forward refuelling points, carrying 155-mm Howitzers and collecting downed aircraft are among the roles which the smaller helicopter finds difficult or impossible. After wiser councils had prevailed following analysis of Kangaroo 89, Australia revealed plans for converting four Chinooks to CH-47D standard, with funds to be provided by trading back the others to Boeing for the US Army National Guard. After further indecision in July 1992 the programme was approved in August of that year, then increased to include all 11 Chinooks. Complete refurbishment involved in CH-47D conversion will reduce operating costs and give the AAAC a further large boost in air mobility, the offset being that the extra Chinooks will replace part of the RAAF's Caribou fleet.

Australian Army Aviation Corps

UNIT	EQUIPMENT	BASE
1 DIVISION		
1 Aviation Regiment (Reconnaissance)		
161 (R) Squadron	JetRanger	Holsworthy
162 (R) Squadron	JetRanger	Townsville/ Laverack
171 (OS) Squadron	JetRanger	Oakey
5 Aviation Regiment (Air Mobility)		
A Squadron	Black Hawk, Iroquois	Townsville/ Garbutt
B Squadron	Black Hawk, Iroquois	Townsville/ Garbutt
173 (GS) Squadron	Nomad	Oakey
TRAINING COMMAND		
School of Army Aviation	JetRanger Nomad, Black Hawk, Iroquois	Oakey
ADF Helicopter School	Squirrel	Fairbairn

Above: It is now planned to refurbish all 11 surviving RAAF Chinooks, modify them to CH-47D standards, and return them to service with the army.

Above: The Pilatus PC-6 Turbo Porter has now been withdrawn from Australian Army service, replaced by the indigenous Nomad.

New Zealand

Royal New Zealand Air Force

The RNZAF's present status may be visualised by recalling that the most exciting development in combat aviation over the past two decades has been the recent rebuilding of ageing McDonnell Douglas Skyhawks to ensure the type achieves at least 30 years in front-line service. In contrast to NATO forces which enjoyed a build-up during the 1980s before the cuts of the post-Warsaw Pact era, New Zealand's equivalents have been in slow but accelerating decline for many years, if their investment in hardware is used as a yardstick. Even in the 1970s, only 8.1 per cent of the NZ defence budget was assigned to buying equipment (compared with the 40-45 per cent achieved by the UK) and though 15 per cent was the target for the late 1980s, economic decline has squeezed both this and the total amount spent on defence.

Such has been the pressure on the armed forces that the Conservative government, which had been elected in 1990 to replace the anti-nuclear administration of the previous six years, was forced to begin its term with a reluctant 10 per cent cut in the defence budget. Defence spending as a proportion of gross domestic product has shrunk from 2.1 per cent in 1988 to 1.6 per cent in 1993. That hardly bodes well for the future, when it is recalled that the meagre spending level set in 1989 was based on the presumption that the worst-case operation over the next 30 years would be the rescue of a handful of NZ nationals caught up a minor armed clash between two Pacific island states.

Administratively, the RNZAF is divided into Operations Group and Support Group, the former having gained flying training units

at the expense of the latter in mid-1993. Seven squadrons, including one with naval connections, constitute the combat and transport component of Operations Group at Auckland, while ground training, stores and miscellaneous functions are the responsibility of Support Group at Wigram. Air forces are tasked with policing the 200-nm (230-mile/370-km) exclusive economic zone and responding to any small military emergency within the Antarctic or those Pacific areas for which Wellington is responsible.

Additionally, the RNZAF is equipped for disaster relief, support of scientific settlements in Antarctica and support of UN peacekeeping operations. In the latter connection, BAe Andovers have been present in Iran to supervise the peace with Iraq between 1988 and 1990, and more recently in Somalia from January to May 1993, when they flew 233 sorties as part of the force attempting to re-impose civil order. Two-thirds of the Somali deployment costs had to be met by the defence budget, despite their being quite clearly a matter for the overseas aid account. Operations Group squadrons are located on North Island, at Hobsonville and Whenuapai (collectively known as RNZAFB Auckland since 1965), plus Ohakea. Wigram and Woodbourne on South Island are the ground training bases of Support Group, and Gisborne is an exercise base with no permanent facilities or resident squadrons.

New Zealanders readily refer to themselves as 'Kiwis' in reflection of the national emblem which, accordingly, forms the centrepiece of the RNZAF's aircraft identity roundel. In the case of toned-down camouflage the red kiwi appears on a blue disc,

Above: Skyhawks are the mainstay of the RNZAF. The original TA/A-4Ks and ex-RAN TA/A-4Gs have been brought to a common standard under the Kahu Upgrade.

Above: No. 5 Squadron operates six modified P-3B Orions under the local designation P-3K. The centrepiece of the squadron's gull badge is worn on the fin.

Left: The badge of the RNZAF Strike Wing, which includes the A-4 units.

Above and above left: No. 75 Squadron operates A-4Ks decorated with the squadron badge of a Tiki superimposed on crossed hammers, flanked by diamonds (yellow on red when presented in colour). No. 75 is the front-line Skyhawk unit, with No. 2 acting as OCU.

Above: No. 75 Squadron's badge is carried in very toned-down style on the intakes of the unit's Skyhawks. The squadron provides the 'Kiwi Red' aerobatic display team.

Above: This patch is commonly worn by RNZAF Skyhawk pilots.

Above: This unofficial No. 75 Sqn emblem incorporates the unit's Maori motto.

Above: No. 2 Squadron's three TA-4Ks and three A-4Ks operate from Nowra in Australia, providing target facilities for the Australian fleet and acting as the New Zealand Skyhawk OCU. This is particularly ironic, since several of the unit's aircraft were previously RAN A-4s.

Above: This unofficial No. 2 Squadron badge reflects its current fleet support role.

Above: No. 2 Squadron's official badge is a winged spear.

Above: The P-3K designation is a local one, standing for P-3 Kiwi.

Above: The P-3K is a P-3B equipped with FLIR, new avionics and radar.

Above: New Zealand's Orions still wear the smart but relatively conspicuous grey and white colour scheme in which they were delivered. The aircraft were delivered in 1966 to replace Sunderlands, and were upgraded to P-3K standards in 1983.

Air Power Analysis

minus the intermediate white. Up to and including the 1970 delivery of the first Skyhawks, New Zealand employed the standard RAF-type roundel with only the addition of a silver leaf within the central red disc. Aircraft serial numbers are prefixed 'NZ' and assigned in four-figure batches, some of

which reflect the aircraft's designation, such as NZ7271-7272 for the two Boeing 727s. In other cases, batches of 100 are reserved for each type of aircraft, combat equipment having used NZ6101, NZ6201, NZ6301 and NZ6401 as starting points for the Canberra, Skyhawk, Strikemaster and M.B.339.

No. 14 Squadron's official badge is a hawk; its aircraft wear white diamonds.

Operations Group

Availability of Australian navy T/A-4G Skyhawks at give-away prices was a welcome boost for Operations Group, allowing it to form a second squadron with these useful if dated aircraft. The choice in the early 1980s had seemed to lie in replacement of the 1970-vintage aircraft by the Lockheed (then General Dynamics) F-16 Fighting Falcon, McDonnell Douglas F/A-18 Hornet or outsider Northrop F-20 Tigershark. However, an expanded fleet made a wide-ranging refurbishment a financial practicality, and thus was born Project Kahu (Hawk). The original aircraft were 10 A-4Ks and four TA-4K combat-capable trainers bought for No. 75 Squadron at Ohakea in 1968, one of each having been lost before upgrading. Initially equipped with AIM-9H Sidewinder AAMs for air defence, the A-4Ks switched emphasis to anti-shipping operations and were retrofitted, from October 1982, with Stencel SIII-3R ejection seats in place of the Douglas Escapac.

At a cost of $A28.2 million, New Zealand obtained eight A-4Gs and two TA-4Gs, together with the complete Australian inventory of spares up to engine size. All were delivered in July 1984, allowing the formation in December of No. 2 Squadron at Ohakea with five TA-4s and three A-4s for operational conversion and tactical reconnaissance. These began passing through the Kahu programme from 1987 onwards. Approved by the NZ government in May 1985, Kahu was launched in March 1986 with a programme management contract to Lear Siegler (later Smiths Industries). The latter brought in local companies Safe Air of Blenheim as the main sub-contractor, plus Fisher & Paykel and Pacific Aerospace for fabrication of parts.

Kahu's prime purpose has been to give the Skyhawk improved maritime attack, air-to-air and close air support capabilities, not least through the addition of Westinghouse AN/APG-66NZ radar in the nose. As suggested by its designation, the latter is a modified version of the F-16 Fighting Falcon's radar which has an antenna reduced in size to fit in the confined space, and also an additional mode for surface search. All wiring and old avionics have been stripped out of the A-4s and replaced by equipment including a Ferranti 4510 HUD/WAC, CRT displays, Litton LN-93 ring-laser gyro INS, VOR/ILS, digital flight control system, HOTAS controls, General Instrument AN/ALR-66 radar warning receiver and Tracor AN/ALE-39 chaff/flare dispensers. To the implied increase in navigational accu-

racy and weapon delivery which these changes impart is added a broader spectrum of armament than the 'iron' bombs and Zuni rockets previously used. New options include Hughes AGM-65D/E Maverick ASMs, GBU-16 laser-guided bombs, CRV-7 rockets and AIM-9L Sidewinders.

Avionics trials began in a TA-4 early in 1985 while, a year later, another A-4 returned to flying at the US Navy's Pensacola rework facility as the 'prototype' structural upgrade aircraft. Undertaken in parallel with the avionics programme (and in New Zealand for the remaining aircraft) this refurbishment included a zero-life re-spar for a further 18 T/A-4s, plus new control surfaces, new landing gear and the addition of a braking parachute. Re-lifed, and with nav/attack systems not far short of the F/A-18 Hornet, the initial 'production' conversion of the Kahu programme (a TA-4K) was flown in June 1988 and was handed over 13 months later. Smith's and the RNZAF undertook this and the second upgrade before passing the work to Safe Air, which performed the remaining conversions at Woodbourne and Blenheim. The Kahu avionics programme cost $NZ140 million; the structural improvements an additional $NZ69 million.

The loss of an A-4K in October 1989 reduced the number available for Kahu update to 21, of which five are trainers. First redeliveries were made to No. 2 Squadron, which then passed a batch to No. 75 after a working-up phase, and started re-equipping for a second time. The first Kahu loss (fourth RNZAF A-4 overall) occurred in July 1992. Ex-RAN aircraft may be differentiated by the serial numbers NZ6211-6218 and 6255-6256, which follow the earlier A-4/TA-4 allocations. A-4Ks were delivered with an 'avionics hump', but such has been the progress with miniaturisation of avionics since then that it was removed during the update. The nose avionics compartment is now tightly packed, so much so that the original design for an undernose cooling air scoop proved inadequate in trials at Tindal RAAFB in 1990 and had to be modified. All Skyhawks are currently known as A-4Ks and TA-4Ks, although such a far-ranging modification from the original standard of A-4K would normally have deserved a new suffix letter. Colours have been changed to wrap-round, low-vis grey and green camouflage with Type-B (white omitted) national insignia.

No. 75 Squadron - a unit tracing its lineage directly from the RAF's No. 75 which was manned by New Zealanders from 1940 to 1945 - has the badge of a tiki (a Maori

One of three No. 14 Squadron Strikemasters retained for ground instructional use. The other seven survivors went to Aermacchi in part payment for the squadron's new M.B.339s.

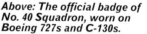

Above: The official badge of No. 40 Squadron, worn on Boeing 727s and C-130s.

Above: This emblem was seen on a No. 40 Sqn C-130, significance unknown.

Above: For many years New Zealand's Andovers wore this brown and green camouflage scheme, which replaced the original brown and sand RAF scheme.

Above: For humanitarian missions in Somalia at least two RNZAF Andovers were painted white overall. The Andover has proved rugged and reliable and has plenty of life left.

No. 14 Squadron's Strikemasters were withdrawn prematurely in December 1992, after a series of structural failures.

Above: Two of No. 14 Squadron's new Aermacchi M.B.339CBs, which have now entirely replaced the much-loved Strikemaster, or 'Blunty'.

Above: The RNZAF 'Macchis' wear the same low-visibility grey and green camouflage as the upgraded Skyhawks, although national insignia and squadron markings are not toned down. The 'Macchis' can be armed with the AGM-65 Maverick and have modern defensive systems.

Above: One of No. 40 Squadron's Hercules is marshalled to its parking spot at McMurdo Station in Antarctica, one of the squadron's regular destinations.

Left and above: No. 40 Squadron applies its badge to both its five C-130H Hercules and a pair of Boeing 727-100Cs. Replacement of these by Boeing 767s has been mooted.

Above: Four of No. 42 Squadron's Andovers have worn this very smart VIP colour scheme, with the full unit crest on the fin. Two aircraft are VIP configured, two are in semi-VIP fit.

Above: The latest Andover colour scheme is similar to that worn by the upgraded Skyhawks, even down to the toned-down insignia. At least two aircraft have been repainted.

One of 10 RNZAF Andovers has now been withdrawn from use, and serves as a spares source for the survivors. The type's long airframe life should ensure many more years of service.

An informal No. 42 Squadron zap portrays a ferocious-looking Andover.

One of three Cessna 421s was sold in late 1990 as an economy measure. They were used by No. 104 Flight at Woodbourne. Their withdrawal has meant extra work for No. 42 Squadron.

totem) before crossed mining hammers. No. 2 Squadron aircraft carry a figure 2 overlaid with the official badge of a winged spear. The 'Kiwi Red' national aerobatic team is provided by No. 75 Squadron and, as mentioned under the Australian navy heading, No. 2 Squadron is on a five-year detachment to Nowra for provision of target facilities, beginning in March 1991. Two thirds of the hours flown by its three A-4Ks and three TA-4Ks are devoted to the RAN and most of the remainder to converting RNZAF pilots, but it also participates in the occasional exercise with the RAAF and army. No. 75 Squadron's regular visits to Australia for joint exercises are used as a means of rotating A-4s through the Nowra detachment, the No. 75 complement being 12 A-4Ks and two trainers. Both squadrons have a pair of 'Hotshot' cockpit procedures/systems familiarity ground training aids.

The second combat aircraft type is the Lockheed P-3K Orion, used only by No. 5 Squadron (badge: a soaring albatross) at Whenuapai. Operating anywhere between the equator and the Antarctic, No. 5 performs long-range maritime patrol and anti-submarine warfare training, fisheries resource surveillance, SAR, medical air transport and support of anti-shipping operations by the Skyhawk force. It also undertakes occasional Northern Hemisphere operations both with treaty partners in South East Asia and in the UK or Canada for ASW competitions with fellow countries of the British Commonwealth. Five P-3Bs were delivered to the squadron in 1966 as replacements for Short Sunderland flying-boats and upgraded to P-3K standard in the 'Rigel 1' programme. The first upgrade, by Boeing in the USA, was completed in September 1983, while Air New Zealand modified the others between October 1983 and May 1984. They now have a Boeing Universal Display & Control System, Texas Instruments AN/APS-126 radar, Litton LN-72 INS, Omega navigation and – the external distinguishing feature from P-3B – AN/APS-36 FLIR in a turret under the nose. A sixth P-3B, which had been traded in to Lockheed by the RAAF, was bought in 1985 and completed its P-3K conversion in June 1986. (The K is for Kiwi and is not an official US DoD designation.)

'Rigel 2' was to have upgraded the acoustics processing equipment by 1991 but was delayed 'indefinitely' by financial problems, as has been the planned addition of Harpoon anti-ship missiles. Interest has now switched to Project Kestrel, an exploratory study revealed in mid-1993. Kestrel concentrates on the fact that airframe lives will expire in about 2000 as a result of flying in the area around New Zealand, which is claimed to be among the worst in the world for low-level air turbulence. If refurbishment at RNZAFB Woodbourne proves cheaper than buying new-built aircraft from the recently reopened Orion production line at Marietta, Georgia, the P-3Ks will gain new wings, fresh skinning on the fuselage centre-section and replacement horizontal stabilisers.

While also carrying armament, the Aermacchi M.B.339CBs of No. 14 are

advanced flying and basic weapons trainers for trainee pilots in general and future Skyhawk crew in particular. The squadron has recently completed phasing out the BAC Strikemaster Mk 88, or 'Blunty', an initial 10 of which were received in 1972, followed by six more in 1975 to replace Skyhawks in the Operational Flight. Nine replacement mainplane sets were supplied from the UK in 1986-87 when fatigue cracks were discovered, but the problem repeated itself more seriously in 1990. By then, Project Falcon had been initiated to study the type's replacement and decided upon Training Flight aircraft being phased out in 1990 and those of Operational Flight in 1995. Delayed by submission to no less than eight committees, selection of the Aermacchi M.B.339 was seen as the ideal solution, combining advanced trainer capability with modern avionics and proven structural integrity. With one Strikemaster grounded and half the surviving 14 subject to a ban on high *g* manoeuvres it was decided to retire the whole batch as soon as possible. A further loss in October 1991 (when the fleet had flown 75,000 hours) and two more groundings the same year accelerated the urgency of replacement, while a third crash followed in October 1992. The remaining 10 were withdrawn shortly before Christmas 1992 and seven handed over to Aermacchi as offsets for the M.B.339 purchase. Three others joined the earlier retirements as ground training airframes

The 18 replacements – known simply as 'Macchis' when in service – were obtained in a package also including technical training, spares support and possibly sub-contract work for local firms. This was a bargain at $NZ266 million, although funding was so tight that the government unsuccessfully attempted to curtail the order after deliveries had begun. The first three arrived in New Zealand in a dismantled state in March 1991 and were formally handed over on 19 April. The remainder have followed at three per half-year, the last in September 1993, all of them flown and accepted in Italy before being broken down into major components for transport to the Antipodes. 'Macchis' wear low-vis camouflage but with full-colour national insignia, and carry 'fighter bars' of a white diamond on a black rectangle on each side of the fuselage roundel. No. 14 Squadron's badge of a kia (an indigenous bird) appears on the forward fuselage.

RNZAF's combat capability has been raised as a result of the latest additions, for the 'Macchi' can be armed with AGM-65 Mavericks and protect itself with a Tracor AN/ALE-40 chaff/flare dispenser and Elettronica ELT-555 jamming pod. It also has the HOTAS controls and HUD of modern combat aircraft to ease the transition to Skyhawks. 'Macchis' began their first 'wings' training course in 1993 and students now fly 115 hours on the aircraft. Since July 1993, 'Macchis' have been operated jointly with the co-located Pilot Training School, and it is PTS instructors who administer the advanced course. Graduates destined for Skyhawks stay on with No. 14's Operational Flight for a further 12-18 months and about 300 hours to

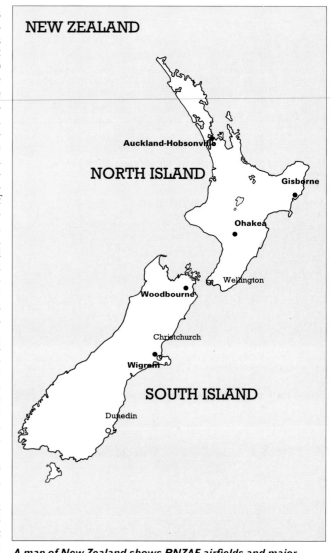

A map of New Zealand shows **RNZAF** airfields and major cities. Airfields are located in both North Island and South Island.

Above: A pair of Bell UH-1Hs of No. 3 Squadron. The squadron operates some 14 Hueys, all upgraded to UH-1H standards, two permanently detached to Wigram.

Above: Most of No. 3 Squadron's UH-1Hs now wear a toned-down grey and green colour scheme. Two Hobsonville-based aircraft stand SAR alert at Auckland and Christchurch.

Above: UH-1s from No. 3 Squadron are periodically deployed to Antarctica, where they operate in an overall-orange colour scheme, as seen here.

Above: A Nitesun searchlight can be fitted to the Huey. This is particularly useful for night SAR missions.

Above and right: No. 3 Squadron's Hueys carry a simplified, silhouette version of the unit's crouching Maori warrior badge, on a red disc on the tailfin.

Above: No. 3 Squadron maintains seven of its Wasps in airworthy condition for operation from the navy's 'Leander'-class frigates. Three arrived in 1966, with an ex-RN attrition replacement in 1974. Six more came in 1982-83 (two for spares), with three more spares ships in 1985 and four ex-RN aircraft in 1989.

Above: One of No. 3 Squadron's airworthy Wasps overflies Hong Kong harbour. These operate from four 'Leander'-class frigates.

Above: The Bell 47G-3B-1/2 Sioux remains in use primarily for training, No. 3 Squadron having reabsorbed these from the CFS in 1988.

become accustomed to combat flying. Training has been affected by flight restrictions resulting from engine surging by the Rolls-Royce Viper 680-43 turbojet which powers the 339. Modification of the fuel control unit by the RNZAF's workshops at Woodbourne was due to begin in November 1993.

Two squadrons, Nos 40 and 42, provide the RNZAF's fixed-wing transport from their base at Whenuapai. The largest is No. 40 (badge: a compass rose) operating five Lockheed C-130H Hercules and two Boeing 727s. Delivered in 1965, the initial Hercules was also the first production 'H' version of the C-130 to fly, all being in service by the end of 1968. As with Hercules the world over, tasks vary from the mundane to the highly unusual. The squadron flies a twice-weekly domestic passenger/freight service around RNZAF bases and regularly visits the UK, Middle East, US, Australia and Pacific islands, while work for the army includes tactical landings, air-dropping and parachuting. Beginning in November of each year, No. 40 launches Operation Ice Cube to deliver mail, food and scientific equipment from Christchurch to McMurdo Station, Antarctica, making approximately 15 round trips over two months. 'One-offs' have included two Hercules operating alongside the RAF C-130K detachment in the Gulf War (560 sorties and almost 700 flying hours between 20 December 1990 and 12 April 1991); Operation Pluto airlifts of passengers between North and South Islands during seamen's strikes; and 'free-fall' planting of trees on Chathams Island.

Requirements to visit South East Asia and the Pacific prompted the purchase of jet equipment in the form of two 727-100Cs, plus a third solely for spares breakdown, all secondhand. Delivered in May/June 1981, the duo received military avionics and additional fuel sufficient for 2,100-nm (2,415-mile/3886-km) stage lengths with maximum cargo. Typical loads include eight freight pallets, or 108-122 passengers or 52 VIPs/staff. In 1985, plans were considered for obtaining Boeing 737s as aerial tankers, as an alternative to converting a pair of Hercules. Subsequent KC-130 schemes similarly failed to mature, with the result that the Skyhawk has no local tanker into which it can plug its fixed refuelling probe. Latest replacement plans for the 727 are based on the possible lease of a couple of civilian Boeing 767s.

No. 42 Squadron (badge: a bird perched before a globe) was yet another unit to benefit from a bargain offer. In 1976-77, 10 low-houred HS Andover C.Mk 1 rear-loading freighters were delivered to the RNZAF at a price, including two years' worth of spares, of $NZ213 million. Until No. 1 Squadron was disbanded in December 1984, six Andovers were used for army support, freight carrying and maritime surveillance, fitted with extra fuel tanks and UHF and TACAN from the Bristol Freighters they replaced. No. 42 continued with two passenger and two VIP aircraft for tactical transport, aeromedical evacuation, inshore patrol and SAR, but gradually built up to six and, now, nine aircraft, which are also used by the Parachute Training and Support Unit to train army paratroopers, as well as the

'Kiwi Blue' demonstration team of RNZAF instructors, formed in 1990. Five Andovers are in utility configuration (the sixth having entered long-term storage in 1992), two are VIP aircraft, and the remaining pair is in a 'semi-VIP' fit. Demands for the aircraft have increased since the three Cessna 421 Golden Eagles of No. 104 Flight at Woodbourne were sold late in 1990 for economy reasons.

In addition to their RAF tropical colours, Andovers have variously worn camouflage of tan and two-tone green; VIP white and grey with blue cheat line; grey and two-tone green; and overall United Nations white. Recently, a few have joined the Hercules fleet in adopting low-vis grey/two greens plus red and blue national insignia. It had at one time been proposed to sell the Andovers to raise cash for new transports, but the lack of a civilian airworthiness licence for the type gave it a negligible resale value and the plan was abandoned. Recent airframe surveys have confirmed earlier estimates of a 100,000-hour structural life, and as the lead aircraft had flown only 19,000 hours by 1993, many more years of service are foreseen.

All helicopter operations by the RNZAF are concentrated within No. 3 Squadron, which applies to them the badge of a crouching Maori warrior. Of the five Bell UH-1D and 10 UH-1H Iroquois received by the RNZAF, mostly in 1966-70, all but one remain in service, the former upgraded to 'H' configuration in 1981-82. Seven of the helicopters were temporarily unserviceable in 1990 when cracks were discovered in a tail boom spar. An interim repair has allowed them to resume operations pending a planned upgrade of the Iroquois fleet, although this has yet to be funded. No. 3 is tasked with tactical air support, battlefield support, aeromedical evacuation, SAR and helicopter conversion training, as well as naval operations, described below. The squadron and 12 of its UH-1s are located at Hobsonville; the remaining two (four until July 1993) are in a permanent detachment at Wigram on South Island, where they are used for SAR and army support. The Wigram-based machines are all equipped with rescue winches, as is the pair from Hobsonville which maintain a 24-hour SAR alert at Auckland and Christchurch.

Occasional detachments are made to Antarctica, where Operation Snowbird has involved a single UH-1 being air freighted to Scott Base, McMurdo Sound, by No. 40 Squadron Hercules for the summer seasons of 1985, 1989, 1990 and 1992. Although not a Snowbird detachment, two Iroquois assisted the US Navy base at McMurdo in 1992. For such operations, the helicopters are painted in the 'Orange Roughy' scheme of overall orange. In New Zealand they wear the grey and two-tone green colours which have replaced brown and two greens. The change of colours coincided with the previously-mentioned fatigue problems, resulting in some interesting combinations of old and new camouflage as serviceable tail booms were swapped around.

In the Naval Support Flight of No. 3 Squadron are the Westland Wasp HAS.Mk 1 torpedo-carrying and utility helicopters acquired from the UK to operate from 'Leander'-class frigates obtained from the same source. The two original, new-built vessels are HMNZS *Waikato* and *Canterbury*, while in 1982-83 *Wellington* (ex HMS *Bacchante*) and *Southland* (ex HMS *Dido*) were added, together with four surplus RN Wasps (and two more for breaking down as spares sources). They joined the survivors of four earlier Wasp deliveries and were augmented by three more spare parts machines in 1985 and four in 1989, although only seven are maintained in airworthy condition, including two assigned to training at Hobsonville. In unarmed guise, Wasps also operate from the survey ship HMNZS *Monowai* and the tanker HMNZS *Endeavour*. Project Amokura is the Wasp replacement which is timed to coincide with delivery of two 'Anzac'-class frigates (also on order for the RAN) during the 1990s.

In July 1993, a reorganisation of flying training resulted in No. 3 Squadron regaining the four Bell 47G-3B-1/2 Sioux it has passed to the Light Rotary Wing Flight of the Central Flying School in 1988. At Wigram, they had trained instructors and provided 12-week rotary-wing conversion courses, these duties now being undertaken entirely 'in house' at Hobsonville by the expanded squadron.

The training changes effected in July 1993 have involved the Flying Training Wing moving from Wigram to Ohakea and simultaneously transferring allegiance from Support Group to Operations Group. Most senior of the aviation units newly transposed to North Island is the Central Flying School, where instructors destined for fixed-wing duties at the co-located Pilot Training School (PTS) initially fly in NZAI CT-4B Airtrainers. Until they were sold on the civilian market in February 1993, four virtually identical AESL T6/24 Airtourers equipped the CFS, but only the 18 New Zealand-built CT-4Bs now remain in the CFS/PTS pool from 19 deliveries begun in 1976. Two Airtrainers form the CFS's 'Red Checkers' aerobatic team, adorned with red and white checks on the engine cowling. Additionally, CFS acts as guardian of the RNZAF tradition, in that its Historic Flight operates single airworthy examples of the Avro 626, DH Tiger Moth and North American Harvard.

PTS has 14 Airtrainers for its six-month/100-hour basic pilot training courses, the syllabus having been modified from the previous one of 133 CT-4 and 85 Strikemaster hours. Graduates passed until recently to No. 14 Squadron for 100 hours of advanced instruction on M.B.339s, but since the move of basic training to Ohakea the instructors for the pre-'wings' M.B.339 phase have belonged to the PTS. On qualification as pilots, graduates are only then selected for fast-jets, transports or helicopters. Those in the first-mentioned stream remain with No. 14 for more M.B.339 time; transport co-pilots are converted by the appropriate squadron; and helicopter candidates by No. 3 Squadron.

A further means of obtaining transport

Left and above: The crests of the Central Flying School and Pilot Training School.

Above: The last of four AESL T6/24 Airtourers has now been withdrawn from use, leaving 18 almost identical Airtrainers in service with the Pilot Training School.

Above: The best way of telling an Airtrainer (seen here) from an Airtourer is by the canopy, which hinges upward instead of sliding aft.

Above: A single Tiger Moth is maintained in airworthy condition by the CFS Historic Flight. This aircraft wears wartime overall-yellow training colours.

Above: The PTS and CFS Airtrainers wear a smart light grey colour scheme, with red wingtips and empennages. The huge canopy gives an excellent all-round view.

Above and below: The CFS at Ohakea mans the 'Red Checkers' team.

Above: The badge of NATTS was worn on the fins of the now-retired F27s.

Above: The 'Red Checkers' display team often flies as a synchronised pair, but a larger team, as seen here, has also flown displays in six fully marked-up Airtrainers. The team is manned by CFS instructors who practise and fly displays in their spare time.

Above: New Zealand's F27-100s were offered for sale in 1993, after New Zealand began joint navigator/AEO training with Australia, using RAAF HS.748s.

Above: Another aircraft used by the CFS Historic Flight is this North American Harvard. Harvards remained in RNZAF service until the end of 1976.

Above: This de Havilland Vampire serves as a gate guard at RNZAF Ohakea. It wears the distinctive markings of No. 14 Squadron, with which it once served.

conversion ended on 17 July 1992 when the Wigram-based Navigation, Air Electronics & Telecommunications Training Squadron (abbreviated as NATTS) was disbanded and all telecommunications training became ground-based with No. 2 Technical Training School at Wigram. NATTS flew three Fokker F27-100 Friendships which had been bought from Air New Zealand and upgraded with revised cockpits (Series 500 standard), Omega, weather radar and an INS. Fitted with a four-seat (including one instructor) navigation console and Air Electronics Officer's station, they were redelivered from February 1980 onwards in anticipation of a 15-year life. In addition to navigator and AEO training, the Friendships handled their own aircrew conversion and were available for transport (20 seats remained) and maritime surveillance (two observation windows and pylon tanks for six-hour patrols). In 1993, the Friendships were offered for sale after short-term storage and the RNZAF and RAAF began joint training of navigators on Australian BAe 748s.

The RNZAF's non-flying elements remain with Support Group and include the Aviation Medicine Unit and Staff College at Whenuapai; No. 1 Repair Depot, No. 4 Technical Training School and General Service Training School at Woodbourne; and Nos 2 and 3 Technical Training Schools, Command Training School and University Officer Cadet Flight at Wigram. The last-mentioned base is to close by 31 December 1995, its ground units transferring to Woodbourne in the middle of that year. The RNZAF Museum remains at Wigram, although a new wing was opened at Ohakea in 1993. No. 1 (the only) Repair Depot handles all the RNZAF's third-line maintenance while No. 4 TTS was expanded following the

closure of No. 1 TTS at Hobsonville in 1992 and now includes all engineering instruction as well as safety and armament training. A logistics base at Te Rapa, near Hamilton on North Island, was closed on 27 March 1992 and the assets of No. 1 Stores Depot distributed to several bases. Finally, RNZAFB Shelly Bay, near Wellington – though currently under threat – is an administration and accommodation base with some minor resident units and no airfield.

Operations Group

UNIT	EQUIPMENT	BASE
Operations Wing - Ohakea		
No. 2 Squadron	A-4K/TA-4K Skyhawk	Nowra (Australia)
No. 14 Squadron	M.B.339CB	Ohakea
No. 75 Squadron	A-4K/TA-4K Skyhawk	Ohakea
Operations Wing - Whenuapai		
No. 3 Squadron	UH-1H Iroquois, Bell 47G Sioux	Hobsonville
Naval Flight	Wasp HAS.Mk 1	Hobsonville and at sea
Detachment	UH-1H Iroquois	Wigram
No. 5 Squadron	P-3K Orion	Whenuapai
No. 40 Squadron	C-130H Hercules, Boeing 727	Whenuapai
No. 42 Squadron	Andover C.Mk 1	Whenuapai
Flying Training Wing - Ohakea		
CFS	Airtrainer	Ohakea
PTS	Airtrainer, M.B.339CB	Ohakea

INDEX

INDEX

Picture acknowledgments

Front cover: Ted Carlson/Fotodynamics. **4:** Aldo Ciarini, Marcus Fulber, Paul Jackson. **5:** Fermin Gallego Serra, Michel Fournier, Aldo Ciarini (two). **6:** Bob Archer, Richard Gennis, Sikorsky. **7:** Peter R. Foster (two), Roger Lindsay. **8:** British Aerospace, Gerry Turner, via Roger Lindsay. **9:** Billington, Lindsay Peacock, R. Mateboer. **10:** Alan Key (three). **11:** Fermin Gallego Serra (two), Eurocopter. **12:** Mike Reyno, Bob McIntyre, Ted Carlson/Fotodynamics. **13:** Jeff Rankin-Lowe, Ted Carlson/Fotodynamics, Renato E.F. Jones (two). **14:** Ted Carlson/Fotodynamics, via Jeff Rankin-Lowe, Ted Carlson/Fotodynamics (two). **15:** Greg L. Davis, Gilles Auliard, Ted Carlson/Fotodynamics. **16:** Department of Defense (DoD), Tim Ripley. **17:** DoD (three), Tim Ripley, Marco Papisca. **18:** RNLAF via Tim Ripley, DoD. **19:** DoD, Marco Papisca, Tim Ripley, Bob Archer. **20:** Tim Ripley (four), Marco Papisca. **21:** Tim Ripley. **22:** A.B. Ward, Tim Ripley, DoD. **23:** Tim Ripley (three), DoD (two). **24:** IAI. **26:** David Donald (two). **27:** Boeing, A.B. Ward, IAI, David Donald. **28:** John Gourley (three). **29:** via John Gourley (three), John Gourley. **30-31:** Sikorsky. **32-33:** Randy Jolly. **34:** Randy Jolly, David Donald, Ted Carlson/Fotodynamics. **35:** US Air Force (two). **36:** US Air Force via Robert L. Lawson, Don Spering/AIR (two). **37:** Fairchild-Republic, Don Spering/AIR. **38:** Don Spering/AIR (three). **39:** via Robert L. Lawson. **40:** Peter R. Foster, David Donald, US Air Force. **42:** Don Spering/AIR (two). **43:** Randy Jolly, Jeff Rankin-Lowe, US Air Force (two). **44:** David Donald, Randy Jolly. **45:** US Air Force via David Donald, US Air Force. **46:** Peter R. Foster, David Donald, via Robert L. Lawson. **47:** Don Spering/AIR (three), Ben Knowles via Robert L. Lawson, Randy Jolly (three). **48:** Peter R. Foster, US Air Force (two). **49:** Rick Linares, Ted Carlson/Fotodynamics, Randy Jolly. **50:** Randy Jolly (two), Jeff Wilson. **51:** Yves Debay, Jeff Rankin-Lowe, Gary Frederick via Robert F. Dorr. **52:** 706th TFS, Randy Jolly (three), David Donald (five). **53:** Randy Jolly (three), 706th TFS (two), David Donald (three), Mal Gault. **54:** Yves Debay (two), Tim Ripley, Rick Linares, Randy Jolly (two). **56:** Jim Rotramel, Randy Jolly (two). **57:** US Air Force (two), Ted Carlson/Fotodynamics, Jelle Sjoerdsma. **58:** Tim Ripley, Ted Carlson/Fotodynamics, Randy Jolly. **59:** Randy Jolly. **60:** David Donald, Randy Jolly. **61:** Jim Rotramel (three), Randy Jolly (two). **62:** Randy Jolly, Mal Gault, Jim Rotramel. **67:** Randy Jolly (two), David Donald, US Air Force (two). **68:** Fairchild-Republic, US Air Force, David Donald (four), Jim Rotramel, Mal Gault. **70:** Randy Jolly, Don Spering/AIR, David Donald (three), Peter R. Foster. **71:** William J. Mondy, Michael Grove via Robert L. Lawson, Randy Jolly (two), Yves Debay (two), Ted Carlson/Fotodynamics. **72:** Yves Debay, Wallace T. Van Winkle, 706th TFS, Randy Jolly (four), Don Spering/AIR. **73:** Randy Jolly (three), USAF via Tim Ripley, Peter R. Foster, Don Spering/AIR, Ted Carlson/Fotodynamics. **74:** David Donald (three), Randy Jolly. **75:** Jim Benson, Mal Gault, Paul Carter (three), Gilles Auliard. **76:** Don Spering/AIR (three), Mal Gault, Andrew H. Cline, Paul Carter, Jeff Rankin-Lowe. **77:** Mal Gault (three), Peter R. Foster (two), Randy Jolly, David Donald (two), US Air Force. **78:** 354th TFW, Don Spering/AIR (two), Michael Grove via Robert L. Lawson, Peter R. Foster, US Air Force. **79:** Jeff Rankin-Lowe, Yves Debay, David Donald, Don Spering/AIR (two), Mick Roth via Robert L. Lawson, Randy Jolly. **80:** Don Spering/AIR, Randy Jolly (two), Paul Carter, Mal Gault (two), Renato E.F. Jones, Ted Carlson/Fotodynamics. **81:** Don Spering/AIR, Tim Laming, Randy Jolly, Bob Archer, Ted Carlson/Fotodynamics. **82:** Robert F. Dorr (two), Randy Jolly (three), Paul Carter, Andrew H. Cline, Peter R. Foster. **83:** Mal Gault, Don Spering/AIR (two), Ted Carlson/Fotodynamics. **84:** Frank Rozendaal (three), Nguyen Xuan At via FR. **85:** Nguyen Xuan At via FR, via FR. **86:** via FR, Nguyen Xuan At via FR (three). **87:** Frank Rozendaal (three), Nguyen Xuan At via FR. **88:** Frank Rozendaal (three), Nguyen Xuan At

via FR. **89:** Nguyen Xuan At via FR (four). **90:** Paul R. Bennett, via Paul R. Bennett. **91:** Peter Steinemann (three), Salvador Mafé Huertas, Angelo Saini via SMH. **92:** Peter Steinemann (two), Chris Brooks/Aerophoto, Greg Meggs, Photolink. **93:** Chris Ryan, Tieme Festner, Hans Nijhuis (two), Robbie Shaw (two), Ben J. Ullings, Antoine Roels. **94:** Salvador Mafé Huertas, Peter Steinemann, Paul Jackson. **95:** Dassault (four), Peter Steinemann (three). **96:** Dassault, Michel Fournier, Peter Steinemann (two). **97:** Peter Steinemann (three). **98:** Peter Steinemann (two), Paul Jackson (three). **99:** Dassault (two). **100:** Peter R. Foster (three). **101:** Martin Baumann, Chris Ryan, Jean-Jacques Petit (two), R. Housden via Paul R. Bennett, Jelle Sjoerdsma. **102:** FB (three), Paul Jackson, Jelle Sjoerdsma (two), Dassault via Michael Stroud. **103:** Paul Jackson (four), Jean-Jacques Petit. **104:** Jean-Jacques Petit, Hans Nijhuis, Paul Jackson (two), Dassault (two), Dassault via Mark Styling. **105:** Martin Baumann (two), Philippe Ferretti (three), Jean-Jacques Petit, Peter R. Foster. **106:** Chris Brooks/Aerophoto, Michel Fournier (two), Philippe Ferretti, Paul Jackson, FB, Jean-Jacques Petit, Martin Baumann, Chris Ryan. **107:** Hans Nijhuis, Paul Jackson (three), FB. **108:** Dassault (two), Paul Jackson (two). **109:** Salvador Mafé Huertas (four), IAI. **110:** Salvador Mafé Huertas, IAI, Dassault, Paul R. Bennett, Paul Jackson. **111:** Peter Steinemann (four), Peter R. Foster, Dassault. **112:** Dassault (two), Peter R. Foster, Peter R. March, Peter Steinemann. **113:** Paul Jackson (two), Dassault, L.J. Vosloo (two), Topper (two). **114:** Herman Potgieter (six), L.J. Vosloo, Salvador Mafé Huertas. **115:** Robbie Shaw, Salvador Mafé Huertas, Swiss air force, Ben J. Ullings. **116:** Robbie Shaw (two), Paul Jackson, Paul R. Bennett. **117:** Paul R. Bennett, Robbie Shaw, Jelle Sjoerdsma, Tim Senior, Ben J. Ullings, Jeff Puzzullo. **118:** Robert L. Lawson, Jeff Puzzullo (two), Dassault, Peter R. Foster. **119:** Peter R. Foster (three), via Paul Jackson, Dassault. **120-121:** Jim Benson, Randy Jolly (two). **122:** Randy Jolly (two), **123:** Jim Benson, Randy Jolly. **124:** Randy Jolly (three). **125:** Jim Benson, Randy Jolly. **126:** Randy Jolly (two), Jim Benson. **127:** Randy Jolly, Jim Benson. **128:** Randy Jolly (three). **129:** Jim Benson (two), Randy Jolly. **130:** Greg Meggs, Jelle Sjoerdsma (two), Michael Stroud (two). **131:** Mal Gault, Robbie Shaw, Michael Stroud (two), RAAF, Greg Meggs (two), Sikorsky. **132:** Paul Jackson (three), Andrew H. Cline, Peter Steinemann, Lenn Bayliss. **133:** Peter Steinemann (three), Robbie Shaw, Paul Jackson (two). **134:** Robbie Shaw, Mal Gault, Greg Meggs (two). **135:** RAAF, David Draycott/Airshots, Greg Meggs. **136:** Greg Meggs (four), Robbie Shaw. **137:** Greg Meggs (three). **138:** Greg Meggs (three), Craig P. Justo. **139:** Jeff Rankin-Lowe, Peter Steinemann, Robbie Shaw (three). **140:** David Donald, Jeff Rankin-Lowe, David Draycott/Airshots, Mal Gault, Peter Steinemann. **141:** Peter Steinemann, Robbie Shaw (three). **142:** Peter Steinemann (three), Greg Meggs (two). **143:** René J. Francillon, Paul Jackson, David Donald. **142:** Peter Steinemann (three), Greg Meggs (two), Craig P. Justo. **144:** Craig P. Justo (two), Peter Steinemann (three). **145:** Craig P. Justo (six), Jeff Rankin-Lowe, Peter Steinemann. **146:** Peter Steinemann (four), Robbie Shaw. **147:** Peter Steinemann (six), Jeff Rankin-Lowe, Paul Jackson (three). **148:** Peter Steinemann, Craig P. Justo, Greg Meggs. **149:** Greg Meggs, Mal Gault, Randy Jolly. **150:** Jelle Sjoerdsma, Peter Steinemann (two), Jeff Rankin-Lowe, Robbie Shaw (two). **151:** Robbie Shaw, Peter Steinemann (two), Jeff Rankin-Lowe (five), RNZAF via Jeff Rankin-Lowe. **152:** Robbie Shaw (five), Jeff Rankin-Lowe (three), Peter Steinemann. **153:** Peter Steinemann (three), Jeff Rankin-Lowe (three). **154:** RNZAF via Jeff Rankin-Lowe, Robbie Shaw. **155:** RNZAF via Jeff Rankin-Lowe, Jeff Rankin-Lowe, Robbie Shaw (three), Peter Steinemann. **156:** Robbie Shaw (two), Jeff Rankin-Lowe (two), RNZAF via Jeff Rankin-Lowe. **157:** Peter Steinemann (three), Jeff Rankin-Lowe (two), Robbie Shaw, RNZAF via Jeff Rankin-Lowe.